DAY
by
DAY

with Your Health Coach

DAY
by
DAY

with Your Health Coach

Beverly Chesser

New Leaf Press

Third printing, June 1998

Copyright © 1993 by New Leaf Press. All rights reserved. No part of this book may be used or reproduced in any manner whatsoever without written permission of the publisher except in the case of brief quotations in articles and reviews. For information write: New Leaf Press, Inc., P.O. Box 726, Green Forest, AR 72638.

Library of Congress Catalog Number: 93-86324
ISBN: 0-89221-247-0

Unless otherwise noted, all Scripture verses are from the King James Version.

Printed in the United States of America.

Introduction

At the age of twenty-seven, I was a physical wreck. Diagnosed as having ninety different allergies, onset diabetes, TMJ, and early signs of asthma, I wondered, *How could I have so many physical problems?* I knew the answer.

For ten years, I had totally neglected my health. My eating habits were atrocious; I smoked; and I had no time for exercise. My lifestyle was killing me, and I knew I had to do something about it.

That's when I started fighting back.

First, I stopped smoking. Then I began to educate myself by reading nutrition books and health magazines. At the same time, I started riding an exercise bike, lifting weights, and going to the spa three days a week.

When I joined the spa and began my exercise program, little did I know that my entire life would change. Although it was a constant struggle to build up my sick body, I could feel myself getting better day by day.

Before long, my weak, overweight, and out-of-shape body began to change as I learned how to eat low-fat foods and exercise. With my energy and health restored, the allergies, depression, and asthma faded away. I promised myself to live this way for the rest of my life.

Today, as I write this book, I am fifty-one years old. For the past fifteen years, I have produced a daily television program called "Beverly Exercise" that is now seen on over two thousand local and cable stations. Five years ago, I began recording a nutrition program that is heard on Christian radio stations across the nation.

As I minister to my audiences via television, radio, and in conferences and meetings, I meet people who are suffering from poor health, lack of energy, and low self-esteem. Because I've been there, I know how much they want help.

In the years I have spent researching information for my programs, I have learned that the best way to develop a healthy lifestyle is to discover the source of the problem and then put a plan into action that will develop good health.

Before change can occur, however, we must first understand why we are overweight, out of shape, or sick. That is why I am writing this book for you

— to give you the information you need on a daily basis.

Each day's devotion will provide helpful facts and tips to teach you how to have a healthier lifestyle. In addition, the scriptural portion of each devotion will strengthen your inner man. As your mind and your spirit grow stronger, you will then have the power to discipline your body.

Your body will only respond to what your mind tells it to do. That's why your mind must first be convinced that a certain lifestyle change is crucial to your health. Then, you can tell your body how to put that change into action.

There's only one problem: Your body won't always cooperate. It desires rich-tasting foods; it rebels against physical exercise; and it balks at change. That's where your spirit comes in. Through the power of God's Word and His Holy Spirit, your human spirit can be strengthened to help you discipline your body.

In fact, God can give you the desire and determination to bring about change. With His help you can do anything. "I can do all things through Christ who strengthens me" (Phil. 4:13).

Through daily Scripture reading, you will realize you must present yourself as a "living" sacrifice — holy and acceptable unto God as Romans 12:1 tells us to do. God wants us to be fully surrendered to Him, living a life that brings honor and glory to Him.

Pastor and author, Chuck Swindol, once said that God wants us to be "living sacrifices" by presenting ourselves daily on the altar to God. The only problem with a living sacrifice, he said, is that it keeps crawling off the altar!

That is the purpose of this daily devotional book — to keep us on God's altar every day of the year.

Please use this book year after year as a part of your daily devotions, but don't use it alone. Read the suggested portion of Scripture at the beginning of each devotion or use your own program of daily Bible reading. As you read and meditate on God's Word and spend time with Him in prayer, your life will change dramatically.

Let me help you claim the health and energy God wants you to have. Pray this prayer with me:

Dear Lord, today I dedicate my life to You. I want to be that living sacrifice that You ask me to be. Please help me to live in a way that will bring honor and glory to You. Amen.

You *can* be the best total person for Jesus Christ — body, mind, and spirit.

Beverly Chesser
Your Health Coach

❖ January 1 ❖

A New Day
Read: Psalm 118

> This is the day which the Lord hath made; we will
> rejoice and be glad in it (Ps. 118:24).

If you're like me, you need all the help you can get when it comes to keeping your body in shape, educating your mind, and strengthening your spirit. It's a constant battle that requires daily attention. That's why, day by day, you and I will be learning new information to keep our motivation at its peak. We will also be reviewing old facts and reminding ourselves of points we may have forgotten as the year goes on.

This may be the first day of the new year, but it is also the beginning of a new day. As we start this year off together, let's take one day at a time. If we look too far ahead or set expectations for ourselves that exceed our ability to perform, we will only become discouraged and give up.

Lord God, as I begin this new year, I rejoice
knowing that You have made this first day as
a day of new beginnings for me.

❖ January 2 ❖

The Early-Bird Advantage
Read: Psalm 63

> O God, thou art my God; early will I seek thee . . . (Ps. 63:1).

Try setting aside the first hour or so of the day just for God and yourself. Before the clutter and hassles of daily life begin to pull you in a dozen different directions, come away for time alone with God.

The psalmist David speaks of waking up in the morning "thirsting" for God. How wise it is to drink from the fountain of life early in the day and thereby gain strength for whatever lies ahead. God sees ahead and, if you give Him time, He can prepare you for what each day holds. Seek Him when you will have the least amount of interruptions because it is usually in the silence that God speaks to our hearts.

Exercise is another activity that seems to work best for me in the early morning. After taking time to refresh and strengthen my spirit, I then devote time to refreshing and strengthening my body. So jump out of bed early and refresh your spirit and body. Chances are, you will be more faithful in your devotions *and* in your exercising if you will do this.

O God, my heart longs to be with You. Help me to discipline
myself to spend time with You each morning,
listening to Your voice.

❖ January 3 ❖

Who Comes First? Read: Matthew 6:24-34

Seek ye first the kingdom of God, and his righteousness;
and all these things shall be added unto you (Matt. 6:33).

At the same time that I was starving myself with dieting, I was also exercising about four hours a day and wouldn't go to bed at night until I had jogged five miles. I thought, *If a little exercise is good, then a lot is better.*

One day I proudly announced to the women at my church exercise class, "I hope everyone thinks I'm thin enough now. When I weighed this morning, I was only 96 pounds!"

To my dismay, one lady replied, "Beverly, you're still not skinny!" Her words rang in my ears the rest of the day. That night, as I lay in bed, I saw myself lying in a coffin. As the people filed by, I heard that same woman say, "She starved herself to death, but she still ain't skinny."

I realized Satan was also trying to destroy me with my addiction to dieting, going on a binge, and exercising. My weight and my body had become my god, and I knew I had to make Jesus Christ the center of my life again. Are you putting God first?

*Heavenly Father, I want to put You first. Help me to
make Jesus Christ the Lord of all areas of my life.*

❖ January 4 ❖

A Winning Combination Read: 1 Corinthians 6:9-20

For ye are bought with a price: therefore glorify God in your
body, and in your spirit, which are God's (1 Cor. 6:20).

After I realized I had gone overboard with dieting and exercise, I began to seek the Lord about how to bring balance into my life. He started to show me that it's okay to miss a day of exercising and that overeating once in while is not the end of the world. I realized that my body belongs to God anyway, but that it is my responsibility to take care of it — without going off the deep end!

God loves you and wants only the best for your life. During this year, we will be learning how to glorify God in our bodies in a way that is balanced and effective for maintaining our health. Our times together will focus on what I have come to see as the winning combination for health: a low-fat diet and regular exercise. By consistently — but not rigorously — making this your goal, you will achieve what you've been striving to do for years: lose weight, feel better, and stay healthy.

*Heavenly Father, I want to glorify You in my body and my spirit.
Help me to always remember that I belong to You.*

❖ January 5 ❖

The Binge Cycle   Read: 2 Peter 1:1-11

. . . Add to your faith virtue; and to virtue knowledge;
and to knowledge temperance; and to temperance patience;
and to patience godliness (2 Pet. 1:5-6).

At one time in my life, I got so carried away with thinness that I measured every bit of food and ate only 600 calories a day. I would keep this up for several days at a time and then find myself eating everything in sight. Afterwards, I'd feel worthless and determine to get control again and not eat any more then my allotted 600 calories.

I didn't know that a binge begins with starving and that I was setting myself up to repeat the same vicious cycle over again. I lacked the knowledge to know how to eat properly, but with God's help He taught me how to be patient and develop good eating habits.

Lord, as I gain more knowledge about how to eat, help me to
develop self-control and the patience to persevere.

❖ January 6 ❖

Why Exercise?   Read: 1 Timothy 4:1-8

For physical training is of some value, but godliness
has value for all things . . . (1 Tim. 4:8;NIV).

Is exercise worth the effort? Some diet books claim that exercise does not burn enough calories, noting that jogging for twenty minutes only burns 180 calories. What they fail to mention is that exercise changes your body so that you burn calories during and *after* exercising. For every twenty minutes of exercise, you reap calorie burning results for up to four hours later! Now there's a bargain!

In a fit body, the benefits of exercise operate day and night. Why? Because exercise stimulates your metabolism so that everything you do during a day — washing dishes, grocery shopping, walking to the office — burns more calories than a person who does not exercise.

Exercise also makes dieting more successful. The well-exercised body responds more quickly and with less muscle loss to the stress of dieting.

Is exercise worth the effort? Absolutely. Even the Bible considers physical training to be of value. Our goal, of course, is godliness in all we do. So let's exercise godliness while we exercise our bodies, making it a special time of fellowship with God.

Lord, use the time I spend exercising to benefit me
both physically and spiritually.

❖ January 7 ❖

Too Busy to Exercise?

And whatever you do, whether in word or deed,
do it all in the name of the Lord Jesus, giving thanks
to God the Father through him (Col. 3:17;NIV).

You may be a fast-paced executive, a career woman, or a busy mother — or all three! Whatever your job, you probably spend your days running around the office, jumping in and out of the car, chasing kids, folding laundry, and on and on it goes. Surely, all that activity must count as exercise, right? No, work is not exercise. These interrupted spurts of activity require only 50 percent of your muscle power, leaving the other 50 percent wasting away.

But there's good news! You do not have to sweat and strain to burn fat. Twenty minutes a day of moderate — even fun — exercise is more than enough to get you in shape and keep you there. Surely, you can find twenty minutes for a brisk walk around the block! That's a perfect way to get your body in shape and clean the cobwebs out of your mind at the same time.

If you exercise in the name of the Lord and for His glory, He will bless it for your good.

Lord, help me in everything I say and do
to bring glory to Your name.

❖ January 8 ❖

Forget Your Failures

Read: Philippians 3:12-21

. . . Forgetting what is behind and straining
toward what is ahead (Phil. 3: 13;NIV).

You've tried exercising before, but you didn't stick with it. Now you're afraid to commit to a daily exercise program again. Forget the failures of yesterday.

Like the apostle Paul, we must forget what is behind and push ourselves forward. It's easy to get bogged down in defeat and discouragement. But, with God's help, you can press on toward the goal for which God has called you.

Even if you stop and start exercising a hundred times during the next year, don't give up. Just start again and keep it up as long as you can.

Press on toward achieving a healthy body that is pleasing to the Lord. Keep striving for physical fitness that will bring glory to God and give you the energy to live a full and active life for Him. Move forward to becoming all that God created you to be — in your body, mind, and spirit.

Lord, forgive me for giving up in the past. Help me to
begin again today to do what You have called me to do.

❖ January 9 ❖

Creeping Obesity   Read: Psalm 37:1-22

Commit thy way unto the Lord: Trust also in him:
and he shall bring it to pass (Ps. 37:5).

After the age of twenty-five, the body's metabolism slows. That means that the rate at which calories are used by your body decreases. During childhood, puberty, and adolescence, your basal metabolism remained high. Once growth was complete, however, your energy needs dropped sharply. Around that time, you probably became busy with family and career. That's when many adults slip into "creeping obesity."

With the demands of adulthood, you may have neglected to program exercise into your lifestyle. Your activity level has decreased, but your eating patterns have probably remained the same. Now you may find yourself broad in the hips and heavier around the waist and stomach. If this has happened to you, it's time to reverse the "creeping" process and get started on a new course of action.

Heavenly Father, I commit my way to You. Help me to make the lifestyle changes that will give me a healthier body, mind, and spirit. I am trusting You and know You will bring this to pass.

❖ January 10 ❖

Why Exercise?   Read: Revelation 3:1-22

Him that overcometh will I make a pillar in
the temple of my God . . . (Rev. 3:12).

You may wonder, "Why can't I just go on a diet without exercising?" Let me explain. Body fat is tenacious — it holds on as long as possible. In fact, the fatter a person is, the more the body tends to try to remain fat. New scientific studies have shown that fat cells don't just sit around waiting to be fed — they fight for food!

Once your body reaches its "fat plateau," it will do everything possible to stay at that set point. Your body doesn't want to lose weight. That's why exercise is so important to weight loss. When you exercise everyday, the weight you lose through dieting will be more fat and less muscle. Your muscles burn calories. If you combine walking with a wholesome, low-fat diet, you will not be hungry and the weight you lose will be mostly fat. Then you'll have a lifestyle of eating and exercise that you can live with.

Lord, help me to overcome those obstacles in my life that are keeping me from becoming all that You want me to be.

❖ January 11 ❖

Are All Calories Created Equal?   Read: Psalm 37:23-40

Delight thyself also in the Lord; and he shall give thee
the desires of thine heart (Ps. 37:4).

For years, food experts thought that all calories were created equal. Today, we know that is not true. Calories that come from fatty foods like butter, sour cream, and oils are converted to body fat more easily than calories from carbohydrates or protein.

When you eat complex carbohydrate foods like fruits, vegetables, and whole-grain breads, your body has to work harder to break them down and in the process burns more calories. That means fewer calories are stored as fat. In fact, for every 100 calories of fat, your body burns up only 3 calories during digestion. That leaves 97 calories stored in your fat cells. On the other hand, your body burns up 23 calories digesting 100 calories of carbohydrates, leaving just 77 to remain as body fat.

If you limit your fat intake to less than 30 percent of your total calories, the calories you *do* eat will burn up much more quickly.

Lord, the desire of my heart is to be healthy and fit.
Teach me how to put You and Your Word first in my life.

❖ January 12 ❖

Getting Filled Up   Read: Ephesians 5:1-21

Be ye not unwise, but understanding what the will of the
Lord is . . . . be filled with the Spirit (Eph. 5:17-18).

A young mother who had been a faithful viewer of my television program, "Beverly Exercise," called to tell me she had stopped exercising and had gained 35 pounds.

"Beverly," she said, "this morning I decided to start trying to lose weight. Instead of eating a stack of pancakes when I fed the children, I ate only one."

I thought to myself, *Why have a pancake at all?* Although some pancake mixes are lower in fat than others, it's the butter and syrup heaped on top that does the damage. The total calories from fat in a serving of pancakes stacks up to a whopping 40 to 60 percent!

Remember, eat only foods that have less than 30 percent of their total calories from fat. Start your day off right with a nutritious, low-fat breakfast of oatmeal or bran flakes with fresh fruit and skim milk. That kind of breakfast will keep you going long after the pancakes and syrup have been digested.

Lord, help me to be wise and able to understand Your will for me
in every area of my life. Fill me with Your Holy Spirit.

❖ January 13 ❖

Sticking to the Basics   Read: Psalm 119:33-48

Teach me, O Lord, to follow your decrees
then I will keep them to the end (Ps. 119:33;NIV).

Losing weight is like football — it's a game of "basics." As your health coach, I want you to focus on the basics. That's the most effective way to win the "battle of the bulge!"

Here are the basics for losing weight and keeping it off:

1. Eat slowly. It takes time for the body to feel full.
2. Remove all high calorie foods from your refrigerator and pantry. Stock them with healthy foods instead.
3. Eat less fat. Limit use of butter, salad dressings, oils, and cheese.
4. Eat more complex carbohydrates: fruits, vegetables, whole grains.
5. Bake and broil meat. Never fry anything. Steam or microwave vegetables.
6. Use skim milk and low-fat or non-fat dairy products.
7. Exercise regularly.
8. Seek out enjoyable activities that don't involve food.

Stick to the basics, and you'll be successful.

That is my prayer today, Lord. Help me to stick to the basics
of Your Holy Word, the Bible, for the rest of my life.

❖ January 14 ❖

Why We Overeat   Read: Matthew 10:24-42

Even the very hairs of your head are numbered. So don't be afraid;
you are worth more than many sparrows (Matt. 10:30-31;NIV).

People overeat for different reasons. Some are depressed and lonely; others have no self-control; some feel unloved, and others are fearful. I know because I've turned to food for all of those reasons. But we all know food is not the answer to our problems. In fact, overeating only makes matters worse.

Let me introduce you to the person who set me free from my bondage to food. He's the one who has every hair on your head numbered. Why? Because He loves you and is interested in every detail of your life. If He takes the time to count the hairs on your head every day (they come and go, you know) then He cares about your feelings and your needs. You are of great value to God. Let Him heal your hurts and loneliness and take away your fears. He loves you and wants to help you in every area of your life.

Jesus, I know You care about me and the little details of my life.
I ask You to take away my fears and put my trust in You.

❖ January 15 ❖

What Makes You Fat?

Read: Psalm 73

Thou shalt guide me with thy counsel, and afterward
receive me to glory (Ps. 73:24).

The average American consumes as much as eight times more fat per day than his/her body needs. In fact, one tablespoon of vegetable oil provides all the daily fat our bodies need. Most of the fat we eat is stored as fat on our bodies.

Foods high in fat remain in your stomach longer after you eat them than low-fat foods. Your stomach empties within three hours following a meal, but French fried potatoes may still be in your stomach the next day!

Fat makes you fat because it slows the digestion and absorption of food. In experiments where animals were fed a totally fat diet, they had zero metabolism after eating. Their body activity fell so low, it was as if they had not eaten at all. Why? Because the body has to put forth very little effort to break down fat for storage.

The next time you hold a chocolate bar in your hand or reach for those potato chips, remember — *the fat you eat is the fat you wear.*

*Lord, as I seek to change my eating habits,
please guide me into the truth and help me to gain the victory.*

❖ January 16 ❖

Finding the Hidden Fat

Read: 2 Corinthians 4:1-15

. . . Let light shine out of darkness . . . (2 Cor. 4:6;NIV).

If I asked you to name several high-fat foods, you'd probably list butter, sour cream, and ice cream. What about peanut butter? Yes, you're right, 60 to 80 percent of its calories come from fat. That means, if a tablespoon of Skippy has 100 calories, up to 80 percent of those calories are fat calories! And tartar sauce? It is 95 percent fat calories!

Would you consider eggs a high-fat food? You probably know they're high in cholesterol, but did you also know they are in the 60-80 percent fat calorie range? If you scramble only the white of an egg, your fat intake is reduced to below 20 percent. That's what we're looking for! Foods that are under 30 percent fat. Bagels are another low-fat food that have only 0-20 percent fat calories. A homemade biscuit, however, has 40-60 percent of its calories in fat. Whole-grain bread, without the butter, would be a much better choice. Almost all fruits and vegetables fall within the 0-20 percent fat range, and you'd do well to make them an essential part of your low-fat diet.

*Thank you for your Word, Lord,
so I don't have to walk in the darkness.*

Fat Souls   Read: Proverbs 11

The liberal soul shall be made fat: and he that watereth
shall be watered also himself (Prov. 11:25).

When God's Word speaks of being "fat," it is referring to our souls and not our bodies. How do you become "fat in the Lord?" As one writer put it: Be F-aithful, A-vailable, and T-eachable. I take that to mean we should be faithful to read God's Word; available to be used by the Holy Spirit; and able to be easily taught by God and by others.

What about those who water? The New International Version of the Bible translates it this way: "He who refreshes others will himself be refreshed." That means as you gain new information on nutrition, share your knowledge with others. As we do that, God will give us opportunities to share our faith with others, too. As you begin to share with others what God has done in your life, you'll be refreshed both within and without — and your soul will be fat instead of your body!

Lord, help me to be faithful, available, and teachable
so I can reach out to others with the good news of salvation.

Who's the Boss?   Read: Psalm 61

From the end of the earth will I cry unto thee, when my heart is
overwhelmed: lead me to the rock that is higher than I (Ps. 61:2).

When you think of the typical "boss," do you picture an overweight fellow who washes down his lunch with a soda and walks around with a cigar hanging out of his mouth?

According to a recent study, however, the top business executives pay more attention to their health than any other segment of society. Only 10 percent of them smoke, and almost half are ex-smokers. Four out of five have regular physical check-ups, and their blood pressure is in the normal range. Two out of three exercise regularly, even though they may work long hours.

What about you? Do you make time for exercise? Have you stopped smoking? Are you eating a low-fat diet? If you don't take care of yourself, no one else will do it for you. Personal health is your own responsibility.

Maybe you don't know where to begin, and the thought of completely changing your lifestyle overwhelms you. Look to the Lord for help and put Him in control of your life. He is much greater than you or me.

Lord, please give me the strength to turn from
destructive habits and form new healthy ones. Thank You.

❖ January 19 ❖

Clean Living   Read: Deuteronomy 11:13-32

> Fix these words of mine in your hearts and
> minds . . . so that your days . . . may
> be many . . . (Deut. 11:18,21;NIV).

Want to live a long life? If you're a smoker, the single most important thing you can do to live a longer, healthier life is to quit smoking.

"But I don't smoke or drink," you say. You are like most Americans who live good, clean lives, but who have one major fault — the way they eat. That's why your choice of diet can influence your long-term health prospects more than any other action you might take. What should you do? 1. Eat more complex carbohydrates. 2. Eat more fiber-containing foods. 3. Eat more foods rich in iron and calcium. 4. Eat less fat and salt.

Dietary factors play a role in some of the leading causes of death for Americans, including heart disease and cancer. It's time you cleaned up your act all the way and started focusing on eating right. Most important, however, is your relationship to God and obedience to His commands.

Lord, help me to keep Your commands and live in a
way that will prolong my life and bring glory to You.

❖ January 20 ❖

Fish, Not Steak   Read: 1 Timothy 4:9-16

> Watch your life and doctrine closely . . . (1 Tim. 4:16;NIV).

Eating fish instead of steak at dinner in the evening could sharply cut your risk of a heart attack the next morning. New studies suggest that high-fat meals — like steak and French fries — put the blood into a hypercoagulation state within six or seven hours, raising the risk that dangerous artery-clogging blood clots will occur.

Researchers realize that the short-term effect of high-fat meals on blood clotting can affect some people. Low-fat meals, however, can quickly reverse the problem. In fact, if you take fat out of your diet, you don't have to wait years to lower your risk of heart disease. You can begin with your next meal and avoid serious consequences the next morning. All it takes is a little more thought about what you eat.

By paying attention to yourself and your body's needs, you can ward off heart attacks and live longer. That will give you more time to teach others about Jesus Christ.

Lord, help me to pay close attention to the things I do and say.

❖ January 21 ❖

Cholesterol — Friend or Foe?　　　Read: 1 John 4:1-6

> Dear friends, do not believe every spirit, but test the spirits
> to see whether they are from God . . . (1 John 4:1;NIV).

With so much talk about cholesterol, many people believe that it is public enemy number one. That is simply not true. We need it in order to live. But the liver makes all we need. We don't need to add any.

The cholesterol produced by our bodies and that which we eat is carried through our bloodstream in molecules called "lipoproteins" (fat plus protein). There are two forms — one is bad and the other is good. The bad form is carried to the liver, and is called LDL. The good form, HDL, is carried from the liver for discharge from our body. Too much bad LDL causes clogged arteries.

Actually, it's not only cholesterol-laden calories that we need to avoid, but also cholesterol-boosting fat calories. You see, a product can be labeled "no cholesterol" and still have cholesterol-boosting fat. Be wise! Always look on the label for the fat content.

God's Word tells us not to be so gullible about everything — especially in spiritual matters. We need to test every new doctrine or teaching to make sure it lines up with Scripture.

Lord, show me how to determine what is truth
so I can know what is truly from You.

❖ January 22 ❖

Water, Water, Everywhere　　　Read: John 7:32-39

> . . . Jesus stood and said in a loud voice, If anyone is thirsty,
> let him come to me and drink (John 7:37;NIV).

Water, water, everywhere, but not a drop to drink." This ancient seaman's problem is not ours in America. We have plenty of drinkable water, but the problem is we don't drink it.

Just because it is wintertime and the weather is cooler doesn't mean it's time to forget about water. In the hot summer months, when you can feel the sweat pouring off, it's easy to drink 6 to 8 glasses a day. But when in cold weather, water isn't as appealing.

That's the way it is with us, too. When our hearts turn cold, we don't sense our need of a Saviour. Jesus, however, doesn't force us to come to Him. He invites us, hoping we will accept the offer of His love and salvation.

Jesus, I need You in my life. I come to You and accept
You as my Lord and Saviour.

❖ January 23 ❖

Dying of Thirst?   Read: John 4:1-26

Whoever drinks the water I give him will never thirst . . . (John 4:14;NIV).

In the colder months, there are several situations in which additional water is required.

When you exercise or do winter sports: Exercising causes you to perspire and body fluid is lost — even in cold weather. *If you are sick:* Dehydration is always a threat with illness. Fever and diarrhea can also deplete the body of water. *If you are dieting:* Your kidneys work harder than usual when weight loss is occurring.

Dehydration is deceptive. Your body's water level can be low without your realizing it. Thirst is not an adequate reminder of your need for water. Instead, you need to force yourself to think about drinking more water.

Sometimes we have to force ourselves to think about spiritual matters, too. Jesus knows that every person has an emptiness inside that only He can fill. That's why He can offer us "a spring of water welling up to eternal life." Have you accepted His offer? Don't wait until you're dying of thirst!

Jesus, I accept Your offer. Let the water of Your Holy Spirit spring up within me and quench my thirsting soul.

❖ January 24 ❖

Water for the Journey   Read: Genesis 21:1-20

Abraham rose up early in the morning, and took bread, and a
bottle of water, and gave it unto Hagar . . . (Gen. 21:14).

Anyone who's crossed a desert knows you'd better take water along with you. Abraham knew that, too, and gave Hagar what she needed for her journey. Later, God miraculously supplied Hagar's need for water in order to save Ishmael. God also knows what you need for your journey through life. Sometimes He may use others to meet your needs; other times He sends a miracle. One thing is for sure, He is faithful to provide for you along the way.

Your body needs water — and plenty of it — every day. In order to get an adequate amount, some of my viewers tell me they take along a travel mug of water with them in the car when they are running errands. Others keep a glass of water with them at their work station or, when they're at home, nearby on the kitchen counter.

Water is essential to keeping your body working right and cleansing out toxins. Drinking water is a habit you need to develop.

Lord God, I trust You to provide everything I need for my journey through life. I know You are always faithful.

❖ January 25 ❖

Beating the Blues Read: Psalm 42

> Why are you downcast, O my soul? Why so disturbed within me? Put
> your hope in God, for I will yet praise him . . . (Ps. 42:11;NIV).

This time of the year a lot of people find themselves fighting "the blues."
The holiday season is over and life has settled back into a normal routine. To
make matters worse, you may have gained weight with all the celebrating, and
now you're battling discouragement. It's easy to turn to food for solace. But
don't give in to your cravings. If you do, you may overeat and end up feeling
more depressed than before.

When the blues drive you to eat, but you're not really hungry, try
something comforting (but calorie-free) like an herbal tea. If you're hungry as
well as blue, eat nonfat frozen yogurt, then go for a walk. It takes about ten to
twenty minutes for the carbohydrates to enter your bloodstream. So by the time
you return from your walk, your desire to binge will be gone.

Remember, you can't binge away the blues but you can praise them away!

Heavenly Father, deliver me from these feelings of hopelessness
and discouragement. Help me to put my hope in You.

❖ January 26 ❖

I Was Hungry Read: Matthew 25:31-46

> For I was hungry and you gave me something to eat, I was thirsty
> and you gave me something to drink . . . (Matt. 25:35;NIV).

Allowing yourself to get so hungry that you feel starved can set you up
to overeat. When you are really hungry, you are likely to eat too fast and too
much. What can you do when you are starved? Begin your meal with soup.
Soup can help tame your appetite.

In a research study, one group of people was given soup and the other
group was given cheese and crackers, which were equal in calories to the soup.
Then both groups were given a full meal. Those who had eaten the tomato soup
ate 25 percent fewer calories!

Why did the soup work better? Because it takes up a larger space in the
stomach, and most of its calories come from carbohydrates rather than fat.
Carbohydrates are more satisfying. In addition, hot soup provides a psychological feeling of well-being that relaxes a nervous, gnawing appetite.

Most of us don't know what real hunger is. Instead of focusing on your
own desires or problems, look for ways to help others who are in need.

Jesus, forgive me for being so concerned about myself.
I ask You to use me to help others who are in need.

❖ January 27 ❖

Taking Responsibility   Read: Romans 8:1-17

> If the Spirit of Him who raised Jesus from the dead is living
> in you, He . . . will also give life to your mortal bodies
> through His Spirit, who lives in you (Rom. 8:11;NIV).

How many times have you tried to diet and failed? Is there a secret to losing weight and keeping it off? Yes. A study found that people who had lost 20 percent of their body weight and kept it off had one thing in common: They accepted the responsibility for losing the weight. They realized that nobody or no program was going to do it for them: they had to do it themselves. They were the ones who succeeded.

As Christians, however, we don't have to "do it ourselves." It's true we still have to take responsibility for the way we eat and exercise, but we have an added advantage — the power of God's Holy Spirit. He can help you lose weight and live a healthy lifestyle of eating right and exercising. If you know Jesus Christ as your personal Saviour, recognize the strength that you have today.

> *Lord God, I need Your help to lose weight and maintain a healthy*
> *lifestyle. Fill me with the power of Your Holy Spirit.*

❖ January 28 ❖

Finishing What We Start   Read: Luke 14:25-35

> Suppose one of you wants to build a tower. Will he not first
> sit down and estimate the cost to see if he has enough
> money to complete it? (Luke 14:28;NIV).

How many of us have started a weight loss program and not completed it? Or kept it up until we lost weight and then quit, regaining every pound?

This problem was the basis of a study conducted by researchers who wanted to know the long-term "success rate" of weight-loss programs — including protein diets, carbohydrate diets, and diet support groups. They found that most people had not lost very much weight. Further review showed the weight-loss programs didn't help keep weight off. Many times, however a weight-loss program can get you eating right and exercising. You may need a structured program to help you reach your goals. Before you begin, however, sit down and decide whether you have the money, the determination, and the spiritual strength to finish the task of losing the weight and keeping it off. Then, ask the Lord to help you see it through to the end.

> *Lord, give me wisdom to know what it will take for me*
> *to succeed at losing weight.*

❖ January 29 ❖

Losing for Good

Read: Luke 9:18-27

> For whoever wants to save his life will lose it, but whoever
> loses his life for me will save it (Luke 9:24;NIV).

Almost anyone can lose a few pounds if they put their mind to it. But what about losing all your excess weight and keeping it off for the rest of your life? That's the hard part.

Why are some people able to lose weight and keep it off? Do they have certain characteristics in common? Yes. Research has found that those who succeed at keeping off lost weight have a sound knowledge of nutrition, exercise regularly, and are self-motivated.

The bottom line in long-term weight loss seems to be a strong desire to bring healthful habits into your life. It may be tough, but it's not impossible. It simply requires a lifelong commitment to a higher quality of life.

God loves and cares for you. That's why He sent His Son, Jesus Christ, to be your Saviour. If you give your life to Jesus, you will find more peace, love, joy, and fulfillment than you ever dreamed possible.

Lord Jesus, thank You for giving Your life for me on
the Cross. I now give my life to You.

❖ January 30 ❖

Cleaning Up Your Act

Read: Psalm 51:7-19

> Cleanse me with hyssop, and I
> will be clean . . . (Ps. 51:7;NIV).

Shortly after I was saved, God showed me that I had a gluttonous spirit. In a restaurant, I had carefully ordered fried chicken breast — no dark meat for me! The waitress mistakenly brought me a huge thigh. I remember looking at that chicken thigh in absolute dismay. I really wanted the white chicken breast. Why, I had been waiting for it all morning!

My reaction clearly showed me that I had let my flesh get out of control in my lust for that chicken breast! That may seem like a small problem, but it signaled to me that I needed to be cleansed of that gluttonous spirit toward certain foods.

God doesn't expect instant perfection from us, but He does want obedience. As He shows us, little by little, the sin in our lives and we confess it, victory will come. It won't happen overnight, but, as we look to God, He begins a work in our lives.

Dear Lord, show me any area of my life today
that needs cleansing.

❖ **January 31** ❖

Fleshly Lusts

Read: 1 Peter 2:3-12

> Dearly beloved, I beseech you as strangers and pilgrims, abstain
> from fleshly lusts which war against the soul (1 Pet. 2:11).

Let's face it: Food is one of the most common fleshly lusts. Lusting after food is sin and can bring on gluttonous acts. I believe this grieves the Lord. Many times this kind of lusting leads to overeating and going on a binge. As a result, many people, especially women, fall into the trap of anorexia and bulimia in a pursuit to be thin.

Let's learn to approach our food as fuel for our body and not as a way of satisfying our flesh. After all, God's Word commands us to "abstain from fleshly lusts." Why? Because these kinds of wrong attitudes and behaviors can attack our soul and may eventually keep us from a pure relationship with God.

Remember, God wants the very best for your life. That's why it's important to obey all His commands.

Lord Jesus, give me the power, through Your Holy Spirit, to
abstain from lusting after food and other sinful desires.

❖ February 1 ❖

A Walk on the Light Side

Read: Romans 10

*. . . The man who does these things will
live by them (Rom. 10:5;NIV).*

Did you know that a simple walk around the block could help save your life? It's true. According to the American Heart Association, even leisurely activities can have an effect on your heart and your life — whether they are light, moderate, or intense.

A *light* activity is anything from bowling to raking leaves. *Moderate* activities include gardening or ballroom dancing, and *intense* activities are back-packing, jogging, fast walking, and shoveling snow.

The higher the activity level, the lower the rate of heart disease, but even lower levels of physical activity still provide some protection from heart disease. Those who had sedentary lifestyles, however, had the greatest risk of developing problems. Exercise — even light activity like daily walking — can help prevent disease.

Life is too short to waste it sitting around watching TV and eating junk food! Get up and get moving. It could save your life *and* your soul!

*Lord, help me to keep Your commandments and be
mindful of how I live my life.*

❖ February 2 ❖

Creeping Obesity

Read: Proverbs 28

*He who trusts in himself is a fool, but he who
walks in wisdom is kept safe (Prov. 28:26;NIV).*

When we are young, the muscles in our body are long and lean with very little fat. As we get older and become less active, however, fat can invade the muscles, making them short and squat.

In fact, muscles can become so saturated with fat that they just can't hold anymore. Where does the fat go? To the outside of the muscle. The scales, however, do not reflect this change because the fat that is replacing muscle weighs less than muscle.

When the muscle has finally wasted away, we realize that we are getting fatter! This is called "creeping obesity" because it creeps up on you, and you don't even know it!

God's Word gives us wisdom for practical, everyday living. Wisdom tells us to exercise these bodies. It is foolish to destroy them by inactivity.

Lord, teach me to be wise and not foolish.

❖ February 3 ❖

Working Together   Read: Ecclesiastes 4:1-12

Two *are* better than one; because they have a good
reward for their labour (Eccles. 4:9).

You can reverse "creeping obesity" with exercise and a proper diet. The two go together. Exercise will cause your muscles to be developed, toned, and increased. And there is an added bonus! As the muscle gets leaner, your metabolism speeds up, and you burn more calories. Why is that? Let me explain. Since you have lost muscle and replaced it with fat, you have also lost your calorie-burning power. Why? Because producing muscle uses up more calories. That's why you need to do more than reduce the amount of food you are eating.

Dieting without exercise doesn't work. Why? Because it causes you to lose the fat that is right under the skin and does nothing to the fat that has replaced the muscle.

Some things naturally work well together, like diet and exercise. You and God are also an unbeatable team. If you work together with Him, you'll have a good return on your efforts.

Lord, help me to work together with You to
accomplish Your purposes for my life.

❖ February 4 ❖

Fat-Burning Bonus   Read: Deuteronomy 8

He gave you manna to eat
in the desert . . . (Deut. 8:16;NIV).

You can increase your fat-burning potential in two simple, yet effective ways. *First,* eat breakfast. Some experts say your body burns calories at a slower rate as you sleep. Breakfast is your metabolism's wake-up call, kicking it into the calorie-burning mode. If you don't eat something in the morning, you may ultimately burn fewer calories throughout the day.

Second, don't sit around after you eat. A moderate workout right after a meal can give you a fat-burning bonus. If you take a brisk three-mile walk on an *empty* stomach, you'll burn about 300 calories. If you go walking on a *full* stomach, you not only burn those 300-plus calories, you also burn another 15 percent of that total. That's another 45 calories! Sounds like a good deal to me.

Just make sure your workout is nothing more than a brisk walk.

Like the Israelites in the desert, we need to gather the "manna" from God's Word, so we'll have everything we need for the day.

Lord, I come to You this morning, looking to You to meet my needs.

❖ February 5 ❖

Fat Burners   Read: Ecclesiastes 9:1-12

> Whatsoever thy hand findeth to do,
> do it with thy might . . . (Eccles. 9:10).

What's the best fat burning exercise? Research has shown that exercises that vigorously work both your arms and legs are better fat burners than exercises like running or walking that involve only your legs. Cross-country skiing rates highest in lab tests for burning the most calories per minute because you use your legs, upper body, and even your torso.

Stationary rowing and stationary bicycles with levers you push and pull with your arms as you pedal also rate high.

When it comes to low-to-moderate exercise, like walking or stationary cycling, the longer you do it, the more fat you burn. The number of calories you burn in three minutes of moderate exercise is equal to about the number you'd burn during one minute of intense exercise.

Find the exercise that works best for you, and then do it unto the Lord with all your might! That's the secret to physical and spiritual growth.

Lord, help me to strive to do my best at everything I do.

❖ February 6 ❖

The Slender Gender?   Read: Genesis 1:26-31

> So God created man in his own image . . . male
> and female created he them (Gen. 1:27).

Did you know that men and women differ in weight gain? She skips the fatty desserts and hits the gym four times a week to stay fit and trim. Her husband, however, eats the same as she eats but rarely exercises — and still looks pretty good. Who said life was fair?

The truth of the matter is: Women need more exercise than men just to stay trim. Why? Men have more muscle mass to start with, and this means they burn more calories when they exercise.

Apparently, God designed men and women to fulfill specific purposes. So instead of complaining, let's appreciate the differences and use our uniqueness to bring glory to Him. If, however, we want our husbands to shape up, then we have to embrace a healthy lifestyle ourselves, including exercise. Walking, jogging, or riding bikes is a great way for couples to spend time together and get in shape at the same time.

Thank You, Lord for the special differences You
designed into us as men and women.

❖ February 7 ❖

Never Too Old   Read: Luke 2:21-40

There was also a prophetess, Anna . . . she was eighty-four.
She never left the temple but worshiped
night and day, fasting and praying (Luke 2:36-37;NIV).

If activities that a few years ago posed no problem have lately seemed to tax or drain your strength, your problem may be loss of muscle tissue.

I recently came across an article in which a female sports gynecologist told how her grandmother and great aunt lived to be in their mid-nineties. Although they were really quite healthy women for their ages, they became helpless due to self-imposed inactivity. Because of their fear of slipping on ice and breaking a hip, they chose to hibernate in their house all winter. Neighbors did their outdoor chores and shopping. The women did not even go to church.

After months of such inactivity, they became too frail to climb stairs. So they settled on the first floor. Always bored and tired, they spent their days snacking, catnapping, and watching television. After a couple of such winters, they no longer had strength to enjoy summer activities such as gardening.

As long as we can, we must stay active — both physically and spiritually, serving the Lord even in our old age as Anna did.

Lord Jesus, help me to continue to serve You — both
spiritually and physically — throughout my life.

❖ February 8 ❖

Five a Day   Read: Genesis 1:1-19

. . . Let the land produce vegetation: seed-bearing plants and trees
on the land that bear fruit with seed in it . . . (Gen. 1:11;NIV).

Despite the fact that the state of California is known for its production of fruits and vegetables, its residents seldom take advantage of this wonderful produce. Only half of the people in California eat a piece of fruit each day, and one-third eat no vegetables on any given day! As a result, the California Department of Health Services began a "5 a Day for Better Health" campaign to encourage Californians to eat five servings of fruits and vegetables daily.

This is excellent advice for all of us! Complex carbohydrates (fruits and vegetables) are cholesterol free, low in fat, low in sodium, high in fiber, and low in calories. That's why eating more fruits and vegetables helps prevent heart disease and cancer. Now that's good news! Make sure you are having five servings of fruits and vegetables a day. God created fruits and vegetables for us to enjoy, most of which even come with their own wrappers!

Thank You for creating fruits and vegetables for us to eat.

❖ February 9 ❖

Overeating Remedy   Read: Genesis 1:20-31

> Then God said, "I give you every seed-bearing plant on the
> face of the whole earth and every tree that has fruit with
> seed in it. They will be yours for food" (Gen. 1:29;NIV).

Do you have a tendency to overeat? If so, you may be interested to know that pectin, a natural, water-soluble fiber, is useful in treating overeating in obese people because it slows the digestive process. Where do you find pectin? In fruits like apples, grapes, grapefruit, berries, and plums.

During a study, pectin was added to the meals of nine overweight people. As a result, their stomachs emptied slower, and they felt full more quickly. Because of this, they ate less and lost an average of 6.6 pounds over a period of one month.

Because pectin also aids digestion, it helps you feel full so you do not overeat. By simply including fresh fruit in your diet, you will feel more satisfied.

God, the Creator of our bodies, gave us different kinds of fruit to eat. Let's take advantage of this God-given food that is low in fat, sodium, and calories.

*Lord God, thank You for providing fruit for us to eat. Please
give me a desire to include more fruit in my diet.*

❖ February 10 ❖

Trial or Challenge?   Read: John 16:17-33

> . . . In this world you will have trouble.
> But take heart! I have overcome
> the world (John 16:33;NIV).

The Scriptures are quite clear that there is a suffering that comes to each of us. None of us is immune. Our attitude in the midst of trials, however, often determines the outcome. If you consider your trial as a challenge to overcome, God can use it to help you grow both spiritually and personally.

Do you have a weight problem? Are you struggling with an addiction to food, smoking, alcohol, or some other sin? Try to think of it as a challenge that, in the process of conquering it, can be used to make you a stronger person. You'd be amazed at how God can turn your weakness into His strength.

If you allow God the freedom to work in your life, you'll discover that the area that was once the weakest has become your strong point. I know because it happened to me!

*Heavenly Father, help me to see my trials as opportunities for
You to work Your will in my life. I submit myself to You.*

❖ February 11 ❖

Live Life!   Read: John 10:1-10

... I have come that they may have life, and have it
to the full (John 10:10;NIV).

What causes compulsive dieting or gaining? It is almost always the result of an underlying problem. Maybe you were overweight as a child with critical parents. Maybe your emotions are out of balance, or maybe you have very low self-esteem.

If you withdraw from others for the sake of a diet, you are on the road to addictive behavior. Be realistic. Allow diet, exercise, and nutrition to be a balanced part of a normal lifestyle. Don't wait until you lose weight to live! That kind of thinking is destructive and usually brings about more weight gain.

By getting out and enjoying life, you will have more to think about other than food. Don't allow food and dieting to become your life!

Jesus came to give us life — an abundant life that He wants us to live to the fullest. Ask Him to come into your life. He has wonderful things planned for you!

Dear Jesus, thank You for coming so that I could have eternal life
in heaven and a fulfilled life here on earth. I give my life to You.

❖ February 12 ❖

Encourage One Another   Read: Hebrews 10:19-31

Let us not give up meeting together, as some are in the habit of
doing, but let us encourage one another ... (Heb. 10:25;NIV).

Yesterday we talked about the need to enjoy life. Part of abundant living involves associating with other people. In fact, social reinforcement is necessary, even crucial, to living. Dieting is not! When other people reinforce you, you feel better about yourself and are more likely to succeed in any endeavor you undertake — including losing weight. If you isolate yourself, there is no chance for reinforcement.

That's why you especially need the fellowship of other Christians. You need their encouragement, and they need yours. Don't get out of the habit of going to church just because you are overweight or on a diet or feel you have nothing attractive to wear. Ask God to give you the courage to obey His Word and go to church. The blessings you receive — and are able to give others — will strengthen and encourage you to become the person God created you to be.

Lord, forgive me for not wanting to go to church.
Give me the courage to face others so they can
encourage me. And help me to be a blessing to them.

❖ February 13 ❖

Simple Ways   Read: Proverbs 14:1-18

> The wisdom of the prudent is to give thought to their
> ways, but the folly of fools is deception (Prov. 14:8;NIV).

How many grams of fat do you need each day? Women need between 20 and 40 grams, and men need 30 to 60 grams. Most people, however, eat at least twice that much fat! How can you lower your fat intake? Here are a few simple ways.

Eliminate two of the main sources of fat calories in our diets — cheese and mayonnaise. This will also help reduce your cholesterol levels. Eliminate fast food items from your diet. These are loaded with fat. Eat simple, low-fat meals. *Breakfast* would include fruit, cereal, skim (not low-fat) milk. A good *lunch:* water-packed tuna and whole-grain bread. *Supper* may consist of fish or some other lean meat, such as turkey or chicken, vegetables, potato, rice, or pasta (seasoned without butter), and fruit. Use wisdom to establish new eating habits. That's the sign of a prudent person.

> *Lord, help me to think about the way I eat and*
> *be wise enough to make changes for the better.*

❖ February 14 ❖

Valentine Chocolates   Read: Psalm 78:17-31

> They ate till they had more
> than enough, for he had given them
> what they craved (Ps. 78:29;NIV).

It's Valentine's Day and to many women that means receiving a box of chocolates! Some receive this gift with pleasure, others with panic. Why? Because, many say, "I'm addicted to chocolate!" One piece, and their diet goes down the drain.

Is it possible to be addicted to chocolate? Yes. Scientists believe the craving for sweets is similar to the craving for opiates like morphine.

What is the best way to get over chocolate cravings? Go cold turkey, and get the substance completely out of your system! For one full week don't eat chocolate or any foods with sugar and/or fat. Instead, eat fruit for dessert. Drink lots of water. Take deep breaths. Exercise every chance you get. For some people, it's the only way to break the addiction.

Some people joke about their addiction to chocolate, but Scripture teaches us that it is no laughing matter.

> *Lord, help me to bring my cravings under*
> *the control of Your Holy Spirit.*

❖ February 15 ❖

A Pleasing Aroma   Read: Leviticus 3:1-17

> The priest shall burn them on the altar as food,
> an offering made by fire, a pleasing aroma.
> All the fat is the Lord's (Lev. 3:16;NIV).

In the animal sacrifices spoken of in the Old Testament, and specifically the fellowship offering, the fat of the animal was always reserved for God. It was never consumed by the priest or by the worshipper. It belonged to God.

This is a principle we can use to help remind us of our need to avoid fat. As you sacrifice fat in your diet, give it to God. Make a point of saying that you gladly sacrifice this part of your food to God so that you can be a temple that is pleasing to Him. He will reward your decision. Your sacrifice will be a sweet-smelling savor to God!

Begin today to give that fat to God — the fat in your foods and the fat in your body. He alone can change you so that you can become all He desires you to be!

Lord, I gladly sacrifice the fat in my diet to You so You can make my body a temple that is pleasing in Your sight. I offer to You all the fat that I like to eat as a sacrifice of love to You.

❖ February 16 ❖

Food — an Idol?   Read: 1 John 5:21

Dear children, keep yourselves from idols (1 John 5:21;NIV).

The Amplified Version of the Bible translates this verse by saying we should keep ourselves from anything that would take God's position from first place in our life.

When "weight control" becomes the main goal in life, the main topic of our conversation, or the main focus of your day, then you are on a dangerous road. You may have gone beyond simply setting a goal of losing weight, and are now taking dieting to an extreme. The goal may have been for athletic reasons, for social reasons, even for medical reasons, or to have better health. But if taken to the extreme, problems can result.

That's why God's Word tells us to keep away from making idols in our lives. Has your diet become your god? Are you making sacrifices (unrealistic ones) to it? If so, you can begin again today. Give God first place and allow Him to produce balance in your life today!

Lord God, forgive me for making losing weight more important then You. Help me to make You Lord of every area of my life.

❖ February 17 ❖

The Thief
Read: John 10:10-21

The thief comes only to steal and kill and destroy . . . (John 10:10;NIV).

An unbalanced focus on dieting and losing weight often leads to eating disorders. An eating disorder can result when dieting begins to equal, in your mind, beauty and success. Not dieting then begins to mean failure. When you try to achieve internal well-being by external means, the result will eventually be bondage and depression.

The two most common eating disorders are anorexia and bulimia. The anorexic will deny she is losing too much weight and continue to suffer for the cause of being skinny. And the skinnier the better.

Diet doctors define bulimics as people who binge on food, then force themselves to vomit.

If these symptoms sound familiar, get help right away. These are serious disorders that can lead to death. Don't allow Satan to steal your health or destroy your life.

Lord, help me to get my heart and mind and spirit focused on You.
Keep me from falling prey to Satan's attempts to destroy my life.

❖ February 18 ❖

A Living Sacrifice
Read: Romans 12:1-8

Therefore, I urge you, brothers, in view of God's mercy, to offer
your bodies as living sacrifices, holy and pleasing to God
this is your spiritual act of worship (Rom. 12:1;NIV).

Have you worshipped God today? When we offer our bodies as a living sacrifice, that is spiritual worship. It is also our reasonable service. Now *that* is a great reason for keeping in shape and watching what we eat. Not that we will make nutrition our God. No. But the reason we choose to be good stewards of our bodies is out of worship and service to God who dwells in our body, His temple.

In an eighteenth century document called *The Manual for Interior Souls*, the author states, "We must go to our meals in the spirit of holy simplicity paying more attention to God than to what we eat." We need to offer our bodies as a living sacrifice and make our eating a time of spiritual worship.

In view of God's mercy toward us, how can we do anything less than try to please Him in everything we do — including eating.

Lord God, I offer my body to You as a living sacrifice.
I ask You to take it and make it holy and pleasing
in Your sight. I love You, and I worship You.

❖ February 19 ❖

Pure Motives

Read: Daniel 1

> But Daniel resolved not to defile himself with the royal
> food and wine, and he asked the chief official for
> permission not to defile himself this way (Dan. 1:8;NIV).

There are lots of reasons for us to diet and exercise: to look good for our husbands; to fit into that new bathing suit; to impress the ladies at the office; to stay healthy and free from disease. While not all of these are selfish reasons, they can be as fleeting as the weight that is lost. Our motivation for losing weight and staying healthy must be based on something more consistent than vanity and what we think is important at the moment.

As a young man, Daniel, not wanting to disobey the dietary laws of God's law, decided not to eat the king's rich food and wine. He was motivated — not out of legalism — but out of a desire to please and obey God. I suggest that you approach the selection of the foods for your diet in the same way. Then your motives will remain pure; you will not become legalistic; and God will give you success in changing your eating habits.

Lord God, purify my motives for wanting to lose
weight and look good and stay healthy. May all I
do be done out of love and obedience to You.

❖ February 20 ❖

Miracle Drug?

Read: Matthew 8:1-17

> . . . He took up our infirmities and carried our diseases (Matt. 8:17;NIV).

There is a powerful prescription doctors are now handing out to their older patients. It lowers cholesterol, blood pressure, and reduces the risks of heart disease and cancer. It makes you stronger, helps you look better, and boosts your spirits. Some medical experts say it may even slow the aging process itself.

A new miracle drug you ask? No, it's exercise, and it's about time you start taking some. Some doctors now say that getting regular exercise is the most important thing you can do to prevent heart disease and other ailments. Studies show that exercise can substantially reduce your chances of dying of heart disease, cancer, or other causes.

God's Word says that we can ask — and expect — Jesus to heal us when we are sick. But we must also work *with* Him and not *against* Him by eating right and exercising.

Jesus, I know You can heal me of my infirmities and my diseases.
Help me to work with You to bring about my healing.

❖ February 21 ❖

Too Much Earwax?   Read: Psalm 34:15-22

> The eyes of the Lord are on the righteous and his ears
> are attentive to their cry (Ps. 34:15;NIV).

Did you know that earwax is a good thing? It prevents infection by trapping dust and other foreign matter. Earwax also lubricates the inside of the ear, helping prevent itching and dryness.

Under normal circumstances, a little bit of earwax is always being removed from the ear canal by the movement of the jaw in talking or eating. Trying to remove earwax with a cotton tipped swab is dangerous. You can push the wax farther down into the ear canal or injure the eardrum.

If, however, the glands that produce earwax are overactive, too much can be produced. Wax can obstruct the canal, causing itching, ringing in the ears, dizziness, or hearing loss. Over-the-counter products designed to soften and remove earwax can be helpful, but you should check with your doctor first before using them.

It is wonderful that God's ears are always open to hear our faintest cries!

> *Lord, thank You for always watching out for me*
> *and always listening to my prayers.*

❖ February 22 ❖

Getting Tested   Read: 1 Peter 1:1-12

> These have come so that your faith . . .
> may be proved genuine . . . (1 Pet. 1:7;NIV).

If you've never had a test to determine your cholesterol level, you need to do so as soon as possible. Call your family physician or the Health Department for information on where you can get a test for cholesterol.

When you have blood taken for cholesterol testing, make sure you are seated 10 minutes before the test. The reading could be off 5 percent if you have been standing. If you are on medication, have a virus, or are pregnant, let the tester know. If the blood is drawn from your finger, don't let them squeeze your finger. That dilutes the blood sample, thus lowering the results.

Life is full of tests. Even God sometimes tests our faith. Why? So *we* can determine the level of our faith. When the results are known, we will know whether our faith in God is strong or weak. If it is weak, then we can take steps to strengthen our faith for the next test.

> *Father God, help me to face the trials of life with joy*
> *and pass the tests of faith with perseverance.*

❖ February 23 ❖

Safe Levels   Read: Proverbs 18:1-10

> The name of the Lord is a strong tower; the righteous
> run to it and are safe (Prov. 18:10;NIV).

What is a safe cholesterol reading? Two hundred or less. If your cholesterol level rises above 200, your risk increases more and more. If your tested level is under 200, you are doing fine; but you still need to stick with a diet and exercise program to keep your cholesterol low.

If your level is above 200 you should change your diet immediately by adding cholesterol-fighting soluble fiber and by reducing your intake of fats — especially saturated fats and dietary cholesterol. Be aware of the other risk factors: being a male, family history of coronary heart disease, cigarette smoking, high blood pressure, diabetes, and being overweight.

We can do everything possible to eat right and stay healthy, but even that holds no guarantees. We must look to the Lord as our source of strength. When we do, He promises to keep us safe. Let's run to Him today!

> *Lord, You are my strong tower. I know whenever*
> *I turn to You for help, I will be kept safe.*

❖ February 24 ❖

The Good and the Bad   Read: 1 Kings 3

> Give therefore thy servant an understanding heart to judge thy people,
> that I may discern between good and bad . . . (1 Kings 3:9).

The desirable range for cholesterol is between 130 and 199. Borderline high is considered between 200 and 239. High is 240 and up!

If your cholesterol reading is over 200, you should have a lipoprotein analysis done by your doctor's office. This analysis will let you know how much of your blood cholesterol is composed of LDL cholesterol, which contributes to cholesterol build-up in the artery walls, and how much is derived from HDL, which cleans cholesterol from the bloodstream. The LDL "bad" cholesterol should be *under* 160 (preferably under 130). HDL "good" cholesterol should be *over* 40.

The answer to the cholesterol challenge is to increase the *good* cholesterol. How? By regular, vigorous exercise, losing weight, and giving up smoking. To decrease the *bad* cholesterol, LDL, you must change your diet. Since your body is already producing all the cholesterol it needs, it makes good sense to avoid all dietary cholesterol and saturated fats.

> *Lord, give me the wisdom to discern between those foods and*
> *actions that are good for me and those that are bad.*

❖ February 25 ❖

A Good Investment   Read: Mark 4:21-33

> . . . The kingdom of God is like . . . a mustard seed, which is the
> smallest seed you plant in the ground (Mark 4:30-31;NIV).

Tests reveal that lowering your cholesterol level even as little as 15 percent will result in lowering your heart risk by 30 percent. The facts prove that if you take one step to improving your cholesterol level, the benefits will be double what you did. That's a big return on a small investment!

If you're overweight, losing weight can raise your HDLs by 5 to 6 points. Moderate regular exercise, at least three times a week, will raise HDLs. For post menopausal women, estrogen supplements can raise HDL 4 to 5 points.

Although it is the smallest seed of all, it becomes the largest plant in the garden. Begin today to plant the seed of God's Word into your heart. As you do, you will reap double returns on your efforts and eternal rewards for your soul. Allow His Word to work in you today!

*Heavenly Father, I thank You for Your Word. Help me to plant it
in my heart so it can grow to be a blessing to many others.*

❖ February 26 ❖

Preventing Depression   Read: Psalm 30:8-12

> You turned my wailing into dancing; you removed my
> sackcloth and clothed me with joy (Ps. 30:11;NIV).

If you're depressed, don't just sit there — do something! If you have been down in the dumps, that's the best advice you can get.

Did you know that exercise helps relieve the symptoms of moderate depression? Psychiatrists have evidence that exercise may *prevent* these symptoms. People who get at least moderate exercise (enough to lose weight or lower blood pressure) may cut their risk of depressive symptoms by half.

How does exercise block the blues? It increases the production of substances that transmit messages between nerves. The more of these you have the less likely you are to be depressed. Exercise also causes your brain to produce opiates that makes you feel better. Best of all, exercise wards off depressive symptoms simply by raising your self-esteem! That's enough to make anyone want to go out and exercise!

The *best* medicine for depression is knowing Jesus Christ as Lord and Saviour. Only He can turn our sorrow into dancing and our sadness into gladness! Not even exercise can do that!

*Jesus, I ask You to turn my mourning into
dancing and my sadness into gladness.*

Boost Your Brain Power

Read: 2 Timothy 1

For God hath not given us the spirit of fear; but of power,
and of love, and of a sound mind (2 Tim. 1:7).

Do you sometimes find yourself unable to concentrate? If so, try reaching for an apple or a bunch of grapes. These fruits, along with other foods like pears, leafy vegetables, and nuts, are a good source of boron.

A recent study found that increasing volunteers' daily boron intakes produced striking changes in their brain wave patterns. Subjects on diets extremely low in boron were less alert. Experts believe 3 to 5 milligrams of boron per day fuels mental functioning. The typical U.S. diet of refined foods, meats, dairy products, and grains delivers only about 1 milligram. Several daily servings of fresh fruits and vegetables will bring levels up to par.

Our Heavenly Father knows exactly what we need. Not only has He given us spiritual power that enables us to have a sound mind, but He created foods for us to eat that would help our brains to function better. God is so good.

Thank You, Lord, for giving me a sound mind that
is free from fear and full of love.

Orderly Eating

Read: Acts 24

Paul discoursed on righteousness, self-control
and the judgment to come . . . (Acts 24:25;NIV).

Did you know that the more we exercise, the more we want to exercise? And the less we eat, the less we want to eat? These are proven facts. This principle is okay in moderation, but a person with an eating disorder or someone with compulsive, obsessive behavior usually goes overboard.

The key is balance. Exercise and diet are only a part of our life. When your eating is normalized, then changes can be made — moderately. Routine regular exercise is good, but the motive should be to build not to punish. A healthy attitude is the most important factor in developing a healthy body.

With a balanced attitude, we can develop good habits and maintain self-control. Destruction occurs when compulsion and obsession are behind our actions. Be a wise woman/man and keep everything in perspective. After all, there is a "judgment to come!"

Lord, help me to keep a balanced attitude
toward eating and exercising so that others
will know that You are in control of my life.

❖ March 1 ❖

Why Fiber?

Read: Psalm 22

The meek shall eat and be satisfied . . . (Ps. 22:26).

Everyone's talking about fiber these days. TV ads sell fiber products you can drink and cereals you can eat. What's so great about fiber? For one thing it satisfies the appetite. High-fiber foods must be chewed, and this allows more interaction with your taste buds so you have more satisfaction.

Because your stomach has to turn fibrous foods into liquids, it takes your stomach a long time to produce all the digestive juices, hormones, and enzymes. As a result, your stomach feels full longer and sends out signals that say, "Don't send more. I'm not through digesting what you have eaten."

You need 25 grams of fiber a day. You can add more fiber to your diet by eating more whole grains, fruits, and vegetables. Then, you will feel satisfied on fewer calories and less hungry for fattening foods. Once you learn how to eat the natural foods that God created, you will begin to enjoy a new sense of well-being and satisfaction in your life.

Lord, teach me to eat the foods You created and that will satisfy me.

❖ March 2 ❖

Only the Finest!

Read: Psalm 81

But you would be fed with the finest of wheat . . . (Ps. 81:16;NIV).

Fiber falls into two basic categories: soluble and insoluble. Both are needed for good health and weight loss. *Soluble* fiber is the kind that dissolves in water. Oat bran is the most famous form of soluble fiber, but this fiber is also found in beans, barley, and some fruits and vegetables like squash, apples, citrus fruits, cauliflower, cabbage, strawberries, and potatoes.

Soluble fiber slows the digestion of foods, so you're not hungry so soon. In large amounts it can lower cholesterol and keep blood-sugar levels steady. This is very important for dieters. On a low-fiber diet, your metabolism runs up peaks and down valleys, causing sudden energy losses and jittery feelings that can trigger going on a binge.

Insoluble fiber is the type found in whole-wheat flour and bran, whole grains, vegetables, and in many fruits like apples and pears. It's a bulking agent, so it prevents constipation. Wheat has long been a staple in the diet of God's people, the Israelites. Surely, we who live in America, where we have access to so many good foods, should be eating the "finest of the wheat" instead of bleached, fiber-less flour!

Thank You for creating exactly the kinds of foods our bodies need.

❖ March 3 ❖

Go Easy Read: Leviticus 25:1-22

The land shall yield her fruit, and ye shall eat your fill,
and dwell therein in safety (Lev. 25:19).

Don't make the mistake of increasing your fiber too rapidly. Instead, start adding foods like apples, beans, and whole grains to your diet. Increase your fiber gradually until you are eating five daily servings of fruits and vegetables, and six daily servings of grains (meaning whole-grain cereals, beans, cooked whole grains, breads, and pasta). The highest fiber-rich foods are legumes (beans and peas) and fruits like apples, prunes, raspberries, and pears.

People who are losing weight need to make a special effort to select the highest-fiber foods. Lettuce is 90 percent water. That's why you're usually hungry soon after eating a salad. A potato, however, will really fill you up.

God promised the Israelites that once they entered Canaan, they would have plenty to eat and feel full and satisfied. That same promise can be yours if you eat the natural foods God has provided for us.

Lord, I claim this promise for myself — that I will eat
my fill and be satisfied with the foods You have created.

❖ March 4 ❖

Strong 'Til the End Read: Deuteronomy 34:1-12

Moses was a hundred and twenty years old when he died,
yet his eyes were not weak nor his strength gone (Deut. 34:7;NIV).

Muscles that aren't used, grow weak quickly. Muscle weakness in older people causes them to become frail and susceptible to falling. It can eventually lead to their needing constant care from others. When you increase your muscle strength through exercise, it is easier for you to climb stairs, get off a chair, lift grocery bags, and get in and out of the car — everything you need to do to remain living at home longer when you get older.

The wonderful news is that muscle loss can be reversed. Researchers have found that loss of muscle mass from aging is reversible through weight training. Twelve men ages sixty to seventy-two increased their thigh strength by almost 200 percent and their muscle size by 15 percent using weight-training machines for eight weeks.

There's no reason why you can't live to a ripe old age like Moses, who was strong and healthy until the day he died.

Lord, help me to follow You as Moses did. Give me
sharp eyes and a healthy body for as long as I live.

❖ March 5 ❖

Preventing Cancer Read: Micah 6

> He has showed you, O man, what is good. And what does
> the Lord require of you? To act justly and to love mercy
> and to walk humbly with your God (Mic. 6:8;NIV).

Isn't it wonderful that we don't have to wonder about what God wants us to do? He has made it very clear and spelled it out very simply in the Bible.

The medical profession has also made it very clear in the past few years what we need to do to stay healthy. It's not as confusing as many people seem to think. Studies have shown that three big factors have at least a moderate effect in preventing cancer:

1. Keeping at the right weight.
2. Exercise.
3. A positive mental attitude.

Why is maintaining your right weight important to reducing your risk of cancer? Because studies have linked obesity with increased risk of colon, breast, prostate, gallbladder, and female reproductive-system cancers. You'd be willing to lose weight to avoid these kinds of cancers, wouldn't you?

Lord, You have showed me what is good and what You required of me. Help my to walk humbly with You and obey Your Word.

❖ March 6 ❖

You Can Do It! Read: 2 Timothy 4:16-18

> For the Lord stood at my side and gave
> me strength . . . (2 Tim. 4:17;NIV).

Yesterday, we talked about three important factors that affect your risk of getting cancer. Today, let's talk about the second factor: exercise.

First of all, exercise is essential in controlling obesity. So that means you get two factors for the price of one! Researchers have found that women who were involved in athletics during their teens and twenties seem to have a lower incidence of breast cancer. People with desk jobs and in-active lifestyles are at higher risk of colorectal cancer. Exercise will help cut their risks for cancer.

The American Cancer Society recommends regular exercise as part of its cancer-prevention program.

If you haven't yet started to exercise, make today the day! Remember, you can do anything through the power of Jesus Christ, who lives within you.

Lord Jesus, give me the strength I need to make the changes in my life that will improve my health. Thank You.

❖ March 7 ❖

Do This and Live!   Read: Luke 10:25-41

. . . Jesus replied, "Do this and you will live" (Luke 10:28;NIV).

Maintaining a positive mental attitude was rated as "important" by 54 percent of the doctors who were surveyed concerning cancer risks. People with a positive mental attitude seem to take better care of themselves; they smoke less and have better eating habits and exercise.

How do you maintain a positive mental attitude? The key word is found in our Scripture reading for today: "love." Loving God involves your whole being: all your heart and soul and strength and mind.

If your mind is focused on loving God, you can't help but have a positive mental attitude. Loving others is also crucial to keeping your mind healthy. In fact, Jesus said that, if you love God and love others, you will live. Not only will you live longer by reducing your risk of disease, but you will live forever through the gift of eternal life. Who could ask for anything more?

Heavenly Father, help me to love You with all my heart,
soul, strength, and mind so that I might live.

❖ March 8 ❖

Exercise and Cancer   Read: Ecclesiastes 7:1-14

Wisdom, like an inheritance, is a good thing and benefits
those who see the sun (Eccles. 7:11;NIV).

Is exercise really effective against cancer? Yes, especially colon cancer. A report published two years ago found that those who were highly or even moderately active had a 50 percent lower risk of colon cancer than those who were less active. *Active* men were defined as those expending more than 1,000 calories per week in recreational activity — the equivalent of jogging or playing tennis two hours a week or walking 10 miles a week.

In addition, a twenty-one-year study of eight thousand Japanese men in Hawaii suggested that those who were physically active at home or at work were as much as 70 percent less likely to develop colon cancer than the sedentary men. Similarly, studies of Swedish men and women show that being sedentary may increase the risk of colon cancer more than threefold.

Physical activity and a low-fat, high-fiber diet may account for much of the reduction in the risk of colon cancer. Harvard researchers, however, reported that exercise seemed to have a protective effect — independent of diet. It appears, that exercise — like wisdom — is a good thing!

Lord, give me the wisdom to benefit from the
knowledge I am learning day by day.

❖ March 9 ❖

Early Training   Read: Proverbs 22:1-15

Train up a child in the way he should go: and when he
is old, he will not depart from it (Prov. 22:6).

While children are young, it is so important to teach them healthy eating. We need to teach our children, from an early age, to eat good balanced diets. Why? Because heart disease and many other dreadful illnesses begin in childhood.

Kids taste for foods are developed in their early years of life. If you start now to feed them foods that are low in salt and fat, they will learn to enjoy those foods later in life, too. If you give them fruits and raw vegetables as snacks instead of chips and cookies, they are more likely to choose nutritious snacks when they grow up.

Kids also learn by example. If they see you eating right and exercising, they are more likely to do so themselves. Find time to take walks together. Go to the park. Be an active family. You teach your children by the lifestyle that you live. Train them. Don't nag them.

*Lord, help me to train my children to have healthy eating and
exercising habits. Let me be a good example for them.*

❖ March 10 ❖

Lower Cholesterol   Read: Psalm 48

For this God is our God for ever and ever; he will be
our guide even unto death (Ps. 48:14).

If you are trying to lower your blood cholesterol, you know that you should eat more fiber. But not all types of fiber affect cholesterol. Which of the following foods *won't* help lower cholesterol levels? (a) oat bran, (b) wheat bran, (c) kidney beans, (d) grapefruit, (e) apples. The answer is (b) wheat bran.

It is still a good idea to eat wheat bran. All plant foods contain some of both basic kinds of fiber — insoluble and soluble. The fiber in wheat bran and whole wheat is primarily insoluble, and this fiber helps prevent constipation and may protect against colon cancer. Soluble fiber, however, the kind found in oat bran, legumes, and fruits helps lower blood cholesterol, primarily the LDL ("bad") cholesterol. These facts may help guide you to make wiser choices if your cholesterol level is high.

We have a "Heavenly Guide" for our lives. As we begin each day we need to meet with our Guide and get directions for the day.

*Lord, I want You to be my guide today
and every day as long as I live.*

❖ March 11 ❖

Fat Makes You Fat!   Read: 1 Corinthians 13

When I was a child . . . I thought like a child . . . When
I became a man, I put childish ways behind me (1 Cor. 13:11;NIV).

Diet experts tell us that it is not just the calories that count when you are trying to lose weight. The source of those calories is what is important.

Fat is the most fattening nutrient in our diet. Fat calories contain 9 calories per gram; protein and carbohydrate contain 4 calories per gram. In other words, 100 calories of bread won't do you any harm, but 100 calories of cheese melted on top will. Another example is potato chips. Ten chips pack more than 10 grams of fat, while the same amount of pretzels has very little fat.

Fat makes us fat. Your body has to work hard to break down protein and carbohydrate calories, but it stores fat. But, the good news is: When you don't eat fat, your body pulls it out of your fat cells. That's how you burn up the fat you have already accumulated!

By giving just a little thought to what you are eating, you can force your body to burn up that extra fat it has stored away.

Lord, help to be wise and give thought to the way I eat.

❖ March 12 ❖

An Inquisitive Mind   Read: Ecclesiastes 7:15-29

So I turned my mind to understand, to
investigate and to search out wisdom and
the scheme of things . . . (Eccles. 7:25;NIV).

Did you know that jelly beans, pretzels, fudge sauce, and cracker jacks are low in fat? For example, when you get a sweet craving for chocolate have some nonfat yogurt with a couple of tablespoons of chocolate sauce. (Smucker's chocolate fudge sauce has only 1 gram of fat per 2 tablespoons, while a 1.45 ounce Hershey bar would have a whopping 13 fat grams.)

People don't feel like they are on a diet when they can eat this way. The word isn't restraint when it comes to eating. The word is freedom — be free to eat foods that are low in fat. Look for foods that have one gram of fat in desserts.

We need to be as wise as King Solomon, who had an inquisitive mind and who enjoyed searching out innovative ways of doing things. If you ask the Lord to help you, He will give you new and creative ways to satisfy your desires and lose weight at the same time.

*Lord, give me an inquisitive mind that will
search for new ways to eat and be satisfied.*

❖ March 13 ❖

Keep Moving
Read: Job 22:19-30

Accept instruction from his mouth and lay up
his words in your heart (Job 22:22;NIV).

Our "spiritual" heart needs instruction in order to know how to live in a way that is pleasing to God. That's why our ears need to know what God has said in His Word, the Bible.

Our physical hearts also need special care in order to function as God designed them to do. But only 8 percent of Americans fifty years and older exercise enough to strengthen their hearts. This is so sad because there is evidence that exercise improves the quality of life in middle and later years and even affects life expectancy.

Movement, even modest levels of it, are beneficial. Just keep moving, and you'll reduce your heart disease risk by 30 percent. And that means all types of movement: yard work, dancing, walking, cycling, swimming, golf, tennis — you name it.

The good news about exercise is that you don't have to run marathons to reap the health benefits of exercise. Movement — thirty to sixty minutes of it three to four times a week — will not only strengthen the heart directly, it will also improve the ratio of "good" HDL cholesterol to "bad" LDL cholesterol, and in some cases, it will even lower high blood pressure.

Lord, give me a heart that is open to receiving
instruction from You and Your Word.

❖ March 14 ❖

Older and Better
Read: Isaiah 50

The Sovereign Lord has given me . . . to know the word
that sustains the weary . . . (Isa. 50:4;NIV).

Let's face it — we all grow weary at times from the pressures of life. We are human. Even the most dedicated Christian faces moments of distress and discouragement. Jesus did when He walked on earth.

But what we must understand and hold on to is the fact that we have a Heavenly Father who never grows weary. He truly understands our weaknesses. He will give power to the tired and worn out and strength to the weak. But we must look to Him, trust Him, and wait on Him to work in our behalf. Someone has said, "God is never early — but He is never late."

Lord, give me the strength and power to live for
You in spite of my weariness.

❖ March 15 ❖

A Rich House   Read: Proverbs 19:1-14

House and riches are the inheritance of fathers: and
a prudent wife is from the Lord (Prov. 19:14).

When a wife despises her husband's authority, the effect upon the children is always disastrous. Her contentious words are like rain leaking through the roof of a house, spoiling the interior. Arabic proverbs list three things that make a house unbearable: a leak of rainwater, a wife's nagging, and bugs.

A prudent wife is from the Lord. A good wife is absolutely necessary for a godly house. She is not acquired, however, as are other possessions which may be worked for or inherited. That's why she is always to be treasured as a gift from God.

Wives, strive to be a wise and submissive helpmate for your husband. Husbands, learn to cherish your wife as a special treasure. If both of you love and respect one another, your house will be rich.

Lord, help me to be the kind of wife/husband that will be a
blessing to my spouse and make our house rich in love.

❖ March 16 ❖

Use It or Store It!   Read: Joshua 24:1-15

. . . Choose for yourselves this day whom
you will serve . . . (Josh. 24:15).

When you replace fats in your diet with calories made up of carbohydrates you get an additional benefit. Complex carbohydrates such as whole bread require the body to work harder to get the energy out of these calories, so some of the calories are actually burned in the processing of these foods in the body. In fact, your body doesn't even like to change carbohydrates to fat. It prefers to keep them in the form of glycogen (that's energy stored in your muscles and liver) so they will be ready for immediate use when you exercise.

This means that carbohydrates should be the food of choice for everyone. The body prefers *to use* carbohydrates, but it prefers *to store* fat. So when you eat a baked potato topped with butter and sour cream, the potato will be burned up before you eat your next meal. The butter and sour cream, however, will likely be stored somewhere on your body.

Life is full of choices, and most of them affect us in one way or another. While choosing the right foods can affect your life today, choosing to serve God will affect you for all eternity.

Lord, I choose to serve You.

❖ March 17 ❖

Use to Get   Read: 1 Chronicles 22

. . . Arise therefore, and be doing, and the Lord
be with thee (1 Chron. 22:16).

In our fifties and sixties our physical bodies will decline in strength and energy unless we follow a good-health regimen of low-fat eating and regular exercise. Much of the aging process can be greatly slowed by keeping the mind and body active.

Our bodies thrive on activity. If you don't like to run, then walk or swim. Tennis and golf provide good exercise as well. When you can, always choose walking over riding and stairs over elevators. Remember: We need to use energy to get energy.

King David, in giving instructions to his son Solomon concerning the building of the temple, told him to "arise and be doing!" Maybe this is a word from the Lord to you today concerning exercise: "Get up and get on with it!"

Lord, I know if I get up and get moving that You will
bless my efforts and give me more energy.

❖ March 18 ❖

Preventing Birth Defects   Read: Psalm 139

For you created my inmost being; you knit me
together in my mother's womb (Ps. 139:13;NIV).

The U.S. Public Health Service recently announced that all women capable of becoming pregnant need to make sure they are getting enough folacin in their diets in order to prevent birth defects. In fact, folacin is now recognized as a major factor in preventing defects such as spina bifida.

As one of the B vitamins, folacin is also called folic acid or folate and comes from the same root word as foliage which is appropriate because the vitamin is supplied by leafy green vegetables. It is also found in legumes, especially dried beans, liver, oranges, peanuts, sunflower seeds, and wheat germ.

A woman should not wait until she knows she's pregnant to start getting folacin into her diet. The defects, when they do occur, happen in the first two weeks of pregnancy. Women need to start building up their folacin stores at least twenty-eight days before becoming pregnant.

God wants you to have a healthy baby, but to do that you have to give Him the nutrients He needs to work with.

Lord, help me to acquire all the nutrients needed for
You to knit my baby together perfectly in my womb.

❖ March 19 ❖

Women and Folacin   Read: Psalm 138

The Lord will fulfill his purpose for me . . . (Ps. 138:8;NIV).

Yesterday we learned how folacin can prevent birth defects, but this nutrient also has benefits for the woman herself. Studies show that folacin may be a significant factor in protecting women against cervical cancer.

You need 400 micrograms of folacin every day. Women who follow a healthy diet, or faithfully take a multi-vitamin, may already be getting the recommended amount. If you are not, then you need to improve your diet or take supplements. Dietary improvements are always the better way since they also supply fiber and other nutrients.

Excess amounts of folacin, however, offer no advantage. If your diet is rich in fruits, vegetables, legumes, and whole grains you should be getting enough. Here are some foods that contain folacin: broccoli, fortified breakfast cereal, orange juice, oatmeal, lentils, and black-eyed peas.

God had a purpose for your life that He wants to fulfill. Let's give Him everything He needs to bring that to pass.

Thank You, Lord, for the wonderful purpose
You have planned for my life.

❖ March 20 ❖

All Who Call   Read: Psalm 86

You are forgiving and good, O Lord, abounding in
love to all who call to you (Ps. 86:5;NIV).

This psalm teaches us how eager God is to hear and answer our prayers. When we are sick, we need to learn to call upon God to heal us. Even a simple cold is not too small a request for God to meet. In fact, it's better to have your cold healed in its earliest stages than to let it become more serious.

A simple cold can lead to painful and dangerous ear infections. But there is one simple way to help prevent them. If you have a cold, blow your nose just one side at a time. On the other hand, if you blow forcefully through both pinched nostrils at once, this creates pressure that can drive bacteria-carrying mucus up the Eustachian tube and into the middle ear. Leaving one nostril free dissipates the force.

Sniffing, on the other hand, poses no problem. And don't worry about bacteria-laden secretions draining down the back of the throat — stomach acid easily kills bacteria.

Lord, I call upon You to help me and heal me,
knowing that You love me and will answer when I call.

Bad Habits   Read: Psalm 106:1-15

> And he gave them their request; but sent
> leanness into their soul (Ps. 106:15).

If we want God to help us overcome our fleshly weaknesses, we must die to self and let Him live through us. Many times people will come to me and say, "I have prayed and prayed to be able to lose weight and nothing happens. I'm just as heavy as ever."

I've thought and prayed about these people. What hinders them and others from receiving deliverance from bad habits? They are Christians, in most cases, who love the Lord, but they are bound by habits such as overeating, smoking, alcoholism, etc. Many times I feel the problem is they are telling God, "Set me free from the consequences of my sin, but don't ask me to give it up." Or, "I want to be thin, but don't ask me to give up my favorite foods." Such an attitude ties the hands of God.

Sometimes God grants selfish requests, but when He does, there is a price to pay. A leanness will creep into the soul of one who prays selfishly. If you want to be set free from your weaknesses, you must allow the Lord to work however He sees fit to bring about your healing and deliverance.

Lord, work in me however You see fit to bring
about my healing and deliverance.

Why Plans Fail   Read: Proverbs 15:22-33

> Plans fail for lack of counsel, but with many
> advisers they succeed (Prov. 15:22;NIV).

Most of us don't plan to fail, but we often do because we try to go it alone and expect God to work miracles overnight. God is never just going to zap your weight problem away. But He will bring nutrition and exercise information to your attention. If you are learning good-health information, it is no accident. That is the Lord intervening in your life in answer to your prayers.

Some people, however, need more than information. They need professional Christian counseling in order to pinpoint the reason for their addictive need for food, cigarettes — even exercise! If you are struggling and can't seem to get deliverance from your addiction, seek out a wise counselor — or even a Christian friend — who can give you the advice you need in order to succeed.

Lord, help me to put into practice the wise counsel I have already
received and make me willing to get more help when I need it.

❖ March 23 ❖

The Right Time   Read: Ecclesiastes 3:1-15

> To every thing there is a season, and a time to
> every purpose under the heaven (Eccles. 3:1).

When is the best time to exercise? That depends.

If 300 people begin exercising tomorrow — 100 in the morning, 100 at midday, and 100 in the evening, a year from now, how many will still be exercising? The answer: 150 — 75 of the morning exercisers; 50 of the midday; and 25 of the evening.

Studies also show that morning exercisers are more likely to stick with an exercise routine than those who choose other times of the day for their workout. If, however, the only time you can exercise is at mid-day or afternoon, keep it up. That's the time when your performance level will be highest. In fact, muscle strength is 5 percent greater at noon than at any other time of the day. Aerobic efficiency, too, goes up by 4 percent in the afternoon.

Remember, exercising any time of the day is better than not exercising at all. Remember, too, that God has a wonderful plan for your life, and He will bring it to pass at the right time.

> *Lord, help me to always be in Your will*
> *and fulfill Your purpose for my life.*

❖ March 24 ❖

Losing Your Taste for Fat   Read: Exodus 16:22-31

> . . . It was white like coriander seed and tasted like
> wafers made with honey (Exod. 16:31;NIV).

The Israelites had to relinquish their desire for the spicy food of Egypt and acquire a taste for the manna that God had provided. Although they didn't like it at first, they soon grew to enjoy the nutritious, low-fat wafers.

If you reduce your consumption of fat, will you lose your desire for it? A new study indicates that women who limit their intake of fat lose their taste for fat. Within six months, many of the two thousand women in the study who cut their fat intake to 25 percent of their calories reported that they found the taste of fat to be unpleasant.

The study suggested that you can retrain your taste buds by substituting low- and nonfat foods for the fatty ones you normally eat. If you can stick with a low-fat diet for six months, you are less likely to return to your old fat-full ways of eating. Why not try it? What have you got to lose?

> *Lord, help me to relinquish my desire for high-fat foods*
> *and to acquire a taste for nutritious, low-fat foods.*

❖ March 25 ❖

Spider Veins

Read: Psalm 145

He fulfills the desires of those who fear him; he
hears their cry and saves them (Ps. 145:19;NIV).

Most of us, especially women, desire to look our best and have an attractive appearance. I believe God wants to fulfill that desire, but we must first be willing to change.

Although doctors say there is no way to prevent spider or varicose veins, our lifestyle can make veins worse. Excess weight is the biggest culprit because those extra pounds put unnecessary pressure on your legs. That's why it is so important to maintain your right weight.

Inactivity also contributes to spider veins. There is nothing better than walking to improve the health of your legs. Walking improves circulation and prevents pooling of blood by strengthening the calf muscle that pumps blood up the leg toward the heart.

There is also a link between smoking and the incidence of varicose veins.

Lord, teach me to fear You in the right way
so You can fulfill my desires.

❖ March 26 ❖

Sitting and Standing

Read: Mark 6:30-44

. . . Come with me by yourselves to a quiet place
and get some rest (Mark 6:31;NIV).

Jobs that require us to sit or stand for a long period of time aggravate the problem of veins. You need to get up and move around if you've been sitting. Or, if you have a standing job, take time to get off your feet and put them up for a few minutes. These suggestions may help minimize the symptoms and prevent mild problems from getting worse:

1. Wear support hose, especially if you are pregnant or have a job where you sit or stand a lot. Even if you don't have varicose veins, the hose will improve circulation and reduce aching.

2. Try to raise your legs above hip level to ease discomfort. Lie on your back with your legs straight up and resting against a wall. Hold this position for a couple of minutes to allow the blood to flow out of the swollen leg veins back toward the heart.

Sometimes we need to heed the words of Jesus and come away with Him to a quiet place. In His presence, we can find rest not only for our bodies but for our souls as well.

Jesus, I will come with You to a quiet place and rest.

❖ March 27 ❖

Cure for Motion Sickness Read: Matthew 4:12-25

Jesus went about . . . healing all manner of sickness
and all manner of diseases among the people (Matt. 4:23).

Ginger may be more effective in preventing motion sickness than the standard medication Dramamine. Nibbling on the root or taking ginger root capsules sold in natural-foods stores is a natural remedy that does not cause drowsiness. I know several people who have found this to be very effective when traveling by car, plane, or ship.

During Jesus' ministry, He spent much of His time healing those who came to Him. In fact, the Bible says, He healed "all manner of sickness." That says to me that Jesus is interested in healing our smallest discomforts and our most serious diseases. Let's learn to trust Him to heal us through His miracle-working power and through the natural substances God has provided for us to use.

Jesus, I ask You to heal me.

❖ March 28 ❖

The Gallstone Risk Read: Jeremiah 31:1-14

. . . I will lead them . . . on a level path
where they will not stumble . . . (Jer. 31:9;NIV).

The more you weigh, the more you pay in lots of ways when it comes to health risks. The Harvard Medical School has recently added one more risk: The fatter your body, the fatter your chance of getting gallstones!

In a study of 89,000 people, Harvard researchers found that the higher a person's weight, the greater the chance of gallstones. Slightly overweight women were found to have a 70 percent more risk of gallstones than women of ideal weight. Very obese women were found to have a 600 percent greater risk!

Why? Gallstones are made of cholesterol! When digestive juices in the gallbladder have too much cholesterol, they form stones. Studies have already shown the link between overweight and higher cholesterol. Other studies have shown higher insulin levels in the overweight, and insulin stimulates an enzyme that produces cholesterol. So, if overweight people produce more cholesterol due to higher insulin levels, then overweight people have more of a chance of having too much cholesterol flowing through the gallbladder during digestion. The result? The formation of stones.

*Lord, help me to do whatever it takes to
get my weight under control.*

❖ March 29 ❖

God's Promise Read: James 4

> Humble yourselves in the sight of the Lord,
> and He shall lift you up (James 4:10).

If you are overweight and want to lose those excess pounds, I want you to claim today's promise from God's Word. As you bring yourself to the Lord with your need to lose weight, He will lift you up to that place where you can be confident in His ability to see you through.

Yesterday, we talked about how gallstones are formed. I know you want to lose weight in order to be healthy and prevent painful gallstone attacks. But how should you go about it? A doctor at Harvard recommends *gradual* weight loss to reduce your risk of gallstones forming if you are already overweight. *Gradual* is the key to success here!

If you follow the weight loss tips discussed in this book, you will lose those extra pounds without having to worry about your diet adversely affecting your health.

> *I humble myself before You, Lord, asking You to*
> *help me lose weight so I can have a healthy body.*

❖ March 30 ❖

Your Reward Read: Psalm 127:3-5

> Children are an heritage of the Lord: and the
> fruit of the womb is his reward (Ps. 127:3).

God's Word tells us that our children are gifts from Him — our inheritance from the Lord. Our most important job is to bring them to know Jesus as their Lord and Saviour. Next, we need to safeguard their health and well-being by providing the love and nourishment they need to grow and mature properly.

I have noticed that when parents become health conscious, they begin to feed their children right. You can help your child learn to make good choices by setting the proper example. Our children do exactly what we do. If we eat junk food, they will eat junk food; if we smoke, we are teaching them to smoke. On the other hand, if they see us eating healthy foods, they are more like to follow our example. If we exercise regularly, they will want to join in, or they will find their own ways of staying physically active.

> *Thank You, Lord, for my children. Help me*
> *teach them more about You so they can come*
> *to know You as Lord and Saviour.*

Eating God's Word   Read: Jeremiah 15:12-21

> Thy words were found and I did eat them; and thy word was
> unto me the joy and rejoicing of mine heart . . . (Jer. 15:16).

We sure do spend a lot of time thinking about food or eating, don't we? Sometimes while we are eating, we are thinking about what we are going to eat next! Why? Because often we are looking to food for comfort. But food does not comfort us, only the Word of God can do that.

Why not "eat the Word of God" instead of that unnecessary snack? Why not feast on God's promises instead of gorging yourself on high-calorie desserts? Your soul needs the nourishment of God's Word, just as your body requires good food to be healthy. If you make reading God's Word part of your daily routine, you will find plenty of reasons for joy and rejoicing!

Lord God, Your Word is better than any food I could eat.
Fill me with the joy that comes from knowing You.

❖ April 1 ❖

Snacking Is Okay?

Read: John 6:1-15

Here is a boy with five small barley loaves
and two small fish . . . (John 6:9;NIV).

Let's face it — kids like to snack; and for good reason. The idea that snacking is bad for kids is a myth. In fact, many pediatricians consider snacking to be important to kids' nutrition and healthy growth development. Why? Because snacking provides growing children 25 to 30 percent of their daily required caloric intake.

Of course, the kinds of the foods kids eat for snacks determines whether they are any health benefit. That's why kids need healthy snacks like low-fat crackers and cookies, cut up vegetables, fresh fruit fig bars, and popcorn.

Limiting between-meal eating isn't good for children. Why? Because sit-down meals tend to be too large for kids, but snacks are just right for their appetites and interest level.

The mother of the boy who gave Jesus his lunch had packed only a small amount, but it was enough for a child his size. Keep that in mind the next time you pack your child's lunch or prepare his plate for dinner.

Lord, show me how to feed my child in a way that will meet their
nutritional needs in the right amounts at the right times.

❖ April 2 ❖

Whose Slave Are You?

Read: Romans 6:15-23

Thanks be to God that, though you used to
be slaves to sin. . . . You have been set free from sin
and have becomes slaves to righteousness (Rom. 6:17-18).

The apostle Paul was ever mindful that God is to be thanked. Why? Because through Christ we are no longer slaves to sin. Instead, we have become the servants of righteousness. Freedom from bondage to Satan means we are feel to serve the Lord who loved us and gave himself for us.

Have you accepted Jesus Christ and the freedom He purchased for you on the cross? Or are you still bound by a lustful desire for food and other harmful habits of the flesh? You don't have to remain as Satan's slave. Jesus came to set you free.

Maybe you are a believer in Jesus Christ, but you don't have victory in certain areas of you life. If you apply God's Word to your heart, you will have the power to live a life that glorifies the Lord.

Thank You, Lord, for setting me free from sin and Satan's
bondage. Help me to yield myself to You as Your servant.

❖ April 3 ❖

Allergy Fallacies

Read: Psalm 119:57-72

Teach me knowledge and good judgment,
for I believe in your commands (Ps. 119:66;NIV).

If you suffer from seasonal allergies, then you know what suffering is. But if you're in "the know" about pollen, you can significantly reduce your misery. Many people think that pollen is at its lowest in the morning. Actually, that's when the pollen count is at its highest. It is lowest in the evening hours and at night. If you are susceptible to pollen, try to plan your exercise routine accordingly.

When you hear the high allergy counts reported during the pollen season, don't necessarily think you're in for increased agony. You need to be concerned not only with the count, but also *which* pollens are involved in the count.

Over-the-counter antihistamines can be helpful, but to be most beneficial, they should be taken *before* symptoms occur. Why? Because it takes forty-eight hours for most antihistamines to become effective.

Having the facts and being informed can help us know how to treat certain health problems. If you have a particular problem, learn as much about it as you can, then ask the Lord to give you good judgment in treating it.

Lord, teach me what I need to know in
order to take care of my health.

❖ April 4 ❖

Dens of Temptation

Read: Ephesians 6:10-20

Put on the full armor of God so that you can take your stand
against the devil's schemes (Eph. 6:11;NIV).

Grocery stores can be dens of temptation if you go into them with your guard down. That's why I suggest you arm yourself with the Word of God when you go food shopping. Memorize today's verse because you may need to repeat it over and over as you push your cart up and down the aisles. If you are determined to "take your stand against the devil's schemes," you will stay away from high-fat, high sugar foods. You also need to make a list and stick to it.

One more tip: Don't shop when you are starved or even slightly hungry. If you do, everything you see will look tempting. If you need to eat, go to the bakery counter and ask for a raisin bagel. This low-fat treat will sustain you for the task ahead and ward off excessive temptation.

Lord Jesus, show me how to arm myself
with the power of Your Word so I can guard
myself against temptation.

❖ April 5 ❖

Keep On Doing Read: James 2:14-26

What good is it . . . if a man claims to have faith but has no deeds? . . .
(James 2:14;NIV).

Exercise generates a tremendous feeling of well-being. It helps ward off and even treat depression, anxiety, and everyday stress. Researchers say exercise is no longer a helpful hobby for older people. It's becoming clear that physical activity is an *essential* daily requirement.

In fact, preparation for healthy, active senior years should begin between the ages of thirty and forty. Walking and lifting weights, under professional guidance and with a doctor's approval, will help maintain and build muscle tissue. If we are otherwise healthy, we can continue to be active even into our nineties. In addition, building muscle tissue enables us to burn more calories and maintain bone density.

Even more important is our need to exercise our spiritual muscles by spending time alone with God each day, reading His Word and talking to Him. As He speaks to us through His Word, we need to apply it to our lives.

Lord Jesus, help me to not only hear and read Your Word but to put it into practice in my life. Help me to be like You.

❖ April 6 ❖

Watching Your Weight Read: Revelation 16

. . . Blessed is he that watcheth . . . (Rev. 16:15).

Have you ever followed a weight-loss program, met your goal, and then the weight slowly comes back on? The experts have found that watching your weight is much easier if you "watch your weight."

Using men who were at high risk for developing heart disease, researchers had them weigh in at regular times at the clinic. By doing this, 70 percent of them were able to keep the weight off that they lost. Why did this regular weigh-in work so well? Because little gains were caught before the extra pounds turned into big gains.

How about you? Do you have a regular time for weighing yourself to see if you are gaining? The perfect time to weigh yourself is first thing in the morning, right after you get up, even before you have your morning coffee. Don't weigh yourself every day; once a week or once a month is enough.

If we spent as much time watching for the return of Jesus Christ as we do watching our weight, we would truly be blessed!

Lord Jesus, help me to focus my eyes on You, waiting expectantly for Your return.

❖ April 7 ❖

Go Ahead and Splurge?   Read: Colossians 2:6-23

Let no man beguile you
of your reward . . . (Col. 2:18).

Many times, when you start losing weight and feeling good you will encounter loved ones or friends who tell you to "go ahead and splurge." Whenever this happens, recall this Scripture quoted for today. Recognize how far you have come and how much better you are feeling.

Don't let someone else throw up a stumbling block for you. The Lord is your judge, and by the power of His Holy Spirit within you, He will show you the food you are to be eating and how to eat it. The Lord will encourage you and give you the strength and power to reach your goal — and your reward!

Lord, give me the strength and
power to resist
pressure put on me by other people.

❖ April 8 ❖

Boron and Your Brain   Read: Psalm 136

Give thanks to the Lord, for he is good . . . and who
gives food to every creature (Ps. 136:1, 25;NIV).

You have probably not heard about the nutrient boron, but it has many benefits that your body needs. Boron affects your mental alertness. In one study, fifteen people were given diets with an adequate supply of this nutrient for fourteen days. Then these same people spent sixty-three days on a low-boron diet. The researchers found changes in the electrical impulses in their brains, which showed a possible decrease in mental alertness while they were on the low-boron diet.

If you have low levels of boron in your body, it could result in poorer performance of a task. Boron is an essential nutrient that also helps keep calcium in your bones. Where do you get boron? Boron is found in apples, pears, grapes, nuts, prunes, raisins, dates, tomatoes, and red peppers. You need to get this nutrient from the foods you eat. Don't try to get boron from supplements.

God made our bodies, and He created the foods we need to make them function properly. That's why we need Him to guide us in eating right.

Thank You, Lord, for giving me
the food I need to be healthy.

❖ April 9 ❖

Healing Scripture   Read: Psalm 30:1-7

O Lord my God, I cried unto thee, and thou hast healed me (Ps. 30:2).

At one point in my life, I had backslidden from good health practices. Because I had moved, I had left behind my church and my own "health coach." I was in a new environment, had stopped exercising, was not careful with my eating. As a result, I had gained 15 pounds.

God's Word convicted me of the sin in my life. I cried out to Him for forgiveness of my sin and for neglecting my body. I was committed to begin exercising and eating right. It didn't happen overnight, but in due time God healed me.

Have you cried unto the Lord with your burden and asked for healing? He will do the same for you, my friend.

O Lord my God, I need You to help me. I can't do this on my own.
Please forgive me and heal my backslidden heart.

❖ April 10 ❖

Lean Hot Dogs?   Read: Leviticus 11

The Lord said to Moses . . . "Of all the
animals that live on land, these are
the ones you may eat" (Lev. 11:1-2;NIV).

The fat content in a "regular" hot dog accounts for 84 percent of its calories! Surely the so-called "light" franks in your grocer's meat case are much lower. Right? Wrong. If you read the labels carefully, you'll find that chicken or turkey franks have an average 73 percent of their calories from fat! Big deal!

The lowest in fat is Hormel Light and Lean, made from beef and pork. They contain 1.3 grams of fat in a 1.6-ounce link. Fat accounts for only 28 percent of the 43 calories per link. Healthy Choice hot dogs — made from beef, pork, and turkey — derive 24 percent of their calories from fat.

Remember, no more than 30 percent of your calories should come from fat. My advice? Stay away from the hot dogs in any form and stick with the leanest of all meats — skinless white turkey breast.

While I don't advocate following the Old Testament dietary laws, I think it's good for all of us to know about them. Surely God knows something about certain meats that we don't know!

Lord, show me which kinds of meat I should eat
and which ones I should avoid.

❖ April 11 ❖

Those Who Wait

Read: Psalm 27

Wait on the Lord: be of good courage, and he shall
strengthen thine heart: wait, I say, on the Lord (Ps. 27:14).

Weight loss comes to those who wait. In a study of over one hundred women on an 800-calorie day, researchers found that some of the participants actually gained weight in the first few days. It wasn't until thirteen days had passed that all the participants were losing weight.

This is the reason people give up. It takes time for weight loss to show up on the scale. People give up trying before the true rate of weight loss becomes evident. By the end of three weeks the weight lost by those in the study ranged from 2 to 28 pounds. The conclusion from this study: Obese individuals would do best to stick with their weight-loss regimen even if it initially seems to be failing.

*Lord, strengthen my heart to wait on You to complete
the work You want to do in me.*

❖ April 12 ❖

Overweight Teens

Read: Luke 2:41-52

And Jesus grew in wisdom and stature, and
in favor with God and men (Luke 2:52;NIV).

Is being chubby as a teenager harmful to your health later in life? Yes, according to a 1988 study. It found that overweight teenagers are more likely than their thin friends to suffer such problems as heart disease, colon cancer, arthritis, or gout by age seventy. Men who were fat adolescents begin to die at a higher-than-usual rate by age forty-five. When they reach their seventies, their risk of death — usually from heart disease — is twice that of those who were normal size as teenagers.

Women also suffer from a variety of additional health problems if they were overweight as youngsters. The new study found that overweight adolescents often have poor health later in life, regardless of whether they became overweight adults.

If you love your kids, pray that they will have wisdom at a young age, as Jesus did. Then teach them to eat right and exercise in order to grow up "in stature" and not "out!"

*Lord, help me to teach my children and
teenagers good eating habits so they can
fulfill Your purpose for their lives.*

❖ April 13 ❖

Exercise Addiction   Read: 1 Chronicles 28:1-10

. . . for the Lord searches every heart and understands every
motive behind the thoughts (1 Chron. 28:9;NIV).

Exercise is good for you; we know that. But did you know it's also
possible to become obsessed with exercise? Some people become "exercise
junkies" who are as addicted as those who abuses drugs.

You may begin innocently enough with jogging 3 miles four days a week.
If, however, you feel compelled to increase the distance to 4 or 5 miles and to
run five, six, or even seven days a week, you may be headed for trouble.

But you don't have to be a long-distance runner to be hooked on exercise.
If you are constantly thinking about how to look and feel better and neglecting
your spiritual life as a result, then it is time to take a closer look at why you
exercise.

If we keep our minds focused on God and His Word, then we won't feel
driven to exercise — or to do anything else for that matter. Instead we will be
filled with His peace and our motives for wanting to look and feel good will
remain pure.

Lord, help me to keep my thoughts and motives
focused on You and not on myself.

❖ April 14 ❖

What's in a Name?   Read: Psalm 9

Those who know your name
will trust in you . . . (Ps. 9:10;NIV).

Granola. Now there's a healthy sounding food. Right? Well, not if the
brand you eat contains 5 to 6 grams per ounce. While granola has a lot of things
going for it, it is typically high in fat. If you look closely, however, you'll find
that there are some low-fat varieties. Kellogg's and Quaker Oats have a 2-
grams-of-fat-per-ounce granola, and Health Valley and Breadshop make one
with only 1 gram per ounce.

How about cantaloupe and honeydew? They're both melons, but by
nutritional standards they don't even compare. Half a cantaloupe contains
more vitamin C than one and a half oranges, and as much beta carotene as half
a carrot. A honeydew contains less than one-third as much vitamin C and very
little beta carotene.

If you put your trust in the Lord, He will never forsake you.

Lord Jesus, I know I can always trust in Your name.

❖ April 15 ❖

Cholesterol Questions Read: Proverbs 10

> Wise men store up knowledge . . . the wealth of
> the rich is their fortified city . . . (Prov. 10:14-15;NIV).

What if you were to reduce the amount of cholesterol you eat from 300 mg. per 1,000 calories (the usually recommended amount) to 100 mg. of cholesterol per 1,000 calories? Would that help much? You bet! It would reduce by nearly half the risk of a fatal heart attack for a middle-aged man. To put it another way, a middle-aged man could add four years to his life expectancy by reducing his cholesterol from 300 to 100 mg.

To do this you would need to get rid of egg yokes, eat small portions of lean mean, poultry, or fish, and avoid fatty dairy products.

If a middle-aged man had other risk factors — elevated blood pressure, smokes a pack of cigarettes a day, has high blood cholesterol, and a high cholesterol intake — and he eliminated each of these risk factors, he could reduce his risk of a fatal heart attack by more than 90 percent. That would mean an increase in life expectancy of more than twenty years!

> *Lord, help me to use the knowledge I am learning to*
> *preserve my life from premature death.*

❖ April 16 ❖

New Muscle Burns Fat Read: Psalm 18:30-50

> It is God who arms me with strength and
> makes my way perfect (Ps. 18:32;NIV).

Dieting is, in a way, self-defeating, because the more you diet, the slower your metabolism gets. Therefore it becomes even harder for you to lose weight.

Muscle, however, burns fat. If you put on new muscle through strength training exercises, you'll perk up your metabolism. The muscle will not only give you an attractive firmer look, it will do wonders toward keeping you lean and trim. Many health experts suggest a workout combining twenty minutes of strength training with twenty minutes of aerobic conditioning.

Here's an extra bonus: Exercise causes us to burn calories both during and even long after our workout. In fact, it causes any activity that we do — like washing dishes, vacuuming, or shopping — to burn more calories. It helps us respond more quickly to dieting and is a great energy booster!

By now, I hope you're on your way to better health and a stronger body. If not, claim today's promise, and get back on track.

> *Lord God, arm me with strength and make my*
> *journey to good health one of constant growth.*

❖ April 17 ❖

What's a Vegetarian?   Read: Daniel 10:1-12

I ate no pleasant bread, neither came flesh
nor wine in my mouth . . . (Dan. 10:3).

Not too many years ago, vegetarians were thought to be a little weird. Today a significant number of people are taking up some form of the practice. Vegetarians are classified in three categories: (1) total vegetarians, who avoid all animal products, (2) lacto-ovo vegetarians, who eat dairy products and eggs, but no flesh foods, and (3) semi-vegetarians, who avoid only red meat, but eat poultry and fish.

There are some advantages to eating a diet high in fruits, vegetables, legumes, and whole grains like: lower risk of certain cancers and heart disease. One of the pitfalls of a vegetarian diet, however, is failing to get all the essential nutrients. For example, the iron that comes from vegetables is not readily absorbed by the body. And vitamin B12 is only available from animal products, and so supplements should be taken. Anyone considering a vegetarian diet should seek out a registered dietitian to make sure such a diet is well-balanced.

The prophet Daniel went on a vegetarian diet during a three-week fast. God may call you to fast for a period of time. A fast, however, doesn't have to mean going without food altogether.

Lord, show me how to fast in a way that is pleasing to You.

❖ April 18 ❖

Water or Soda Pop?   Read: Isaiah 55

Come, all you who are thirsty, come to the waters . . . (Isa. 55:1;NIV).

When we're thirsty, nothing satisfies like water. A lot of people, however, don't like to drink water because of the taste or because it contains too many chemicals. If the water out of your faucet doesn't taste good, buy bottled water from the grocery store.

But don't use the bad taste of water as an excuse to drink soda pop. Why? Most regular sodas contain 8 to 12 teaspoons of sugar in a 12-ounce serving. In fact, all their calories come from sugar. Start replacing sodas (regular and diet) with water. Besides, it's much cheaper than soft drinks and will truly satisfy your thirst without that sugary after-taste.

All of us have an inner thirst within our souls that also needs to be satisfied. And like water, there is only one Source that brings true and lasting satisfaction. That Source is Jesus Christ. He is calling you today to come to Him so He can meet your needs. What will your answer be?

Jesus, I come to You to satisfy the longings of my soul.

❖ April 19 ❖

Ask the Experts   Read: Ecclesiastes 8:7-17

> . . . the wise heart will know the proper
> time and procedure (Eccles. 8:5;NIV).

If you were to ask the experts what's the best way to eat to promote good health and reduce the risk of disease, what do you think they would say? Well, *Consumer Reports* did just that. And here's the consensus of what sixty-eight nutrition experts said about healthy eating:
- Eat seven or more servings of fruit or vegetables a day. (The average for Americans is 3-1/2.)
- Eat no more than three 3-ounce servings of red meat a week. (Americans eat twice that much.)
- Eat fish twice a week.
- Get 20-25 percent of your calories from fat. (The average is 35-40.)
- Eat no more than three egg yokes a week.

As the Bible says, there is a proper time and procedure for everything. The more you know about what to eat and how much, the more success you will have in maintaining a healthy lifestyle.

Lord, give me wisdom to know what, how, and when to eat.

❖ April 20 ❖

TV and Fat Kids   Read: Proverbs 29

> . . . a child left to himself disgraces his mother (Prov. 29:15;NIV).

Does watching TV make kids fat? Yes, according to two reports. Both suggested that excessive TV watching was a major cause in the development of childhood obesity. They found that children who are not obese now will become obese from excessive television viewing. In 1988 the average American child spent twenty-three hours a week watching television. The average American child in 1988 was significantly fatter than children in the 1960s.

Children sitting in front of the TV are inactive. They are not playing or running and burning calories. They burn the same number of calories watching TV that they would burn if they were asleep. Also, the TV is constantly advertising junk food. In one year there are more than eleven thousand low-nutrition junk food ads. During a typical week of prime time television, eating, drinking, or talking about food occurs about nine times an hour.

It's easy to use the television as a babysitter. Parents need to encourage their children to be physically active and to exercise regularly with them.

Lord, help me to encourage my children to exercise
and to monitor what they watch on TV.

❖ April 21 ❖

Yogurt: Cold Medicine?   Read: Isaiah 58

The Lord will guide you always; he will satisfy your needs
. . . and will strengthen your frame (Isa. 58:11;NIV).

Does yogurt have any real health value? Studies at the University of California School of Medicine suggest that it does. Researchers have found that persons who eat live-culture yogurt have 25 percent fewer cold and hay fever symptoms than those who don't eat yogurt. Why is that? Scientists think it may be that yogurt boosts the immune system by stimulating production of gamma interferon.

Yogurt is also a good, low-fat source of calcium, and that helps prevent osterioporis (loss of bone) in women. If you want a healthy frame, be sure you get enough calcium in your diet.

Do you see how small amounts of certain nutrients affect our bodies in different ways? That's why it is dangerous to go on a startvation diet or one that only lets you eat a few selected food items. The Lord will meet all your nutritional needs if You allow Him to guide you as He has promised to do.

Lord, I claim Your promise to guide me,
to satisfy my needs, and to strengthen my body.

❖ April 22 ❖

Diet Pill Side-Effects   Read: Ephesians 5:1-17

Therefore do not be foolish, but understand
what the Lord's will is (Eph. 5:17;NIV).

Do you or someone you know take over-the-counter diet pills for weight loss? If so, is this person often irritable and disgruntled. Does he/she get angry over insignificant things and show signs of severe paranoia? It's no wonder, because the active ingredient in most diet pills is an appetite suppressant that can cause nervousness, rapid pulse, dizziness, and other complaints.

The manufacturers caution against exceeding the recommended amount, mixing the pills with other drugs, or using them in the presence of medical ailments, such as high blood pressure. Still, some people react badly to these pills. The fact that a drug can be purchased without a prescription is no guarantee it is safe or not habit forming.

Diet pills are not the answer to permanent weight loss. If you are using them to suppress your appetite, the side effects may cause you more harm than the few extra pounds you need to lose. The Lord has a better way for you.

Lord, I don't want to be foolish in my efforts to lose weight.
Help me to understand Your will for me.

❖ April 23 ❖

The Fairer Sex?

Read: 1 Peter 3:1-7

Wives . . . be submissive to your husbands . . . .
Husbands . . . be considerate as you live with your wives,
and treat them with respect as the weaker partner . . . (1 Pet. 3:1,7;NIV).

Recent research finds that body weight for both sexes hinges heavily on fat intake. Women, however, need exercise more than men to stay trim. Health differences between men and women are often related to hormones, and this can also affect weight gain in women.

Men expand their waistband primarily by eating too much fat. But men seem to switch to a lower-fat way of eating once the wife starts eating that way.

For both sexes, though, just a 5 percent increase in fat intake can result in a two-pound weight gain over two years. So whether you are a man or woman, exercise is still a great calorie burner and one of the best ways to keep flab off the torso.

God's Word also notes the differences between men and women and how they are to act toward one another as husband and wife. When we come into line with God's Word in every area of our lives, we will find ourselves reaping the rewards.

Lord, help me to obey Your Word and be the
kind of spouse You want me to be.

❖ April 24 ❖

How Fat Makes You Fat

Read: Proverbs 1:24-33

Therefore shall they eat of the fruit of their own way,
and be filled with their own devices (Prov. 1:31).

Does eating fat really make you fat? Yes. Foods high in fat stay in your stomach longer after you eat than low-fat foods. Your stomach almost entirely empties within three hours following a meal, but fried potatoes may still be in your stomach the next day!

Fat makes you fat because it slows the digestion and absorption of food. In experiments where animals were fed a totally fat diet, they had zero metabolism after eating. The activity of the body was so low it was as if they had not eaten at all. No wonder fat makes us fat!

Let's face it: You can eat whatever you want, but if you do, your health — and your relationship to God — are bound to suffer.

Lord, help to not to make my stomach my god,
but to eat only those foods that are beneficial to my body.

❖ April 25 ❖

Fats and Exercise Read: Psalm 92

The righteous will flourish like a palm tree, they will grow
like a cedar of Lebanon (Ps. 92:12;NIV).

Yesterday, we talked about how high-fat foods stay in our stomachs longer. That's also one reason why health experts tell us not to eat fat food and then exercise. Instead, we should eat a piece of fresh fruit or a cup of low-fat yogurt to pick us up about mid-afternoon so we can go to our 6:00 p.m. exercise class. If we ate fat food at 3:00 p.m., it would still be in our stomach at 6:00. The yogurt and fresh fruit are complex carbohydrates, and they digest quickly.

The experts tell us that complex carbohydrates (fruits, vegetables, and whole grains) actually stimulate the body to burn calories and actually speed your metabolism. This is what you want — complex carbohydrates that speed up your metabolism, not fat food that slows it down.

God doesn't want us to slow down either. He want us to keep growing spiritually so we can become strong in the Lord.

Thank You, Lord, for this promise that I will flouish and
grow spiritually as long as I trust in You.

❖ April 26 ❖

Eating Spaghetti Read: Proverbs 18:11-24

From the fruit of his mouth a man's stomach
is filled; with the harvest from his lips
he is satisfied (Prov. 18:20;NIV).

The best way to reduce your fat intake is to replace fat foods with fruits and vegetables and other foods — like pasta or spaghetti. Now we're talking!

Remember, however, that you can turn a wonderful food like pasta or spaghetti into a fat food if you load it with rich meat sauces and cheeses. Instead, put a small amount of tomato sauce on a big plate of spaghetti. This way you will be eating a food that is high in complex carbohydrate and low in fat. Your body will burn this food for energy and not store it as fat.

You will also find that you feel more satisfied when you eat complex carbohydrates because they stimulate insulin in our bodies, and this is what lets our brain know that we have had enough to eat and we get the signal to stop eating. Let's learn to satisfy our need for food and not always be searching for ways to stimulate our appetites.

Lord, teach me to eat and talk in a way that
will satisfy me and bring glory to You.

❖ April 27 ❖

F - I - T   Read: 1 Kings 2

> . . . and observe what the Lord
> your God requires . . . (1 Kings 2:3;NIV).

To benefit most from exercise you need the three components described by the word FIT: F — frequent; I — intensity; T — time. The length of time you exercise and the frequency at which you do it are most important. Intensity will usually follow automatically because your body will adjust to more strenuous exercise as you progress.

Getting started is not that hard; it's keeping it up that's challenging. Maybe you started exercising with the new year and now that you've been at it for a while, you are bored. A change in your routine will help. If you've been jogging, try alternating walking or biking every other day. Or, if your exercise routine has lost it's appeal, buy a new video or switch to playing tennis.

Keep going and going — like the "Energizer Battery." A little bit of drudgery is worth the new level of energy you've acquired through exercising. Don't quit, even if all you do is ride your stationary bike during the evening news! Exercise is for a lifetime. God will reward your persistence.

Lord, give me the strength to keep going
and receive the rewards You have for me.

❖ April 28 ❖

Kidney Stones   Read: Isaiah 43:18-28

> . . . I will even make a way in the
> wilderness, and rivers in the desert (Isa. 43:19).

Painful kidney stones affect over 350,000 Americans each year. The odds of getting a kidney stone are one in ten for women and one in seven for men. Most stones form in persons between the ages of twenty and fifty.

"Stones" — formed from crystallized salts in the upper urinary system — are most prevalent during the warm months of the year when large amounts of body fluid are lost through perspiration. Active people, such as joggers, are particularly at risk, since they often don't drink enough fluids to compensate for excessive perspiration. Others at risk are those who do not drink enough water during the day. Health experts agree that the key to preventing kidney stones is drinking lots of liquids — as much as 8 ounces every waking hour.

God wants to do a new thing in your life. Just trust Him to do what He has said He will do.

Lord, do a new thing in me. Make a way for me through the dry
places of my life and send rivers of healing into my life.

❖ April 29 ❖

Nuts for You?

Read: Psalm 5

> For thou, Lord, wilt bless the righteous; with favour wilt
> thou compass him as with a shield (Ps. 5:12).

Nuts are high in fat, and fat contributes to heart disease. Right? Well, usually. Yet a study of thirty thousand Seventh Day Adventists indicated that people who ate nuts at least five times a week had half as many heart attacks as those who ate nuts less than once a week.

What's even more interesting is that this significant reduction occurred in people who were already at low risk for heart disease because of their healthy eating habits.

Researchers speculate that the fatty acid profile of nuts may favorably alter blood lipid levels. What were the most common nuts eaten? Peanuts, almonds, and walnuts — all of which are high in monounsaturated fat, low in saturated fat, and high in fiber. Just be sure the nuts you choose are salt free, and, as with all foods, moderation is the key. Don't forget, nuts are very high in calories!

> *Thank You, Lord, for blessing me and*
> *protecting me with Your favor.*

❖ April 30 ❖

Smoking and Back Pain

Read: 1 Timothy 5

> The sins of some men are obvious, reaching
> the place of judgment ahead of them; the sins of
> others trail behind them (1 Tim. 5:24;NIV).

Did you know that smokers have a higher incidence of lower-back discomfort? To make matters worse, the longer and heavier they smoke, the greater their risk, according to a study of more than ten thousand people over the age of twenty-five. Stress or structural damage are often the cause, and smoking may contribute to either of these factors, according to a recent medical report. One theory tells us that nicotine may decrease blood flow to the spine, which invites injury to the spongy discs between the vertebrae.

If you still smoke or know someone who does, this is certainly a great reason to quit. Anyone who has had back problems would do almost anything to alleviate the pain.

All of us have sin in our lives that needs to be corrected. Let's look to God to help us repent and change today!

> *Lord, show me those sins in my life that are trailing*
> *behind me so I can correct them before it's too late.*

❖ **May 1** ❖

Mother and Baby   Read: Isaiah 49:8-21

> Can a mother forget the baby at her breast and have no
> compassion on the child she has borne? . . . (Isa. 49:15;NIV).

When a woman gets pregnant she often develops a new interest in her health for the sake of her baby. According to a study, 90 percent of women make major changes in their lifestyles during pregnancy, such as eating better, eating regularly, exercising more, and cutting out caffeine, smoking, and alcohol. But six months after the baby is born, only 10 percent maintain these healthy changes.

Why didn't these women keep up their good health practices? The study cited the fact that there is pressure from advertising, friends, doctors, etc. on pregnant women to make healthy choices. Once they give birth, however, the women felt that this pressure was removed.

If you have had a baby and have reverted back to some old habits, today is your day to revert again — back to health. Why? Because God loves you as much as you love that child. You have as much worth as your baby.

Lord, help me to see that You love me as much as I love my baby.

❖ **May 2** ❖

Storing Up!   Read: 1 Timothy 6

> . . . do good . . . . Laying up in store for themselves a good
> foundation against the time to come . . . (1 Tim. 6:18-19).

When you look at your plate and see fat, remember "the fat you eat is the fat you wear." Most of the fat we eat is stored as fat on our bodies. The average American consumes as much as *eight* times more fat per day than what is actually needed! In fact, our bodies only need the fat equivalent of only *one tablespoon* of vegetable oil each day!

Too much fat causes weight gain and a slowing of the digestion and proper absorption of food. When we eat too much fat, this causes us to store too much cholesterol, and this in turn contributes to heart disease, high blood pressure, stroke, and other serious illnesses.

Most of the fat we eat is ready to be stored in our fat cells. The body has to do very little work to break it down for storage, so very few calories of fat are burned to get it ready for storage.

Instead of storing up fat, let's be more concerned about storing up good deeds that will benefit others and keep us from becoming so self-centered.

*Lord, help me to concentrate on doing good things for
others instead of always thinking about myself.*

❖ May 3 ❖

Sports Drink
Read: Matthew 16:13-28

*If anyone would come after me, he must deny himself and take
up his cross and follow me (Matt. 16:24;NIV).*

You're rushing from the office to the gym for a 7:00 p.m. workout. After a long day at work, your stomach may say "eat." But you know from experience that eating too much before you work out can cause stomach cramps. So pre-treat yourself with a sports drink.

Drinking a good sports drink right before exercising can provide carbo-hydrates for energy, plus lots of liquid and some minerals that you're likely to lose in sweat. Keep in mind, too, that once you start working up that sweat, your appetite will naturally wane due to increased blood circulation.

Sometimes we need to deny ourselves food in order to do what is best for us physically. This is also true in the spiritually realm. If we deny the desire to serve ourselves and instead choose to follow Jesus, the rewards will far outweigh what little we give up.

*Lord, I have decided to deny myself the pleasures of
this world and to follow You, with all my heart.*

❖ May 4 ❖

God's Training
Read: Revelation 3:14-22

*Those whom I love I rebuke
and discipline . . . (Rev. 3:19;NIV).*

Changing ingrained habits is never easy. In fact, it can be downright painful, but in the end it will be worth all the effort and discomfort that we put forth.

If God has shown you a sensible eating and exercising plan and you choose to disobey and "do your own thing," you will surely reap the conse-quences. I believe you lose the joy and peace of obedience whenever you disobey.

Let's thank God for giving us good information and for disciplining us when we need correction. We also need to allow God to train us so we can produce the blessings of right living for His glory and for our good. Open your heart to Him today. He loves you and wants you to succeed.

*Lord, help me to accept Your discipline in my life.
I want You to train me so I produce the
blessings of righteousness for Your glory.*

❖ May 5 ❖

Cardio-Nutrients   Read: 1 Timothy 6:11-17

> . . . God, who richly provides us with everything for
> our enjoyment (1 Tim. 6:17;NIV).

Have you heard of the cardio-nutrients? They are vitamins and minerals that pack an added punch against heart disease. Most of the scientific evidence centers around vitamins C, E, and beta carotene — known as the "antioxidant" vitamins. A large number of studies suggest that people who have a high intake of these nutrients have a lower risk of heart disease and heart attack than people whose diets aren't as nutrient rich.

Vitamin C and beta carotene, the other two promising antioxidants, are readily available in fruits and vegetables, which are core ingredients in a heart-healthy, low-fat diet.

A diet that's very low in fat and cholesterol, however, limits certain foods that are key sources of vitamin E, like eggs and seed oils like sunflower or sesame. That's why it's even more important to eat foods like whole grains, kale, and spinach. But these are only good — not great — sources of vitamin E. Multivitamin/mineral supplements may help protect against deficiencies.

*Lord, thank You for providing everything I need in
order to enjoy life and good health.*

❖ May 6 ❖

Soybeans   Read: Ezekiel 4

> Take wheat and barley, beans and lentils, millet and spelt . . .
> and use them to make bread for yourself . . . (Ezek. 4:9;NIV).

Soybeans may be the food of the future — if not the present. Nutritionists are raving over this bean that has heretofore been grown primarily — at least in the United States — for feeding animals.

The National Cancer Institute has found that persons who eat soybean products have less colon and rectal cancer than those who eat no soy. In addition, substituting soy protein for animal protein in the diet has been shown to reduce the levels of harmful LDL cholesterol.

You can find a variety of soy products in the stores now in the form of tofu, soy cheese, and soy milk. In years to come soybeans will likely be a major source of protein in American's diets.

Beans, lentils, and whole grains have been the basis of most Middle Eastern diets for thousands of years. In fact, God told Ezekiel to make a nutritious bread out of these foods to sustain him for more than a year!

Lord, show me how to eat the way You showed Ezekiel.

❖ May 7 ❖

A Wife's Diet

Read: Titus 2

> . . . train the younger women to love their husbands and
> children, to be self-controlled and pure . . . (Titus 2:4;NIV).

Wives, if you want your husband to lose his "pot belly" and get on a healthy program of low-fat eating and exercising, then it may be up to you to lead the way. A recent study shows there is a strong connection between a wife's diet and exercise program and her husband's eating habits. It was found that wives who eat low-fat are able to influence their husbands into eating right.

On the other hand, if the wives don't watch their fat intake, most of their husbands do not watch their's either. If the person in the family who plans the meals can adopt healthier dietary habits, those habits may then be transferred to others. In other words, husbands and children usually eat what the wife eat.

As wives and mothers, we are mainly responsible for seeing that our family gets nourishing meals. Let's do all we can to not only set a good example with our eating habits but also to prepare food that will keep our husband and children healthy.

> *Lord, help me to feed my family in a way*
> *that will be of value to them.*

❖ May 8 ❖

The Perfect Problem?

Read: Psalm 102

> Hear my prayer, O Lord . . . . Because of my loud groaning
> I am reduced to skin and bones (Ps. 102:1,5;NIV).

There is one problem that we'd all like to have: the need to gain weight! Unfortunately, most of those in this enviable position are recovering from an illness or, like the Psalmist, are too distressed to eat. Others may just be burning up too many calories through exercise.

You can gain weight by eating ice cream, chocolate bars, potato chips — all the foods that are taboo if you're trying to lose weight. But your cholesterol level will shoot up faster than your weight does.

For healthy weight gain, focus instead on foods that are naturally high in calories and fiber but low in saturated fat and cholesterol. Let me suggest a lunch of peanut-butter-and-banana sandwiches (on whole-grain bread). Bananas are high in calories and contain virtually no fat. Peanuts are also loaded with calories. Although most of them are fat calories, the fat is mono-unsaturated, which appears to be heart-healthy when eaten in moderation.

> *Lord, I'm glad I can cry out to You for help*
> *when I am afflicted and distressed.*

❖ May 9 ❖

Take It Away!   Read: Exodus 23:20-26

Worship the Lord your God, and his blessing will be on
your food and water . . . (Exod. 23:25;NIV).

It's becoming more and more clear through scientific research that certain vitamins and minerals, along with exercise and a healthy diet, are associated with lower risk of heart disease.

Also, there's laboratory evidence that suggests that certain nutrients help prevent LDL cholesterol — the bad stuff — from being damaged by mutated oxygen molecules known as free radicals. Free radicals cause changes in LDL that make it accumulate in your arteries, forming the "fatty streaks" that are the first signs of heart disease.

Preliminary research has linked supplemental vitamins and minerals with lower risk of heart disease. They include the B vitamins (B6, B12, and folate), potassium, calcium, and trace minerals like magnesium, chromium, and selenium.

God has promised to bless our food and water. We also need to trust Him to use vitamin and mineral supplements to strengthen our bodies.

Lord, I claim this promise for myself and my family.

❖ May 10 ❖

Apt Words   Read: Proverbs 25:1-13

A word aptly spoken is like apples of gold in
settings of silver (Prov. 25:11;NIV).

Let's look at two common, but not serious, problems and what you can do to correct them and stay healthy.

You crave potato chips. The solution is to switch to lightly salted pretzel chips. They crunch like potato chips, but that's where the similarity ends. Potato chips get about 60 percent of their calories from fat; pretzel chips are only about 15 percent fat. In addition, you save 4 grams of fat for every half ounce your eat. Just don't dip them in some high-fat sour cream or mayonnaise dip!

You've got a cold. Try eating a take-out order of Chinese hot-and-sour soup. A few years ago, a study confirmed what moms have been saying for centuries: Chicken soup can help soothe the symptoms of a cold. No one knows exactly why.

God's Word is full of "apt words" that can make your life beautiful.

*Lord, help me to search Your Word, the Bible,
for the apt words You want to speak to me.*

❖ **May 11** ❖

Turn and Burn

Read: Romans 13

. . . Clothe yourselves with the Lord Jesus Christ, and do not think about how to gratify the desires of the sinful nature (Rom. 13:14;NIV).

When you want to burn fat, you need to eat carbohydrates instead of fat. Why? Because it is much harder for your body to turn carbohydrates into body fat than it is to turn dietary fat into body fat. Because our bodies store fat very easily, it takes a small amount of energy to digest, absorb, transport, and store fat. That means your body doesn't burn many calories when you eat fattening food. Instead, it stores almost all the calories from that food.

When you eat carbohydrates instead of fat, however, your body burns a lot of those calories just getting the food ready for storage. Then, instead of storing the calories as fat, your body turns them into glycogen and stores this in your muscles and liver. This glycogen is quickly used by your body for energy. When you eat foods like fruits, vegetables, and whole grains, these calories are quickly burned, and the remaining calories are turned into glycogen and used by your body for energy.

Lord, help me stop thinking about how to gratify my sinful desires with rich, fatty foods. Help me to be more like Jesus.

❖ **May 12** ❖

A Good Tip

Read: Proverbs 1:1-19

Let the wise listen and add to their learning . . . (Prov. 1:5;NIV).

Yesterday, we learned that eating complex carbohydrates like fruits, vegetables, and whole grains makes it is harder for your body to turn these foods into fat. But there are other benefits, too. Loading your diet with complex carbohydrates means you're probably eating fewer total calories, too. Why? Because one gram of carbohydrate contains about 4 calories, while one gram of fat has 9.

Here's another tip: Stick with small meals throughout the day because larger meals will result in your body releasing more insulin, which causes your body to store fat. Foods that cause more insulin to be released promote weight gain. Why? Because insulin keeps your fat cells from breaking down fat and releasing it into the bloodstream where it can be burned as fuel.

Like the writers of the Book of Proverbs, I want you to remember the things we are learning this year. It might be a good idea to use a highlighter to mark those tips that you don't want to forget.

Lord, give me a mind to remember and put into practice all I am learning this year.

❖ May 13 ❖

A Quick Fix

Read: Joshua 21:43-45

. . . all the Lord's promises . . . was fulfilled (Josh. 21:45;NIV).

Coffee "addicts" can get clobbered with caffeine-withdrawal headaches when they quit cold turkey. But for those who take their coffee in moderation, a strong cup or two can abort a migraine in the making.

Migraines are usually caused by the dilation of blood vessels, and doctors have found that caffeine constricts blood vessels. For best results, however, swallow an aspirin with a caffeine-laced drink. If coffee's not your cup of tea, choose another drink with caffeine, such as cola or black tea.

Don't get me wrong; I'm not advocating coffee drinking. But I think this is an important tip that could help those who get painful migraine headaches. Just remember, in this case, the caffeine is to be used like a medicine and not constantly as a beverage. The better way is to pray and ask the Lord to heal you.

Lord, help me to build my faith by reading Your Word
and to trust You for healing.

❖ May 14 ❖

Working Is Healthy?

Read: Colossians 3:18-25

Whatever you do, work at it with all your heart; as
working for the Lord . . . (Col. 3:23;NIV).

Job-related stress has generally been regarded as a risk factor for men. In fact, it has been assumed the work-a-day life is one of the reasons men don't live as long as women do.

Now the results of an interesting study indicate that when women work outside of the home, they are actually healthier. The study found that women in professional roles smoked and drank less and exercised more than their stay-at-home counterparts. And they had lower blood pressure and lower levels of cholesterol and blood sugar.

The researchers concluded that women who worked outside of the home probably feel more control over their lives, which may mean that they are actually under less stress than women who stay at home. Since the women in this study were well-to-do professional women, it would mean that had less stress because they enjoyed the jobs they were doing. It also made me wonder if they had a housekeeper and a cook to help them at home!

Lord, help me to do all my work — at home and
on the job — as unto You.

The Right Exercise for You

Read: Luke 8:9-18

> . . . those . . . who hear the word, retain it, and by
> persevering produce a crop (Luke 8:15;NIV).

Exercise and perseverance go together. That's why it's important to choose the right form of exercise. If you select a program that suits your lifestyle, your schedule, and your budget, you're more likely to stick with it. Someone has said, "If you like it today, you will do it tomorrow."

Walking briskly provides cardiovascular exercise without straining your muscles. Jogging, biking, swimming, or using a rowing machine are all excellent ways to burn fat and firm your muscles. Aerobic fitness classes or videos make exercising fun and add variety to your daily workout.

Once you've decided on a plan, don't overdo it. Do what you can in the beginning and build up gradually. If you push too hard, you are likely to give up before you even get started. Training takes time. Slow, consistent, and steady is the winning ticket in the game of exercise.

Perseverance also counts in our spiritual lives. It's during times of testing that God is at work molding us into mature men and women of faith. Don't give up!

Lord, help me to persevere and not give up!

Be a Winner

Read: Psalm 60

> With God we will gain the victory . . . (Ps. 60:12;NIV).

As Christians we should never underestimate the fact that God is all-knowing, all-powerful, and in control of our lives. But we should also never underestimate the impact our own thought life can have on us.

Negative thinking is not of God. And negative thinking reaps a negative harvest. I have learned to talk back to my negative thoughts, and it works! All through the Bible, God is impressing us with the truth that through Him we can be winners.

Even if you feel that, up to this time in our life, you have lost one opportunity after another and have missed life's best, it is still not too late for you to experience victory through the name of Jesus. He will restore to you all that Satan has tried to steal — lost dreams and opportunities. Jesus can quickly turn our negatives into positives once we allow Him to live in us and be Lord of our lives. We just have to let Him!

Lord, teach me how to think like a winner and
trust You to bring the victory.

❖ May 17 ❖

Best Calcium Source   Read: Jude 17-25

. . . build yourselves up in your most holy faith and
pray in the Holy Spirit (Jude 20;NIV).

Calcium is bone building material. For children it grows strong bones. For older people, it keeps them strong.

Without an adequate supply of calcium an elderly person's bones become brittle. The condition is known as osteoporosis. That's why doctors often advise the elderly to take calcium supplements. But there's a catch-22 here. As you get older, the body loses its ability to absorb calcium from certain supplements.

The calcium in milk, however, is readily absorbed and is the preferred source of calcium for the elderly. Skim milk, by the way, is higher in calcium than higher-fat milk.

If calcium supplements are taken, most doctors recommend the more soluble form, calcium citrate, as opposed to the less soluble calcium carbonate. Be sure to take them with a meal to boost absorption.

Lord, teach me how to build up my
body and my faith.

❖ May 18 ❖

Keeping Your Teeth   Read: Genesis 49:1-12

His eyes shall be darker than wine, his teeth
whiter than milk (Gen. 49:12 NIV).

Did you know that a balanced diet will help save your teeth? In a recent study with patients who suffer from periodontal (gum disease) disease and plaque, it was found that those who adjusted their diet as well as their brushing habits had significantly less disease and plaque than those who did not.

What kinds of foods were they eating? It was nothing more than good basic food — fruits, vegetables, and whole grains. They were also advised to eat less sugar and more foods containing vitamins C and E, zinc, and folic acid. In addition, they ate more calcium-rich foods and included more grains, fruits, lean meats, and dairy products. They also avoided fatty, sugary foods.

Now that's something you can sink your teeth into. A good diet *does* provide tooth protection.

When Jacob blessed his twelve sons, he blessed Judah with white, healthy teeth. It seems white teeth have always been considered a treasured physical feature. Let's take care of the teeth God has given us by eating a balanced diet.

Lord, help me to take care of the teeth You have given me.

❖ **May 19** ❖

False Teeth?   Read: 1 Corinthians 3:10-23

> Don't you know that you yourselves are
> God's temple . . . (1 Cor. 3:16;NIV).

Yesterday, we talked about how a balanced diet affects our teeth and gums. Teeth may seem a small thing to you. You may even think, *If they fall out, I will replace them.* But, if your diet can help you to save your teeth, it would be fitting and proper to make the changes necessary to get them in order. God, who has even the hairs on our head numbered, is surely interested in how many teeth we have in our mouths and what condition they are in!

God's Word teaches us that our body is the temple of the Holy Spirit. Now in a physical temple, we would think it poor maintenance if we had everything in place, but the windows were yellowed, cracked, and maybe even missing. The same is true with our spiritual temple. We should want to please Him by caring for our own health. Let's make a wise choice for Him today.

Lord, help me to keep Your temple, my body,
in perfect working order, teeth and all.

❖ **May 20** ❖

Trick Yourself   Read: Psalm 51:1-6

> Surely you desire truth in the inner
> parts; you teach me wisdom in
> the inmost place (Ps. 51:6;NIV).

Have you ever said, "My eyes were bigger than my stomach"? Well, it turns out that the way we see things has a lot to do with how much we eat. Did you know you can decrease your appetite and end up eating a lot less just by changing what you see during a meal? Here are some ideas recommended by a diet expert:

• Use smaller plates and bowls. You don't need as much food to fill them up, but you won't feel deprived.

• Eat from several plates as a way of slowing down your eating habits. That will give your stomach more time to signal the brain that it's satisfied.

• Use a place mat instead of a tablecloth to define the area where the food should be. This keeps you from looking beyond your own space.

These are just a few ideas. I'm sure with a little creative thinking of your own, you can find ways to trick yourself into eating less.

Lord, give me wisdom to know how to discipline
myself to eat only what I need to be healthy.

❖ May 21 ❖

Beating the Odds   Read: Ezekiel 18:19-32

For I have no pleasure in the death of him that dieth, saith the
Lord God: wherefore turn yourselves, and live ye (Ezek. 18:32).

D r. William P. Castelli is the first man in his family to turn fifty without
having had a heart attack. Now at age sixty he says, "I'm living proof you can
beat the odds of heart disease — even if it runs in your family." As director of
the Framingham Heart Study, he knew he had to change his lifestyle once he
realized that:
- Smokers have a 70 percent chance of dying of a heart attack.
- High blood pressure increases one's risk of heart attack and stroke by as
much as *five* times.
- High total cholesterol and low HDL cholesterol (the good kind) are
among the strongest predictors of heart disease.

Here's the doctor's advice: stop smoking, get your blood pressure under
control, and lower your total cholesterol and raise your good cholesterol. His
was 270. Since then he's reduced his to 190 and raised his HDL cholesterol
from 49 to 63. He knew if he didn't he'd become just another statistic himself.

Lord, help me to change those areas of my life
that are destroying my health.

❖ May 22 ❖

The Jeans Test   Read: Song of Solomon 2:14-17

Take us the foxes, the little foxes,
that spoil the vines . . . (Song of Sol. 2:15).

O nce a year, on your birthday, try on a pair of jeans that fit you well. On
your next birthday try them on again. If they still fit well, you are keeping your
fat under control.

The Bible teaches that it is the "little foxes that spoil the vines."
Sometimes it is letting the little things go by unchecked that create a big
problem for us. Remember that 150 unneeded calories a day will result in a
weight gain of 13 pounds in a year. You see, if the little foxes are stopped when
they are little, it is easier to get things under control.

Whether your weight needs a little or a big adjustment, God is able to meet
your needs. If you have failed before, God is the God of a second (and third and
fourth) chance. His mercies are new every morning. You can begin again —
and with Him, you can make it!

Lord, I need a another chance to begin again in my efforts to keep
my weight under control. Thank You for being there for me.

❖ May 23 ❖

Commanded to Love

Read: 1 John 4:7-21

Hereby know we that we dwell in him, and he in us,
because he hath given us of his Spirit (1 John 4:13).

Are there people you feel you cannot love? It's true, you can't love them, but the Holy Spirit dwelling within you *can* . If you do not know the presence of God's Spirit and you are not motivated by His Spirit to love others, you should re-examine your experience of salvation.

"And this commandment have we from him, That he who loveth God love his brother also" (1 John 4:21). The two greatest commandments are that we love God with all our heart and with all our soul and with all our mind, and that we love our neighbor as ourselves. And please notice that it is a commandment. It is expected of us. If the Spirit of God truly abides with us, we will obey and demonstrate the kind of love that makes our salvation evident.

Heavenly Father, fill me with Your Holy Spirit
so I can truly love You and love others with all my heart.

❖ May 24 ❖

When to Weigh In

Read: Luke 21:29-38

Be careful, or your hearts will be weighed
down with dissipation . . . (Luke 21:34;NIV).

Do you know the scale can be public enemy number one if you are on a diet? It can bring torment, and weigh-ins can even be addictive! If you are trying to change your eating and exercise patterns, then once a week is often enough to weigh in! Remember, it is the overall trend toward positive behavior that you are after.

How do you stop the scales from luring you onto them day after day? First, keep a record of how often you weigh for one month. Look at that pattern. What did you weigh on day one? On day thirty? Cut back on the number of times you weigh. Try guessing what the scale will say before you step on it. It probably won't be telling you anything new.

A young boy and his playmate were studying the family's bathroom scale.

"How does this thing work?" asked the playmate.

"I dunno," the boy replied. "All I know is you stand up on it, and it makes you mad!"

If that's what weighing every day is doing to you, then it's time to throw the scale away or bury it in the bathroom closet.

Lord, You know my weight now and what I should weigh
in order to be healthy. Make of me what You want me to be.

❖ May 25 ❖

Love One Another   Read: 1 John 3:11-24

For this is the message that ye heard from the beginning,
that we should love one another (1 John 3:11).

Someone has said, "Love is hard to define, but it is so easy to see." True love is seen in our response toward people and toward God.

Let's face it: It's a lot easier to talk about love than it is to demonstrate it. I guess this is why we sing about it and talk about it so much. True love is more than pious speech. It is doing unto others as you would have them do unto you. It is doing for others when they cannot do *anything* for you. It is sometimes being a servant when you know that the recipient of your service is undeserving.

As we grow and mature spiritually we will demonstrate true love in our lives.

*Lord, help me to obey Your command to love others,
even when I feel they don't deserve it.*

❖ May 26 ❖

Sticky, Stickier, Stickiest   Read: 1 John 1

If we confess our sins, he is faithful and just and will forgive us our
sins and purify us from all unrighteousness (1 John 1:9;NIV).

What makes foods most harmful to the teeth? According to the American Dental Association, it's their "stickiness." Starchy foods are worse than sugary ones because simple sugars are quickly washed away by saliva. Starchy ones, on the other hand, tend to stick to tooth surfaces longer creating a breeding ground for bacteria. These bacteria then begin to emit enamel-eroding acids.

Here is a list of twenty-one foods studied by dental researchers as to their stickiness: *Barely sticky:* apples, bananas, hot fudge sundaes, mild chocolate bars. *Moderately sticky:* chocolate-caramel bars, white bread, caramels, creme-filled sponge cake. *Stickier:* dried figs, jelly beans, plain doughnuts, chocolate-caramel-peanut bars, raisins. *Stickiest:* granola bars, oatmeal cookies, sugared cereal flakes, potato chips, salted crackers, puffed oat cereal, creme-sandwich cookies, peanut butter crackers.

You can see why it's so important to brush your teeth after every meal to remove any sticky substances.

We also need to be diligent about quickly confessing and repenting of any sin in our life before it begins to corrupt our entire lives.

*Heavenly Father, I confess that I have sinned against You.
Please forgive me and cleanse my heart.*

❖ May 27 ❖

Stand Fast   Read: Galatians 5:1-15

Stand fast therefore in the liberty wherewith Christ hath made us free,
and be not entangled again with the yoke of bondage (Gal. 5:1).

When you are listening to the controlling, guiding voice of the Lord you are not a slave to cookies or other tempting treats. So often we are just deceived into thinking that we can eat a small amount of a fattening food.

Ask God to show you the items in your diet that are harmful. You may be in bondage to chemicals that are found in addictive food and not even know it. If you seek the Lord's help, He will set you free. In fact, Jesus Christ will give you what you desire most: to eat for the health and strength of your body that you might serve Him all of your days. God's Word will give us victory. We are more than conquerors through Christ who strengthens us.

*Lord Jesus, I believe You have already set me
free to live a life free from bondage to any kind
of food. I give my life and my desires to You.*

❖ May 28 ❖

Arthritis and Exercise   Read: Matthew 15:21-39

And great multitudes came unto him, having with them those
that were lame, blind, dumb, maimed, and many others, and cast
them down at Jesus' feet; and he healed them (Matt. 15:30).

If you have arthritis, should you exercise? Yes. Research shows that aerobic exercise — the kind that gives the heart a good workout like brisk walking — helps people with arthritis. A recent study confirms that aerobic exercise actually *reduces* joint pain.

Exercise also increases strength and the ability to take in air and circulate blood. In fact, it seems that exercise helps to get nutrients into the joints. Exercise also may have a positive influence on the arthritis patient's mood and social activity.

You want to go very easy with your exercise program. Don't force your body, and warm up slowly. I have some specially designed exercises that are low impact and easy to do. Once you begin to exercise every day, your body will get used to it.

If your doctor approves, you may want to try walking, dancing, swimming. You may also want to contact the Arthritis Foundation and ask them about their program called PACE (People With Arthritis Can Exercise).

Lord Jesus, I thank You for Your healing power.

❖ May 29 ❖

Think Thin   Read: Luke 18:18-34

> Jesus replied, "What is impossible with men is
> possible with God" (Luke 18:27;NIV).

Maybe you have been condemning yourself for years for being over-weight. Instead of knocking yourself, begin saying, "With God's help, I can be thin." Or, "With God's help I can overcome whatever habit has me bound." Once you allow your desires to line up with God's desires for you, then truly all things become possible.

How about thinking yourself thin? Picture in your mind how you would like to look and believe it is possible through Christ. He wants you healthy and fit for His service. Then eat a sensible, low-fat diet, coupled with regular exercise of a type you can enjoy. I promise you, if you stick with it, you will not be disappointed. Positive thinking leads to positive talking which leads to positive action, all for the glory of God.

Someone has said: "The pessimist sees the difficulty in every opportunity; the optimist sees the opportunity in every difficulty."

> *Heavenly Father, I believe You desire victory for*
> *me in every area of weakness and that, through You,*
> *I can overcome the negatives in my life.*

❖ May 30 ❖

The God of Comfort   Read: 2 Corinthians 1:1-14

> . . . God of all comfort; Who comforteth us in all our tribulation, that we
> may be able to comfort them which are in any trouble, by the comfort
> wherewith we ourselves are comforted of God (2 Cor. 1:3-4).

As you continue to embrace a new way of eating, desiring wholesome food, and exercising your body, it's easy to begin to feel sorry for yourself. Have you been asking lately: "Why can't I eat the good things instead of being grateful for a better, healthier food plan?"

As you look to God and desire to live a life that glorifies Him, He will comfort you. You will experience a peace and joy that you can pass on to others as they see the changes in your life. Your victory will overflow because your motive is right — to be healthy in order to glorify God in all you do. As a result, your victory will overflow, and you will be used by God to comfort and encourage others.

> *Thank You Lord for comforting me as I exercise*
> *my body and eat better for Your glory.*

Listening to Your Body   Read: Matthew 10:24-42

> Are not two sparrows sold for a penny? Yet not one of them
> will fall to the ground apart from the will of your Father
> . . . you are worth more than many sparrows (Matt. 10:29-31;NIV).

After you've removed the bathroom scale, you may find that you are paying more attention to your body and what it is saying to you. If so, that means you are learning to gauge when you feel hunger and when you feel full. After a while, you will think less about what the scale indicates and more about how you feel.

You will eventually learn to listen to your body and eat only in response to hunger. You'll also know when to stop eating. If you eat quality food and exercise regularly, you will be able to make peace with your body now, no matter what the size. Remember, your worth as a person is not measured by the scale!

Jesus said that "the very hairs of your head are all numbered." Jesus loves you very much. He died to save you because He considers you to be of great worth.

Lord Jesus, thank You for dying on the cross to save me.

❖ June 1 ❖

Fat Kills   Read: Proverbs 16:15-33

There is a way that seems right to a man, but in
the end it leads to death (Prov. 16:25;NIV).

Fat can kill you. Too much fat is the most pervasive problem in the American diet. Americans get almost 40 percent of their calories from fat. Health groups recommend no more than 30 percent — and many suggest keeping it at 25 percent or less. The fat-disease connection has been established in heart disease, some cancers, and diabetes when it is obesity related.

Saturated fat is the number one culprit. It has been linked to elevated blood cholesterol, a contributing factor in heart disease. It causes the body to manufacture cholesterol, which can clog arteries. Remember, too many calories make fat. When calories aren't *needed* by the body they become body fat.

Let's not be so stubborn in our ways that we refuse to accept the truth about fat and disease. If you continue to eat fatty foods and do things your own way, the result may be premature death.

Lord, I know my ways are not right. Help me to change.

❖ June 2 ❖

Made Alive   Read: Ephesians 2:1-10

. . . God, who is rich in mercy, made
us alive with Christ . . . (Eph. 2:4-5;NIV).

If more than 30 percent of your calories come from fat, you're asking for trouble. Obesity and heart disease are just two side effects. So if you're not supposed to be eating high-fat foods, what should you be eating? Fruits, vegetables, and whole grains need to make up approximately 70 percent of your diet. If this represents a radical departure in your eating habits, don't panic. Long-term changes are best accomplished one step at a time.

Start off by making sure you eat *five* fruits and vegetables a day. Start with an increase from one serving to two or three. You can do this by eating an apple in the morning and raw carrots in the afternoon.

Another way to lower your fat intake is to look for healthier versions of the foods you like. Select complex carbohydrates such as grains, breads, pasta, beans, corn, and potatoes because these will easily be broken down by your body. If you make these a regular part of your diet, you will be on the way to a longer, healthier life.

Thank You, Lord, for having mercy on me and giving me
new life through Jesus Christ.

❖ June 3 ❖

Meat and Fat   Read: Leviticus 7:22-38

The Lord said to Moses, "Say to the Israelites: 'Do not eat
any of the fat of cattle, sheep or goats . . .' " (Lev. 7:22-23;NIV).

How can you make sure you are getting enough protein in your diet? Health experts advise against protein supplements and the highly advertised amino acids. So where should you get your protein? The best sources of protein are foods: lean meat, fish, and poultry.

It's a myth to say meat is bad. *Fat* in meat is bad. Lean meat is an excellent source of iron, which helps the blood transport oxygen through your blood, and zinc — which promotes healing.

Eat less hamburger meat, and, when you do eat it, be sure it is the leanest you can find. Begin to consider meat as a small part of your meals instead of the centerpiece.

The Old Testament dietary laws included the eating of certain meats, but the Israelites were forbidden to eat fat. Once again we find that God had the right idea all along!

*Lord, help me to get the right amount of
protein in my diet without eating too much fat.*

❖ June 4 ❖

Small Steps   Read: Job 8

Your beginnings will seem humble, so
prosperous will your future be (Job 8:7;NIV).

While we're on the subject of how to reduce fat intake, let me suggest a few small steps you can take. One good place to start is to switch from whole milk to 2 percent, then to 1/2 percent or skim. From there, you can begin to cut saturated fat in other ways by eating fewer whole-fat animal products such as meat, milk, and cheeses.

The next step is to learn to read labels to determine how many fat grams are in a serving size. Then buy only those products that are the lowest in fat. Just taking it one day at a time, adding fruits, vegetables, and whole grains to your diet and replacing high-fat food with food that has no fat or is lower in fat, will get you into a healthy low-fat way of eating.

Starting out with small changes in your eating habits is the best way to go. In fact, a little at a time is also the way God usually works. Most people think they have to change their complete lifestyle overnight. If you've ever tried to do it, you know it doesn't work. Let's try to do things God's way.

Lord God, bless my first small steps toward low-fat eating.

❖ June 5 ❖

Summer Kidney Stones   Read: Psalm 107:23-35

He turned the desert into pools of water and the
parched ground into flowing springs (Ps. 107:35;NIV).

Summertime is prime time for kidney stones. Why? Because of loss of water through perspiration, which reduces the body's water fluid to a dangerous degree. Kidney stones often form when an excessive concentration of waste products causes the urine to become supersaturated.

What do we need to do to prevent kidney stones? Drink plenty of water. Your body can be two quarts low on water and you won't even feel thirsty. Make sure you drink plenty of water during exercise, especially outdoor exercise. Tennis players have been known to lose 6 pounds of water during a vigorous match. That fluid needs to be replaced. Drink water before, during, and after exercising.

Water is crucial to life no matter where we live on this earth. God, however, has the power to make dry land flourish. He can also do the same for you and your life. Just ask Him.

Lord, cause the dry places of my life to flourish.

❖ June 6 ❖

An Ounce of Prevention   Read: Exodus 15

I will put none of these diseases upon thee . . .
for I am the Lord that healeth thee (Exod. 15:26).

You've heard the saying, "Prevention is worth a pound of cure," well, it certainly applies in the case of kidney stones. Although 12 percent of the U.S. population suffer these painful formations, they can easily be prevented.

Stones can develop from a variety of mineral compounds, but calcium oxalate accounts for most. Oxalate is found in iced tea. This is a popular summer drink, but it has one significant draw-back — it dehydrates. That means it takes the water *out* of you. In fact, if you drink iced tea, you probably need to follow it with a glass of water to replace what you may have lost. To increase the absorption rate of water you should drink it cold and not add sugar or salt to it. Chilled, plain water is the best thirst quencher.

God doesn't want us to be sick. If we follow His commands and do what is right in His sight, we will stay healthy. But, if we do get sick, we can ask Him to heal us.

*Lord, teach me to obey Your commands and
heal those areas of my body that are sick.*

❖ June 7 ❖

Cool Down

Read: Hebrews 10:35-39

You need to persevere so that when you have done the will of
God, you will receive what he has promised (Heb. 10:36;NIV).

After any vigorous exercise, you should go through a cool down phase.
When you stop, your skeletal muscles relax, but your heart continues working
hard to bring the oxygen to your muscles. It continues to pound in your chest.
As a result, the muscles are not able to assist the circulation system in getting
blood back to your heart. Your blood pressure can then drop and you can
become light-headed. You may faint or even worse.

After vigorous exercise, walk at an easy pace for five to ten minutes or
until you are no longer breathing hard. This keeps the large muscles in the legs
active while the blood supply is redistributed. Your cool down time is a crucial
part of your workout. Don't short change your body by being too quick to stop.

We also need patience in our spiritual lives. If we keep doing the will of
God, we will eventually receive what He has promised us.

*Lord, give me patience so that I can continue to do
Your will and receive Your promise of eternal life.*

❖ June 8 ❖

Be Good to Yourself

Read: 1 John 3:1-10

How great is the love the Father has lavished on us,
that we should be called children of God! . . . (1 John 3:1;NIV).

By now, you may be feeling like you are doing everything wrong, and
that you will never be able to change. I suggest you take some time to remind
yourself that you are special because God created you. Compliment yourself.
Think about your good traits and accomplishments, and reward even small
areas of improvement.

Remember, God loves you very much, no matter what your physical —
or even spiritual — condition. If you have accepted Jesus Christ as your
Saviour, then you are a child of God. Surely, your Heavenly Father wants to
help you succeed. You are not alone.

If you have never invited Jesus Christ into your heart and life, I suggest
you turn to the back of this book and read "A Final Word." There I take you
through the steps from the Bible that will show you how to be saved. Once you
do that, you'll find that all the guilt and condemnation about your habits and
lifestyle will be washed away in God's love.

*Heavenly Father, thank You for loving me and making me
one of Your children. Help me to see myself as You see me.*

❖ June 9 ❖

Your Ideal Weight   Read: 2 Samuel 22:26-51

As for God, his way is perfect . . . (2 Sam. 22:31;NIV).

Every woman has a magical number in her mind that she thinks she should weigh. This could be her weight when she graduated from high school or when she got married. For many women this "ideal weight" is an unrealistic expectation, and trying to achieve it can cause a great deal of stress.

One lady confessed that when she got to her goal in weight on a popular weight-loss program, it completely consumed her life. She became a slave to staying at that number on her scale.

Many women even want to get below a certain magic number, and in the process they can become sick and nonfunctional. Let's stop worrying about that "perfect number," and decide for ourselves how much we want to weigh. At what weight do you think you look and feel your best? That's where you want your weight to be.

Only God's ways are perfect. That's why without His help, we will ultimately fail.

Lord, show me how much I should weigh
in order to stay healthy and fit.

❖ June 10 ❖

Your Final Number   Read: 1 Samuel 16:6-13

. . . Man looks at the outward appearance, but the
Lord looks at the heart (1 Sam. 16:7;NIV).

Yesterday we talked about your "ideal weight." Today let me share another way to decide on your proper weight. It is usually the weight you are able to maintain for a long period of time — six months or longer. That would be a stable weight for you. Make your final number the point at which your clothes fit well and you feel best. But don't get fixed there. Instead, allow your weight to average a few pounds up and down. This allows for the natural fluctuation of body fat and water.

Concentrate on how good you feel, not on how skinny you think you should look. Don't judge yourself by someone else. If you envy others who appear to have a better body, destructive habits may develop. Make peace within your heart about who you are in God's eyes, then a healthy attitude will produce a healthy body. Be at peace with yourself today.

Lord, forgive me for envying the way other people look. Help me
to accept myself and be at peace with the body You have given me.

❖ June 11 ❖

Scorched and Withered

Read: Mark 4:1-20

> But when the sun came up, the plants were scorched, and
> they withered because they had no root (Mark 4:6;NIV).

This time of year, we often see a lot of young people sunning themselves to develop a "good tan." Maybe that's why those at the highest risk of sun-caused melanoma experienced sunburns prior to age twenty. In fact, Caucasians suffering three or more blistering sunburns before the age of twenty are at five times the risk as those who never had severe sunburns. Also at risk are those with fair skin, light hair, and light eye color. Unfortunately, the deadliest form of skin cancer — malignant melanoma — is on the rise.

To make matters worse, your skin doesn't repair after sun damage. In fact, the damage done to your skin during the summer months from over-exposure does not heal during the winter. Sun damage is cumulative and may not be apparent for twenty to thirty years. But permanent damage will show up some day in the form of wrinkles, blotches, sagging tissue, or skin cancer.

Let's keep our hearts open to receiving God's Word, so we can be rooted firmly in the truth.

Lord, let the seed of Your Word penetrate deeply into my heart.

❖ June 12 ❖

Sun Blockers

Read: Exodus 13

> By day the Lord went ahead of them in a pillar of cloud
> to guide them on their way . . . (Exod. 13:21;NIV).

Yesterday, we talked about the damage the sun can do to our skin. You may be wondering how this happens. Ninety percent of skin cancer comes from the sun's ultraviolet rays and 80 percent of skin cancer occurs on the head, neck, and hands. Be sure to apply sunscreen or, better yet, sun block to protect your face and exposed areas from damaging UV rays.

Almost half of all non-melanoma skin cancer deaths start as tumors in or on the ear. That's why wearing a hat makes sense! A hat can offer protection if it is made of tightly woven fabric (straw hats don't do any good) and if it has a three-inch brim all the way around. Baseball-type hats don't protect the ears.

As for clothing, tightly woven synthetic materials offer the best screening of UV radiation. Remember, dry fabrics offer more protection than wet ones.

In the desert, the Israelites did not have umbrellas and sunscreen, but they were protected from the scorching sun by the pillar of cloud that God provided.

Lord, be my guide and my protection.

❖ June 13 ❖

Are You on Fire?

Read: Acts 2

They saw what seemed to be tongues of fire. . . .
All of them were filled with the Holy Spirit . . . (Acts 2:3-4;NIV).

Ever wonder why so many south-of-the-border cuisines feature red-hot chili peppers? Because eating spicy foods helps dilate blood vessels, making you sweat. And sweating is part of nature's body-cooling mechanism. As perspiration evaporates, your skin temperature drops.

So if you're really hot, try some spicy hot chili! If you do, you may set off a three-alarm fire in your mouth. When that happens, swish your mouth with milk. Contrary to popular practice, water won't squelch a hot-pepper burn. The chemical component that gives red-hot peppers their bite, is actually dispersed by water, so flushing your mouth with it is likely to spread the burning sensation. Whole milk makes a better fire extinguisher because the milk fat absorbs the chemical component that causes the burn.

There is one fire we don't want to put out — and that's the fire of the Holy Spirit burning in our hearts. Like the early disciples, let's ask God to fill us with the Holy Spirit — and fire!

Lord, fill me with the fire of Your Holy Spirit.

❖ June 14 ❖

The Trap

Read: Proverbs 23:1-3

And put a knife to your throat if you are
given to gluttony (Prov. 23:2;NIV).

I have this verse from Proverbs marked in the front of my Bible because God used it to convict me of the sin of gluttony. At one point in my life, I fell into the trap of eating whenever I got bored or felt blue. I started to gain weight and didn't want to go out to walk for fear my neighbors would notice I was getting fat. The devil used this fear to make me a "captive" in my home.

During my quiet time, my gracious God showed me this verse from Proverbs. I wept over my sin, made a fresh commitment to God to live, eat right, and exercise to His glory. Praise God I have been doing that ever since. In fact, it was out of that desperate situation in my life that my present ministry, Beverly Exercise, was born. God takes our mistakes and sufferings and makes something wonderful out of them.

Lord, help me to see my sin the way You see it,
and give me strength to overcome it.

❖ June 15 ❖

Exercising to Music   Read: Psalm 149

Let them praise his name with dancing and make
music to him with tambourine and harp (Ps. 149:3;NIV).

You've heard it said that music can "soothe the savage beast." Now scientists tell us that music's soothing qualities help us exercise better. They're even calling it "the new scientific training tool."

Studies confirm that exercisers perform better with rhythmic music in the background. Certain musical rhythms stimulate physical movement and even improve muscular coordination. Listening to music increases your endurance, regulates your breathing rate, and helps you establish a mood for physical activity. Exercising to music also lowers your perception of pain and fatigue, making it possible for you to push your body harder.

What kind of music should you select? Tunes with predictable rhythms without extreme changes in beat flow better with your body's biological rhythms. Listening to praise songs is a great way to firm up your muscles and strengthen your spirit at the same time!

*Lord, teach me how to praise and worship You with my lips and
with my body. I want to glorify You with my whole being.*

❖ June 16 ❖

Smoke or Praise?   Read: Psalm 34:1-14

I will bless the Lord at all times: his praise shall
continually be in my mouth (Ps. 34:1).

Did you know that smokers tend to have lower levels of vitamin C in their blood and that they tend to eat fewer vitamin C rich foods? That fact could affect the smoker's ability to ward off colds and flu.

And, if you're a smoker, don't break any bones in your body. Why? Because smoking delays the healing of bones. Of course, you could give up smoking and help the break heal quicker.

Here's more bad news: Smoking is responsible for 85 percent of lung cancer cases in men and is the second highest risk factor for heart attack. Smokers have a 70 percent higher death rate from coronary heart disease than nonsmokers. Male smokers have more fat around the waist than nonsmokers, and these fatty deposits are associated with higher blood pressure, fat, and cholesterol in the blood. Also, hormonal changes can be caused by tobacco.

The next time, you reach for a cigarette, quote today's verse. It is hard to smoke and praise God at the same time!

Lord, help me to praise you constantly.

❖ June 17 ❖

TV and Extra Pounds   Read: Ephesians 4:17-32

> . . . you must no longer live as the Gentiles do,
> in the futility of their thinking (Eph. 4:17;NIV).

A study done at Auburn University found that men who watched more than three hours of TV a day were twice as likely to be overweight as those who watched less than one hour. In fact, the waistlines of the typical American family has already shown that the more hours of TV kids watch, the chubbier they are. The researchers are not sure if TV watching causes obesity or if obesity causes more TV watching. They believe one reinforces the other.

Let's learn to monitor the TV behavior of our children as well as ourselves, and spend more active time taking walks, playing tennis, or doing other things with the family that will keep us active and communicating.

God is calling us not to live the way we used to or as the world does. Let's set higher standards for ourselves now that we are disciples of Jesus Christ.

> *Lord, I don't want to live the way I used to. I want*
> *to live in a way that is pleasing to You.*

❖ June 18 ❖

Get the Fat Out!   Read: Ephesians 5:15-33

> Be very careful, then, how you live —
> not as unwise but as wise (Eph. 5:15;NIV).

Did you know that cholesterol in foods, such as egg yolks, is less of a problem than the cholesterol churned out when the body consumes saturated fat? That's why we need to avoid whole-fat dairy products, and coconut and palm oils. These foods make the kind of cholesterol most likely to clog your arteries.

We need to get the fat out of our diet. Why? Because a high-fat diet increases the risk of some cancers and coronary disease, which accounts for almost half the deaths in America! Even beneficial olive oil — if used excessively — can contribute to all the same problems associated with obesity. We need to stop looking for quick fixes and start eating a variety of foods that pack lots of vitamins and minerals.

Here are a few simple suggestions: Eat less, especially fats and saturated fat. Eat a variety of foods, especially fruits, vegetables, and grains. If you do these things, you'll have the most important nutrition bases covered.

> *Lord, help me to be careful how I live.*
> *Give me Your wisdom.*

❖ June 19 ❖

It's Up to You

Read: 1 Corinthians 9:19-27

> Everyone who competes . . . goes into
> strict training . . . (1 Cor. 9:25;NIV).

Okay, let's get practical. In a healthful, low-fat diet you shouldn't have rich high-fat ice cream for dessert. You probably already know that, but do you know why? Because there are almost 20 grams of fat in a cup of ice cream! But a low-fat frozen yogurt has only 2 grams of fat.

Other lower-fat products on supermarket shelves include: no-fat-added tortilla chips; no-fat dips; lower and no-fat cheeses, salad dressings, and mayonnaise; lower-fat luncheon meats; fat-free cakes and pastries; low-fat cookies; and even low-fat ground beef.

Now that you know the facts, there is one more thing you need to do: You have to *want* to change. Until that happens, you will always be looking for ways to get around eating a low-fat diet. It's up to you. No one can make you change.

Lord, I throw off every reason that is keeping me from eating in
the way I know is right. Please help me to change.

❖ June 20 ❖

Don't Talk Dieting

Read: Mark 10:1-16

> Let the little children come to me, and
> do not hinder them, for the kingdom of God
> belongs to such as these (Mark 10:14;NIV).

Parents, don't talk size and dieting to your children. A child cannot grow properly if you severely restrict his calories. Instead, learn all you can about fat in food. Then teach them, right along with yourself, more about good nutrition. Make sure your child is eating a diet that is about 60 percent fruits, vegetables, and whole grains.

Limit fast food, and don't allow your children to eat in front of the TV. Do away with high-fat snack foods. Avoid fried foods as much as you can, as well as rich desserts. For a treat, remember nonfat or low-fat yogurt. Teach a lifestyle that will keep your child slim and healthy for life.

If your child is overweight, never tell him he is fat. Let your child know that he is loved and accepted just the way he is. Little hearts and minds are being formed. When the time is right, then he will have the desire — and the know-how — to shed the excess weight.

Jesus, help me to show my children the same respect
and love You have for them.

❖ June 21 ❖

Feeling Flush   Read: 1 Peter 1:13-25

. . . your faith and hope are in God (1 Pet. 1:21;NIV).

If you drink too much water will you be flushing nutrients out of your body? No. Water doesn't interfere with the normal absorption of nutrients for several reasons. The water you drink *with* a meal passes quickly through your digestive tract, ahead of the solid food, so it wouldn't even be around to flush any nutrients out of your body. Also, the gastro-intestinal tract is very efficient at digesting and absorbing nutrients. More or less water doesn't affect the process very much.

On the other hand, if you eat a lot of high-fiber foods like bran cereals, you've got to make sure you aren't drinking too *little* water. You need enough fluid to ensure that the fiber moves smoothly through your system. In fact, drinking up to two quarts is well within the range of fluid that you should drink each day to replace what you lose through excretion, sweat, and other bodily secretions.

Lord Jesus, my hope is in You. Keep my heart pure.

❖ June 22 ❖

Spot Reduction?   Read: Matthew 22:34-46

Love the Lord your God with all your heart and with
all your soul and with all your mind (Matt. 22:37;NIV).

Some people think spot exercising alone will eliminate their bulging stomach or hefty hips. It's true that thirty minutes of sit-ups or leg lifts may firm the muscles, but they won't burn enough fat to make much of a difference. Why? Because the muscles in the abdomen don't just burn fat from the mid-section; they burn fat from all over the body.

In order to lose weight from your stomach or hips, you need to do calorie-burning exercises that involve the large muscles in the body — namely the thighs. Walking, jogging, swimming, biking, and aerobic exercises burn the most calories. If you combine large muscle activity with sit-ups and floor exercises, you'll firm up your muscles and burn the fat off those areas that need to be reduced.

Like spot reduction, we often want to pick and choose those areas of our lives that we want to give to God. But, God wants all of us — heart, soul, and mind.

Lord, I give You my heart, my soul, and my mind.
Come into my life and help me to live for You.

❖ June 23 ❖

A Perfect Ten?

Read: Mark 11:20-33

... what ever you ask for in prayer, believe that you
have received it, and it will be yours (Mark 11:24;NIV).

If we think we will find our happiness in an ideal weight, a certain dress size, or a certain look, we will be disappointed. All those things are temporary. Even if we reach the goal, it will still not be enough. The happiness will be temporary as well.

We must learn to base our happiness on One who never changes — God himself. Once we get to that point, then this world has nothing to offer us in the way of true fulfillment.

If our joy is full because of the Lord, then we can say with the apostle Paul, "Whatever state I am in, I am happy because God is there, and I can do anything with Him."

Go to the One who is your joy today, and find true happiness. He wants to answer your prayers and meet your needs. Put your faith in God. He's the only way to truly live happily ever after.

Lord, teach me how to pray with the right motives today.
My hope and trust are in You.

❖ June 24 ❖

Feeling Tired?

Read: Isaiah 40:21-31

But those who hope in the Lord will renew their strength. . . . they will
run and not grow weary, they will walk and not be faint (Isa. 40:31).

I know the perfect remedy for fatigue. Exercise. You may think you are too tired to exercise, but it is actually the lack of exercise that makes you feel tired. Exercise gives you energy. How can that be? Exercise reduces stress and helps all your bodily functions operate more easily. Exercise is also a terrific energy booster. Once you are on a regular program of exercise, mental fatigue, stress, and physical tiredness will disappear.

Decide today to begin a regular program of exercise. It doesn't have to be strenuous. A brisk twenty minute walk twice a day is a perfect way to boost your energy level.

Depression and anxiety can also make you feel tired. If you put your hope in the Lord, trusting him with all your problems, you will soon rise above your difficulties. Remember, if you are over thirty-five and have been inactive for six months, or if you have a health problem, check with your doctor before beginning an exercise program.

Lord, my hope is in You. Thank You for renewing my strength.

❖ June 25 ❖

Older and Fatter?
Read: Psalm 46

God is our refuge and strength, an ever-present
help in trouble (Ps. 46:1;NIV).

Does getting older mean you'll get fatter? Maybe. Why? Because your body's basal metabolism — the rate at which it burns calories at rest — slows down. This is true even though your activity level remains the same. Basal metabolism declines with age primarily because metabolically-active muscle fiber is replaced with metabolically-inactive fat.

To maintain your desired weight as you grow older, you should do three things: (1) Do aerobic exercise (walking, jogging, cycling, swimming, etc.) to burn calories. (2) Cut back on the number of calories you eat, and lower the fat because fat has more calories. (3) Do some resistance exercise (weight training) to maintain muscle density. To do this use wrist and ankle weights for floor exercises. Remember, it is muscle tissue that keeps the basal metabolism rate high.

Remember, too, that God is always there to help us no matter what our age.

Thank You, Lord, for always being there for me.
You are my refuge and my strength.

❖ June 26 ❖

Never Go Hungry
Read: John 6:25-59

Jesus declared, "I am the bread of life.
He who comesto me will never
go hungry . . ." (John 6:35;NIV).

Do liquid diet drink programs work? Obviously not. Just ask Oprah Winfrey! Why don't they keep the weight off in the long run? Because whenever you under-eat, your body only craves food more.

If you embark on a starvation diet or drastically cut you calories in order to lose weight, your own body will turn against you. Your body sees any calorie restriction as starvation and adjusts itself by becoming more efficient with every calorie it burns. After a while, you won't lose weight even if you eat less than 1,000 calories a day.

The most effective way to lose weight is to eat a diet of low-fat foods and complex carbohydrates that burn calories as they are digested.

Jesus wants to satisfy the longings of your soul with His love and His salvation. He is truly the bread of life who can fill the emptiness of your heart.

Jesus, I come to You. Be my Lord and Saviour.

Normal Weight People

*But the noble man makes noble plans, and
by noble deeds he stands (Isa. 32:8;NIV).*

Believe it or not there really are people who maintain a normal weight. How do they do it? Let's look into the lifestyle patterns of normal weight individuals and see what we can learn from them.

A study was done to find out how people of normal weight managed their eating habits and how their lifestyle factors contributed to their success. Here's what this group of normal weight people were doing right:

They ate three meals a day, with most taking in about 1,700 calories. They did not feel they were depriving themselves of food. Most of the group regularly avoided fried food, dessert, or gravy. Other than that, they mostly ate what they wanted and were satisfied with their portions. None of the participants followed a rigid diet. As a result of these habits, they didn't have too much fat on their body, and their cholesterol reading was good. In addition, most of them had a fitness rate from good to superior.

What's the secret of their success? It could be that they "plan" to stay at a normal weight.

*Lord, I commit my weight loss plan to You,
knowing You will help me succeed.*

Deciding to Eat

The fruit of the Spirit is . . . self-control (Gal. 5:22-23;NIV).

Let's take a closer look at this group of normal weight people involved in the study we talked about yesterday. One common characteristic seems to apply to these very disciplined individuals. The study found that the group made conscious decisions about (1) what to eat, (2) when to eat, and (3) how much to eat. They did not binge, but they didn't ever feel extremely hungry either. These people were not starving themselves or just nibbling on salads for lunch to maintain their weight.

It seems that people who really restrain themselves when it comes to eating are more likely to binge. They are tense about what they eat, and when they lose control due to stress or anxiety, it's like the floodgates opening up. On the other hand, those who exercise self-control don't allow food to take control of them. One of the fruits of the Spirit is self-control.

*Lord, fill me with the Holy Spirit and let the fruit of
Your life be formed in my character.*

❖ June 29 ❖

Ordered Lives   Read: 1 Corinthians 14:26-40

God is not a God of disorder
but of peace (1 Cor. 14:33;NIV).

There is one more interesting characteristic about the people who maintained a normal weight. Can you guess what it is? If you said that they had extremely ordered lives, you're right. As a result, they were in control and didn't let life lead them around by the nose. They made their own decisions at their jobs, at home, and at the dinner table. They considered themselves to be reserved and self-regulated; they were not excessive. Moderation in eating, drinking, and exercising — in all aspects of their lives — seemed to be the key to their success.

If you are having trouble maintaining your weight, compare your lifestyle habits to these normal weight people. Take control of your life and make a commitment to yourself. Because God is a God of order, He can help you establish a more disciplined lifestyle.

Lord God, show me how to manage my life in an orderly fashion.
Give me Your peace and Your sense of order.

❖ June 30 ❖

The Secret of Peace   Read: Hebrews 13:17-25

Now the God of peace . . . Make you perfect in every good
work to do his will, working in you that which is
wellpleasing in his sight, through Jesus Christ;
to whom be glory for ever and ever (Heb. 13:20-21).

The world is searching for peace, and they look for it in many different ways — through financial gain, physical beauty, business success. When things are going along smoothly in our lives, the world's peace looks great. But it takes more than that to sustain us when we go through the difficult times. That's when we realize we must have the peace of God — that deep inner peace that only comes from the Creator. God's word tells us how to find this peace.

Where does that deep, inner abiding peace come from? You may be surprised to learn that it comes from obeying God's Word and doing His will. When we do God's will, we have tremendous inner peace. When we are out of God's will, we feel anxious and uptight. Could that be why you are not enjoying God's peace?

Lord God, teach me to do Your will and please
You in all I do. I long to know Your peace.

❖ July 1 ❖

Fiber Scorecard   Read: Genesis 1:27-31

> Then God said, "I give you every seed-bearing plant on the
> face of the whole earth and every tree that has fruit with
> seed in it. They will be yours for food" (Gen. 1:29;NIV).

Generally speaking, for a food to be beneficial to the body, it has to be digested. Fiber, however, is that part of plant material that the human body can't digest because the enzymes in the human intestinal tract won't break it down.

But in fiber's case, its indigestibility makes it beneficial.

Two types of fiber play important but different roles in protecting the body. Insoluble fiber — such as the outer layer of wheat and corn, the skins of fruits and root vegetables, and leafy greens — speeds the passing of waste through the lower intestine, alleviates some digestive disorders, and appears to help prevent colon and rectal cancer.

Soluble fiber — which comes from oats, beans, barley, psyllium, and a variety of fruits and vegetables — helps lower LDL cholesterol (the bad kind) and may help control blood sugar levels.

How much fiber should one eat? The standard recommendation is 20 to 30 grams per day. Some experts even recommend 40 to 50 grams daily.

Nutritionists agree that it's best to get your fiber from natural food sources and to spread your fiber consumption throughout the day.

> *Lord, help me to remember the many benefits of*
> *eating fresh fruits and vegetables.*

❖ July 2 ❖

Try It, You'll Like It!   Read: Song of Solomon 7:10-13

> . . . at our gates are all manner of pleasant fruits, new and old, which
> I have laid up for thee, O my beloved (Song of Sol. 7:13).

Did you know you can boost your meal-induced calorie burn by eating unfamiliar foods? When the body is faced with the same old food, it can digest it blindfolded. But when something new comes down the pike, the body's got to work harder to deal with it. Of course, substituting a high-fat unfamiliar food for a low-fat familiar one defeats the purpose. As long as the foods are similarly low in fat calories, then trying new foods you don't eat often may help burn extra calories.

> *Lord, may I be open-minded as I select new, healthy*
> *foods and glorify You in my eating.*

❖ July 3 ❖

Ready to Exercise?   Read: 2 Timothy 2

... he will be an instrument for noble purposes, made holy, useful to the Master and prepared to do any good work" (2 Tim. 2:21;NIV).

Cats do it; people should, too. Cats stretch. People would do well to learn from them. Stretching has a number of benefits:

Increases the range of motion in certain joints.
Increases muscle coordination by promoting free, easy movement.
Reduces the risk of injury.
Increases body awareness.
Promotes circulation.
Prevents or alleviates some problems.
Prepares the body for strenuous activity.
Feels good.

Don't confuse stretching and warming up. Stretching and warming up are often associated with getting ready for some serious exercise. But the two aren't the same. Warming up means getting the body's core temperature 1 to 2 degrees higher to "soften" muscles and make them more pliable. Stretching should always be done after warming up. Cold muscles are tight, and that invites tears in their fibers. Warming up prepares them for safe stretching.

Lord, as I care for my body, help me to have the energy, alertness, and readiness to do Your will.

❖ July 4 ❖

Freedom from Fat!   Read: 2 Corinthians 3:7-18

Now the Lord is the Spirit, and where the Spirit of the Lord is, there is freedom (2 Cor. 3:17;NIV).

Think back to where you were just a few weeks or months ago. After changing your eating and exercising habits, you've probably begun to see a drop in weight or felt an increase in your energy level. Don't despise the day of small beginnings. Your new life may have begun with a decision to walk after dinner, to substitute fruit for your usual rich dessert, or to drink more water each day. Those small steps, taken consistently over time, lead you to freedom from fat.

Progress may be slow at times, but don't get discouraged. Don't measure your success by what happened today or this week. Remember, it's not where you start but where you finish!

Thank You, Lord, for liberating me from an unhealthy diet and lifestyle!

❖ July 5 ❖

Weight Lifting Can Be Uplifting   Read: Proverbs 14

All hard work brings a profit . . . (Prov. 14:23;NIV).

Lifting weights can be an uplifting experience for your psyche. How can weight training boost your self-esteem? According to Robert Motta, Ph.D., director of the doctoral program in school community psychology at Hofstra University, "Exercise has a powerful impact on the way we view ourselves. It offers one way to attain mastery over a task, while in life's other activities, we might not be so successful."

In addition, resistance training compounds the benefits of mastery by offering almost immediate, powerful feedback — in the form of increased muscle and a trimmer body. Motta says that as you become stronger and more fit, your physical self-worth will improve, "which can have a positive effect on your sense of personal self-worth."

Lord, give me the mental toughness to get
the most out of a workout.

❖ July 6 ❖

The Forgotten Fat   Read: 1 Samuel 4:12-18

When he mentioned the ark of God, Eli fell backward off his
chair. . . . His neck was broken and he died, for he was
an old man and heavy (1 Sam. 4:18;NIV).

We cringe at the word cholesterol because we know that high levels of this fat increase the risk of heart disease. But there's another term that has been called the "forgotten fat." The fat is triglyceride.

Triglycerides and cholesterol climbed to the forefront as the primary fat for heart disease. Recently, however, an international panel of experts decided to take a closer look at this fat, which is routinely checked as a part of a multiphasic blood test. The panel says that one should be concerned about high levels of triglyceride, especially when the total cholesterol level is high (above 200).

Elevated triglycerides increase the risk of developing adult-onset diabetes and heart disease.

Controlling triglycerides is similar to controlling cholesterol: reduce dietary fat, exercise regularly, limit the intake of alcohol, and maintain weight within a normal range.

Lord, give me the strength to forego fatty foods
and sedentary habits that rob me of a healthy life.

❖ July 7 ❖

Why Exercise?   Read: Hebrews 12

> No discipline seems pleasant at the time, but painful. Later on,
> however, it produces a harvest of righteousness and peace for
> those who have been trained by it (Heb. 12:11;NIV).

Why do Americans exercise? Here are the reasons they give:
    80 percent say it makes them feel better.
    50 percent say they sleep better.
    40 percent say it makes them more alert.
    40 percent say it makes them look better.
    40 percent say it makes them live longer.
    33 percent say it enhances their ability to cope with pressure.
    33 percent say it makes them more productive.
    33 percent say it improves their outlook on life.
    33 percent say it boosts their self-image.
    25 percent say it makes them more creative.
On the other hand, here are some reasons others give for not exercising:
    43 percent say they don't have the time.
    16 percent say they don't have the willpower.
    12 percent say they don't feel like it.
    9 percent say they have medical reasons that prevents exercising.
    8 percent say they don't have enough energy.
The overwhelming benefits have motivated me to make exercise a part of
my daily routine. You can, too.

> *Lord, help me to look beyond the rigors of regular
> exercise to the benefits that soon will be mine.*

❖ July 8 ❖

Alcohol — Not Just Calories   Read: 1 Corinthians 6:12-17

> Everything is permissible for me — but not everything is
> beneficial . . . (1 Cor. 6:12;NIV).

If you drink you'll probably gain weight. But it may not be just from the
additional calories. Alcohol also inhibits the body's ability to burn fat.
    Studies in Switzerland determined that when subjects ingested alcohol,
they burned up to one-third less fat. Alcohol apparently slows down the liver's
fat metabolism process. Researchers don't yet know why. Perhaps the body
prefers the alcohol first, or maybe alcohol has some effect on the body's
metabolism of fat in the liver.

> *Lord, help me to live a life of unencumbered service to You.*

❖ July 9 ❖

Pleasant Dreams   Read: Ecclesiastes 5:1-12

The sleep of a laborer is sweet, whether he eats
little or much . . . (Eccles. 5:12;NIV).

A new study tells us that "working out" may help you sleep better. To gauge the effect of being physically fit on sleep, researchers looked at twenty-four men between the ages of sixty and seventy-two. Half of them exercised vigorously at least three times a week for a year or more. Their activities included aerobic walking, swimming, jogging, tennis, and biking. The rest of the group did not exercise. During the study, each group slept at night either following a forty-minute afternoon exercise session or no daytime exercise. The men who did not exercise had more periods of lighter sleep, less deep sleep, and were awake more of the night than the ones who exercised.

This occurred regardless of whether the fit men exercised that day or not — suggesting it's regular exercise that's doing the trick, not just a single workout. On average, it took the inactive group twice as long to fall asleep at night. The inactive group also spent more time awake during the night.

Lord, allow me to work diligently, play heartily, and
sleep soundly as I maintain a balanced life.

❖ July 10 ❖

Alcohol is Poison   Read: Proverbs 23:29-35

Do not gaze at wine when it is red, when it sparkles in the cup,
when it goes down smoothly! In the end it bites like a
snake and poisons like a viper (Prov. 23:31-32;NIV).

The body regards alcohol as a poison. Unlike food and non-alcoholic drinks that are digested in the mouth, stomach, and intestines, alcohol is processed in the liver. It is the liver's function to detoxify poisonous substances introduced into the body.

One fitness journal said alcohol is by definition a toxin.

What does alcohol do to the body? Moderate drinking over extended periods of time causes fat to accumulate in the liver. Heavy drinking can cause inflammation of the liver. This is a condition called hepatitis. When heavy drinking continues, liver cells are damaged by alcohol and replaced by nonfunctioning scar tissue. This condition is called cirrhosis, and it can be fatal.

Alcohol also reduces the body's capacity to absorb such minerals as calcium, magnesium, iron, and zinc, and many of the B vitamins.

Allow me to embrace Your commands, O Lord, knowing
You have made them for my protection.

❖ July 11 ❖

Glorify God in Your Body
Read: 1 Corinthians 6:18-20

*You were bought at a price. Therefore honor God
with your body (1 Cor. 6:20;NIV).*

We should glorify God in every area of our lives. Why? He owns us. We have no right to abuse what belongs to God. Smoking, drinking alcohol, overeating, not exercising, and not getting enough rest abuse a body and spirit that belong to God. Eating healthy is like the Christian lifestyle — we don't get days off for good behavior. It has to be a consistent, daily practice before it has any lasting effect.

I know it's hard to eat the low-fat way at first. Don't think for one moment I don't remember how much I loved the taste of fried chicken, skin and all. But the fat hiding in that delicious treat caused me more distress than giving up the chicken did.

Where is fat hiding in your diet? Do you always cook your chicken without the skin? Do you buy the leanest meats and low-fat or fat-free dairy products? Unless a salad dressing is low-fat or fat-free, it's sure to be packed with saturated, artery-clogging fat. And, of course, desserts are usually loaded with fat. Begin cooking and eating the low-fat way. The life you save belongs to the King of kings.

Lord, remind me that I'm not my own.

❖ July 12 ❖

Ignoring Doctor's Advice
Read: Romans 12:9-21

*Be joyful in hope, patient in affliction,
faithful in prayer (Rom. 12:12;NIV).*

If you're like most, when you're suffering from a cold or fever or influenza or diarrhea, you ignore the most common advice your doctor gives: "Drink plenty of fluids."

You've heard it all your life. But it seems so . . . so . . . unimportant. And most people tend to think they're drinking enough already. But it is important. In fact, not doing so can prolong recovery and contribute to complications.

How can you know if you're drinking enough fluid? Urine should be clear and pale in color. Cloudy or strongly-colored urine is a sign that you're not drinking enough water.

Giving your body adequate water will cleanse your system and put you on the road to better health.

*When sickness comes, remind me to do the little
things that enable You to restore my health.*

❖ July 13 ❖

Enjoy a Deeper Sleep   Read: Psalm 4

I will lie down and sleep in peace, for you alone, O Lord,
make me dwell in safety (Ps. 4:8;NIV).

A computer program that counts individual slow brain-wave patterns indicative of deep sleep found that fit men had significantly more of these waves during the night. Light fragmented sleep is much less satisfying and could affect your daytime alertness and functioning. It could be that exercise, by making you sleep better, can help you function at your peak during the day.

Why being fit might make for a less fitful sleep isn't completely understood. It may be that your body has to compensate for the exercise, and deep sleep serves that restorative function. If you have more tissue breakdown from exercise, sleeping may help rejuvenate bodily tissues. Exercise may also help by regulating your temperature. If you heat your body through exercise, you may stimulate a deeper sleep for a proper cool-down.

The experts say the key is not to exercise too close to bedtime because it takes time to bring the temperature down so you can fall asleep.

Renew and restore me in the night season, O God.

❖ July 14 ❖

Thirst Quenching   Read: Matthew 5:1-12

Blessed are those who hunger and thirst for righteousness,
for they will be filled (Matt. 5:6;NIV).

Drinking water is crucial to weight control. We need at least six, 8-ounce glasses of water daily. Drinking water not only suppresses your appetite but will also decrease the amount of fat and fluid retained by your body. Too often we reach for food when our bodies really crave water.

Always drink water before, during, and after exercise. You may not feel thirsty every time your body needs fluids. During exercise you can quickly become dehydrated without even realizing it. Athletes may lose as much as two quarts of fluid before becoming thirsty. Also, when you drink your thirst will feel quenched long before all lost fluid is replaced.

If you tend to feel "hungry" often, increase water intake and time spent in giving to others. Often the emptiness we try to fill with food is really an emptiness of the spirit that can only be filled by God. The more time spent in the Word, in prayer, and in serving others, the less emptiness we feel. Let the Lord direct you to meaningful tasks and relationships in Him.

*Lord Jesus, fill the empty places in my life with more of You. Show
me those You would have me give myself to in Your name.*

Kids and TV
Read: Proverbs 20

*Even a child is known by his actions, by whether his
conduct is pure and right (Prov. 20:11;NIV).*

If a child goes from watching an hour of television a night to six-plus hours during summer vacation, he may experience a 5- to 7-pound weight gain. That's just from watching the tube alone — that does not take into account the snack food eaten during the TV watching. While watching TV your child is sedentary, burning many fewer calories than if he was moving about. He or she may also be snacking, possibly on the high-fat, sugary substances advertised so often on TV. Along with this metabolic drop you've got a triple whammy (increased eating, lower physical activity, and lower metabolic rate) that can really place the child at risk for obesity and its unhealthy consequences. In fact, research suggests that the chance of a child becoming fat jumps 2 percent with every hour per day of TV watched.

Strongly encourage your child to participate in other activities that involve exercise, and put strict limits on the amount of viewing. You can also talk to the child about what's on the screen. Once the brain starts revving, that may help reverse the metabolic drop.

*Lord, help me to provide my child with wholesome
and healthy entertainment.*

Knowing When to Quit
Read: Psalm 22

The meek shall eat and be satisfied . . . (Ps. 22:26).

Your body thinks that every meal you eat is your last. And in watching people at food bars, I think many of them agree with their bodies.

Your mind knows when you go to bed at night that you will eat breakfast in the morning. It knows that five to six hours after lunch you will have dinner. But nature designed your body to store every bit of extra energy that your last meal provided as fat on the hips, stomach area, back of arms, and thighs. Your body may not think you're going to eat again, but you know you will. So don't eat like it's your last meal.

If the meek shall eat and be satisfied, then we want to be meek or humble, patient, and gentle. If you handle stress with a food binge, get to the root of your problem. Is it anger, restlessness, unforgiveness, or perhaps a need to be in control that drives you to food?

*Lord, prompt me during meals to recognize the difference
between being satisfied and being satiated.*

❖ July 17 ❖

Good Medicine   Read: Proverbs 17

A cheerful heart is good medicine, but a crushed spirit
dries up the bones (Prov. 17:22;NIV).

Recent scientific studies prove the above verse to be true. Today medical research clearly points to a direct connection between mental and physical health.

Norman Cousins beat a crippling, chronic disease of the joints by administering large doses of laughter to himself through watching comedy films. Laughter heals because it replaces fear and stress with serenity. Later Cousins again "laughed" his way to better health after a severe heart attack.

You may have read the heartbreaking stories of the orphans in Romania who were dying from a lack of love. One baby who should have been perfectly healthy just wasted away and died. An autopsy showed that its bones had literally dried up. Why? Its spirit was starved for love, touching, and laughter.

God's people should be the happiest, most giving people on earth. We should make a point of loving the good and joyful things of life and sharing them with others.

Father, grant us merry, giving hearts,
full of faith and hope in You. Amen.

❖ July 18 ❖

Healthy Aging   Read: Proverbs 23:7-18

For as he thinketh in his heart, so is he . . . (Prov. 23:7).

Uncle Ned says he can't do this and he can't do that. When you ask him why, he shrugs and says, "I'm just getting older." A new study suggests that older adults who attribute their health status to getting older have a 78 percent greater risk of dying.

Researchers looked at a group of 1,391 adults, age seventy and older, who experienced difficulties in daily functions. Those who could blame it only on aging had a higher death risk than those adults who could give specific, non-aging reasons for their problem. Once you say a problem is caused by old age, you may resign yourself to thinking it isn't treatable and delay seeking care.

We often talk about prevention in terms of the physical — plenty of exercise and sticking to a healthy diet — but prevention is mental, too. We can't promise optimism will actually make you live longer, but the alternative of giving up may set you up for adverse health in the long run. Keep fighting.

Lord, allow me to view life positively and from Your perspective.

❖ July 19 ❖

Avoid "The Old Person Act"   Read: Joshua 14:6-15

> . . . So here I am today, eighty-five years old! I am still as strong
> today as the day Moses sent me out . . . (Joshua 14:10-11;NIV).

A doctor wrote an article in which he said, "A seventy-five-year old diabetic with heart disease might be sick enough to need a nursing home or well enough to sit on the Supreme Court." There are many judges in their seventies and eighties who may have health problems — but they don't sit all day, eat unhealthy food, and stay up late. You can choose — a nursing home or a productive life.

Wellness begins with an attitude. It begins with avoiding what doctors call "the old person act" of letting yourself become fat and flabby. Proper nutrition is a major factor. Of the ten leading causes of death, five — heart disease, stroke, cancer, diabetes, and chronic liver disease/cirrhosis — are diet-related to some degree. What you do makes a difference. You can choose to enjoy good health even into your golden years.

Lord, give me vigor to serve You all the days of my life.

❖ July 20 ❖

Seven Tips for Better Health   Read: Ecclesiastes 12

> The words of the wise are like goads, their collected sayings
> like firmly embedded nails . . . (Eccles. 12:11;NIV).

Here are some common, everyday tips to help you improve your health:
• Eat breakfast. It's been found that persons who eat breakfast have more energy and are less likely to overeat during the rest of the day.

• Use stairs. Over a year's time, they'll provide a lot of exercise.

• Drink water. Whether you're thirsty or not, six to eight glasses of water a day will lubricate your joints, burn fat, help flush toxins from your body, and help keep your skin soft.

• At least three times a week, find twenty minutes to exercise vigorously.

• Eat fiber. High fiber foods, such as whole grains, fruits, and vegetables, will reduce your risk of colon cancer and heart disease.

• Eat bright. Generally speaking, the brighter colored fruits and vegetables are more nutritious — especially orange (cantaloupes, sweet potatoes, apricots) and dark green (broccoli, spinach, turnip greens, collard).

• Reduce fat. Try to keep fat consumption to 20 to 30 grams a day to help prevent cancer and heart disease.

Lord, remind me that even small changes in my
lifestyle will have lasting effects over time.

❖ July 21 ❖

Managing Your Worries   Read: Psalm 94

When anxiety was great within me, your consolation
brought joy to my soul (Ps. 94:19;NIV).

One expert says you must manage your worries or they'll manage you.

Anxiety can be a normal, even beneficial, reaction to stress. Anxiety increases your alertness and can spur you into action. Mild apprehension can give a performer or athlete that extra "spark" to succeed, but if you are preoccupied with dread, apprehension, or tension, you are too anxious.

If anxiety becomes pronounced, it can express itself in various ways:
- Have trouble falling asleep and staying asleep.
- Dwell on a particular situation and think only about that.
- Feel tense, restless, jittery, dizzy, and sweaty.
- Have trouble concentrating.
- Overeat or lose your appetite.
- Be overly vigilant and startle easily.
- Have a feeling of impending disaster.
- Be depressed.

No matter how anxiety affects you, prayer can be the best way to cope.

Lord, I relinquish my fears and my future to You.

❖ July 22 ❖

High Blood Pressure   Read: Zechariah 4

Who despises the day of small things? (Zech. 4:10;NIV).

Do you know that simple diet changes and a little extra walking will go a long way in lowering your blood pressure? That's the state-of-the art treatment used at the University of Minnesota to lower blood pressure in patients with moderate hypertension. Note — that is moderate hypertension.

This is the same advice for all "healthy" Americans: Lower daily sodium intake to about 1 teaspoon of salt, control weight by obtaining 30 percent of calories from fat, and use a form of non-strenuous exercise such as walking.

This program is the first line of defense for the forty million-plus Americans with moderate hypertension. These changes don't always work for people with a more severe blood pressure problem or those who have had high blood pressure for a while. In these cases, drugs are used.

Remember that a diet/medication treatment allows a person to take lower drug doses. That is why you still want to follow a low-fat diet and exercise.

*Lord, help me not to overlook the simple changes I can
make to lead a healthier, more productive life.*

❖ July 23 ❖

How to Appease a Sweet Tooth

Read: Job 20

*Though evil is sweet in his mouth and he hides it under his
tongue . . . God will make his stomach vomit them up (Job 20:12,15).*

If you can settle for a banana or a nectarine for dessert, that's great. But
if you can't, take your sugar "straight up," without the fat. Try angel food cake
or a couple of plain low-fat gingersnaps. You will have the sweets without the
fat. But sugar stimulates the appetite for some people, so eating sweets actually
makes them hungrier. If sugar affects you this way, you would be wise not to
eat it.

Ask the Lord to give you a taste for the natural sugar found in fresh fruit
and to help you find healthy, low-fat substitutes for dessert.

*Lord, teach me the discipline of moderation in my
eating habits — especially when it comes to sweets.*

❖ July 24 ❖

Conquer Sugar Cravings

Read: Proverbs 2:1-11

*For the Lord gives wisdom, and from his mouth come
knowledge and understanding. He holds victory in
store for the upright . . . (Prov. 2:6-7;NIV).*

Dear Doctor,

I have finally won the war against sugar cravings. I've tried diet
after diet with no success because all of them forbid any kind of
sweets, and I have an incurable sweet tooth.

When I finally learned I was craving fat — not sugar — I began
to count every gram of fat, making sure that not more than 20 percent
of my calories came from fat. I walked briskly for thirty minutes
every day, and in three weeks I had lost six pounds!

This is the only diet that works for me because of my sweet
tooth. I may have to measure my dessert for fat grams, but at least I
can still have it.   — Happy at last

Recap: She counts fat grams and reserves some fat grams for dessert. She
might give up butter, mayonnaise, or red meat so she can treat herself.

The secret to losing weight and keeping it off is lowering the fat in your
diet. Eventually foods that are high in fat will taste too rich for you. For
example, once you get used to skim milk, whole milk will taste like cream.

*Lord, give me insight into nutrition that will
bring lasting results in my life.*

❖ July 25 ❖

Eat Fish Twice a Week
Read: John 21:1-14

> When they landed, they saw a fire of
> burning coals there with fish on it,
> and some bread (John 21:9;NIV).

If you eat fish twice a week, you are less likely to die of a heart attack. While fish is relatively high in fat, that fat is full of health benefits. Fish oil is high in Omega 3 fatty acids that lower cholesterol levels and reduce the blood's tendency to form plaque. But that's not all.

Fish oil serves as a building block for chemical messengers that affect body functions like blood clotting, inflammation, and immunity. It helps the body fight against such disorders as rheumatoid arthritis and cancer.

Its role in preventing the formation of plaque on artery walls works like this: Plaque begins to form at the site of a tiny injury in the wall, and these chemical messengers help the immune system repair the damage quickly before plaque can form.

Our diet has gradually shifted away from fish (containing Omega 3 oils) toward more vegetable oils (Omega 6).

The fish that are high in Omega 3 oil include salmon, rainbow trout, mackerel, herring, sardines, Atlantic bluefish, and tuna.

Lord, help me to reduce my consumption of red meats
by substituting broiled and baked fish.

❖ July 26 ❖

The Scoop on Sweat
Read: Genesis 3

> I praise you because I am fearfully and
> wonderfully made . . . (Ps. 139:14;NIV).

Do men sweat more than women do? Actually it depends on how you look at it. On the one hand, researchers have just discovered that women tolerate temperatures about one degree Fahrenheit higher than men before they begin to perspire. But once women do start to sweat, their perspiration output equals men's. And it's a good thing. Sweating is the most important defense we have against hyperthermia (extremely high body temperatures). Without the cooling effect of sweat, exercising in warm weather would be impossible.

How marvelous our bodies are! The smallest parts remind me of God's intricate handiwork.

Thank You, Lord, for the way You designed my body to regulate
itself in all kinds of weather and in all kinds of activity.

❖ July 27 ❖

Fat Builders

Read: Nehemiah 8:8-12

... eat the fat, and drink the sweet, and send portions unto them for whom nothing is prepared: for this day is holy unto our Lord ... (Neh. 8:10).

What causes your body to store fat?

Calorie counting. Very low calorie diets make it harder for you to control your weight in the long run. Why? Because when you drastically reduce your caloric intake, your body loses muscle as well as fat. Less muscle means a lower metabolic rate, so your body burns calories slower. And people who starve the weight off are more likely to reach a breaking point and binge. They often gain back the weight they lost and then some. You should exercise to add more muscle — which will increase your body's calorie-burning rate — and cut fat, not calories.

Cheesecake — or any other combination of fat and sugar. When sugar hits your bloodstream, your body releases a flood of insulin in response. That insulin triggers your fat cells to open. So the fat in the cheesecake that follows goes right into storage. Reduce the fat in your diet and that won't happen as much. And if you do eat fat, be careful not to combine it with sugar.

Lord, motivate me to reserve high-sugar, high-fat foods for special occasions and not make them a part of my daily diet.

❖ July 28 ❖

Low-Fat Snack Foods

Read: Acts 10:23-48

... I now realize how true it is that God does not show favoritism ... (Acts 10:34;NIV).

The key to healthy snacking is simple: keep healthy snack foods around the house. Here's a list you can take to the grocery store:

- Skim or low-fat milk
- Low-fat or nonfat cottage cheese
- Fruit juices (100 percent juice)
- Fresh fruit/unsweetened applesauce
- Dried fruit
- Raw vegetables
- Nonfat or low-fat yogurt
- Ice milk
- Frozen fruit bars
- Graham crackers
- Cold cereal
- Pretzels
- Popcorn (for air popping)
- Bagels

If you consistently turn to these foods for between meal snacks, you will see your weight begin to drop. If these foods aren't available, drink water or take a brisk walk around the block instead of reaching for a high-fat snack.

Help me to remember that anyone who follows Your laws of health will eventually reap benefits.

❖ July 29 ❖

Pumping Iron   Read: Philippians 4:10-13

I can do everything through him who
gives me strength (Phil. 4:13;NIV).

When you pump iron, your muscles grow with gratitude. But it may be your heart that really owes you a special thanks for lifting weights. New research says that strength training like lifting weights lowers LDL cholesterol.

The researchers had one group of middle-aged ladies lift weights for one hour, three times a week, for five months. Another group continued their exercise program but did not lift any weights. Cholesterol tests before and after the five-month period showed that the women who lifted weights had significant drops in both total cholesterol and LDL cholesterol. The group that did not lift weights had much smaller declines in cholesterol readings.

Researchers think there is a potential for reducing heart disease risk through resistance training. The weightlifters lowered their body fat while boosting their fat-free muscle. If you have access to a gym, include some weightlifting exercises in your workout. The repetitions will improve your cholesterol reading.

As my muscles firm through exercise, remind me that
other good changes are occurring that I can't even see.

❖ July 30 ❖

The End of Bad Habits   Read: Romans 6:1-14

Do not offer the parts of your body to sin, as instruments of
wickedness, but rather offer yourselves to God . . . (Rom. 6:13;NIV).

Do you need some good ideas on how to break a bad habit? We've all been there. After changing our behavior for a month or more, we falter. When we least expect it, we succumb to the bad habit again. Back to eating the wrong foods, back to sleeping in instead of exercising, whatever.

Relapses have been proven to occur to most people within ninety days of breaking a bad habit. Once it was believed that relapse was a part of the person's "inability to resist withdrawal." But most people backslide long after withdrawal symptoms leave, usually when we are right at the threshold of success.

Experts say it is emotional distress. Most people break the good habit and resume the bad one when they feel angry, anxious, depressed, bored, or lonely. This is often why the habit began in the first place — the need to feel pleasure and comfort. The habit may have met this need before, and when the strong need for this feeling occurs again, the habit is resumed.

Lord, help me to be dead to the power and appeal of bad habits.

High Energy Diet   Read: Proverbs 30:1-9

> . . . give me only my daily bread. Otherwise, I may have
> too much and disown you. . . . Or I may become poor and
> steal, and so dishonor the name of my God (Prov. 30:8-9;NIV).

One doctor said some of her patients thought they could "pig out" because they were involved in strenuous exercise daily. But only elite athletes who exercise strenuously for long periods of time need to increase their calorie intake.

You must consider your body's adaptive mechanism. If you ran thirty minutes a day, three times a week as a method of weight control, at some point you will have to either run faster or a longer distance to keep losing weight. When you first started running you burned more calories, but as your body became more efficient you used less energy and burned fewer calories. If you want to continue to lose weight, you will have to either increase the duration of your exercise or decrease the amount of food you eat.

You need 1,300 calories a day. Complex carbohydrates should take up 65 to 70 percent of that amount. This "high energy" diet keeps your glycogen stores up, creating a ready source of energy. If you concentrate on bread, cereals, fruits, and vegetables, you automatically cut the fat content in your diet.

Lord, let me be content in eating only the amount of food I need.

❖ August 1 ❖

Sweet Tooth or Fat Tooth?

Read: Deuteronomy 31

> . . . and they shall have eaten and filled
> themselves, and waxen fat; then will they
> turn to other gods. . . (Deut. 31:20).

Did you know we are not born with a taste for sweets? We develop it. Most people who think they have a sweet tooth really have a "fat tooth." It's a drive for fat that sends you after chocolate bars, double chocolate ice cream, and chewy cookies. The first ingredient on the label might be sugar, but right behind it would be fat.

Research tells us that people with this fat tooth have a programmed desire for a particular mix of carbohydrates, protein, and fat in their foods, and every day they will try to maintain a certain level of fat in their diet. When they grab a sweet they are usually trying to get a level of fat that satisfies that deeper need.

Fat is not only the secret seducer in desserts and snacks, it's also the villain. Fat increases our risk of heart disease and certain kinds of cancer. Sugar is not that bad for you unless you are a diabetic, but the fat can kill you.

Lord, may the way I nourish and care for my body honor You.

❖ August 2 ❖

The Eye-Mouth Gap

Read: Romans 14

> So then, each of us will give an account of
> himself to God (Rom. 14:12;NIV).

A recent study revealed that a group of overweight people ate twice as much as they said they did and exercised much less than they reported.

Studies show that 80 percent of us underestimate our food intake — lean and athletic people as well as the obese. One survey found that adults underestimate their daily diet on an average of about 800 calories. This discrepancy has been called the "eye-mouth gap." People just don't know how much food they put on their plates. If you are trying to lose weight, don't trust your eyes. Weigh or measure the food you eat, at least for awhile, to get a sense of what a serving is. This is less important if you're on a truly low-fat diet, but for high-fat items it's essential. Keep a journal, writing down exactly what you eat and also how much you exercise each day.

Accountability, no doubt a challenging discipline, bears tremendous fruit in the lives of those who practice it. Try it this week and see if it doesn't help.

Lord, allow me to walk in integrity as I
pursue healthy eating habits.

❖ August 3 ❖

Be at Peace   Read: Hebrews 12

> Make every effort to live at peace with all men
> and to be holy . . . that no one misses the grace
> of God and that no bitter root grows up to cause
> trouble and defile many (Heb. 12:14-15;NIV).

As we start each day let's make sure that we are at peace with all men. Is there someone who has hurt you in some way? Has someone's failure to repay a debt upset you? Remember that hurts can grow into bitterness. Unrest in our lives can lead to binges with food. Resentment and bitterness can even cause sickness. Ask Jesus to heal you of this hurt today.

Lord, I bring my relationships before You. Show me if I'm not
at peace with any family member, co-worker, or friend.

❖ August 4 ❖

Calorie Banking   Read: Proverbs 23:19-28

> Do not join those who drink too much wine
> or gorge themselves on meat, for drunkards
> and gluttons become poor . . . (Prov. 23:20-21;NIV).

Is it healthy to skip meals so you can eat more later? "Banking calories" often gets out of hand. These dieters come to the table half-starved so they can "afford" to eat a huge dinner. This "starve-gorge syndrome" can damage your health because it throws off your metabolism and causes you to make poor nutritional choices.

Some people cut their food intake the week before vacation or a major holiday. Experts say this is okay if it's done wisely, but some folks eat only salad and drink diet colas to get ready for a time of eating.

Others work late, don't have dinner until 10 o'clock or later, or are so busy during the day they simply forget to eat. By the time they do get their meals they throw caution to the wind, lose sight of nutrition, and they binge. Without realizing it, they compromise nutrition as much as those who starve and stuff themselves on purpose.

Moderation in eating is more healthy for you, and it produces lasting results.

Lord, remind me that moderation
produces better results than fads and crash diets.

❖ August 5 ❖

Water Robbers   Read: Judges 15:9-20

*. . . When Samson drank, his strength returned
and he revived . . . (Judg. 15:19;NIV).*

Thirst is a sensation that lags far behind the body's needs. Our bodies can be two quarts low on water before we feel thirsty. Water loss from perspiration can quickly lower your body's fluid balance — especially if you exercise in hot, humid weather. Older individuals also need lots of water because their thirst mechanism does not work properly.

Water robbers are coffee, tea, fat, and sugar. Whenever you have these beverages, always follow them with a glass of water. Eating a high-fiber diet also requires water. Keep a bottle of water in the refrigerator, and drink all day long.

You're giving a keynote address. *What do you do for your jitters? Sip a tall glass of water.* Drinking water — at any temperature — can help prevent dehydration, counteracting the dry mouth, sweaty palms, and heart palpitations that accompany high anxiety.

No matter what your age or activity level, you need a regular intake of water to function at your best.

*Lord, remind me to drink water often —
even when I don't feel thirsty.*

❖ August 6 ❖

Fresh or Frozen?   Read: Proverbs 3:1-8

*My son, do not forget my teaching, but keep my commands
in your heart, for they will prolong your life many
years and bring you prosperity (Prov. 3:1-2;NIV).*

You can get more vitamin C from certain vegetables if you pick frozen over fresh. A recent study from the University of Illinois at Urbana-Champaign showed that frozen green beans retained nearly twice as much vitamin C as fresh. That's because produce commonly takes between seven and nine days to get to market, while commercial freezing occurs within hours of picking. Some exceptions to the rule: Fresh broccoli is higher in vitamin C than frozen, even after refrigeration. And the more fragile, leafy choices like spinach and kale must be eaten fresh and as soon as possible to gain the highest C impact.

Increasing your knowledge of nutrition will help you make wise choices when you shop for and prepare food.

*Lord, help me to live a long and healthy life by
making wise choices at the grocery store.*

❖ August 7 ❖

Motivation: Key to Active Lifestyle   Read: Ecclesiastes 11

... childhood and vigor are meaningless (Eccles. 11:10;NIV).

Physical activity is a natural instinct in the young. You have probably said many times, "I wish I had as much energy as that child!"

Children are instinctively active. They hop, skip, jump, and run from place to place. And have you ever watched puppies? They play much more than do older dogs.

As we get older, we tend to slow down. Yet we know that activity is the key to maintaining youthful bodies and energy.

That's why scientists are beginning to recognize that motivation must take over where instinct leaves off.

The older we get the more natural it is to decrease our activity level. So the key to maintaining a high level of activity is to be self-motivated. And the way to do that is to find active things that are enjoyable. It may be playing golf or tennis or gardening or walking through the neighborhood or the shopping mall.

The older we get the more we must all fight the natural instinct to slow down.

Lord, keep me motivated by helping me to combine
exercise with activities I enjoy.

❖ August 8 ❖

Beta Carotene   Read: Psalm 104:10-17

He makes grass grow for the cattle, and plants for man to cultivate
— bringing forth food from the earth (Ps. 104:14;NIV).

The body converts beta carotene, which is found in dark green and orange vegetables, into vitamin A. But it's the chemical's antioxidant properties that have most impressed scientists. Oxygen molecules in the body can damage DNA and protein, setting the stage for cataracts and cancer, and they can turn harmless cholesterol particles into artery-cloggers.

Beta carotene neutralizes these oxygen molecules. In studies at Brigham & Women's Hospital in Boston, persons who took 50 milligrams of beta carotene every other day experienced half the health problems of those who didn't.

Thank You for providing natural foods that
contain so many benefits for us.

❖ August 9 ❖

Good Health for Seniors   Read: Isaiah 65:17-25

> Never again will there be . . . an old man who does not
> live out his years . . . (Isa. 65:20;NIV).

Senior citizens can improve their general health dramatically with just a little exercise daily. This is true even if they're in a nursing home. You certainly don't have to be a bodybuilder to get and stay in better shape, though moderate weight-training has been shown to improve muscle tone and bone density. The important thing is to adopt an exercise program in line with your own physical condition and one approved by your doctor and then follow it regularly.

Staying socially and mentally active contributes to your good health. Involve yourself in activities you enjoy — photography, bowling, tennis, etc. Learning to cope with change and loss and staying involved with family and friends is essential. Don't withdraw under any circumstances.

Volunteering your time to help others is still another excellent way to maintain mental wellness and exuberance for living. Share yourself. You'll be glad you did.

Lord, help me give my life away a little more each day.

❖ August 10 ❖

Cholesterol and Overactive Platelets   Read: Psalm 27

> Wait on the Lord: be of good courage, and he shall strengthen
> thine heart . . . (Ps. 27:14).

The role of cholesterol in clogging arteries of the heart and brain has long been appreciated. Now it appears that's not all that cholesterol does. High cholesterol levels also cause blood platelets to become overactive.

One of the functions of platelets is to release chemicals that either relax or constrict arteries. When platelets become overactive, they can release an excess of an artery-constricting chemical, thus precipitating a stroke or heart attack.

Studies at the University of Iowa involving twenty-two men and women aged twenty-three to fifty, with cholesterol levels ranging from 142 to 277, indicate that cholesterol levels higher than 200 have a tendency to "turn on" platelets.

This is another reason to watch your cholesterol levels.

*Lord, allow me to do the right things to have
a sound heart and body.*

❖ August 11 ❖

A Balanced Life   Read: John 3:1-8

Jesus answered and said to him, "Verily, verily, I say unto
thee, Except a man be born again, he cannot see the
kingdom of God. . . . That which is born of the flesh is
flesh; and that which is born of the Spirit is spirit" (John 3:3,6).

Spirit and flesh are intertwined. Have you ever noticed how much harder
it is to be kind and generous when you don't feel good? Your irritability
increases and little problems become big issues. While it is certainly possible
to be a godly person despite ill health, why burden yourself unnecessarily?
Common sense, exercise, and good nutrition can help you live an abundant life.

We need to care for our flesh as well as our spirit. Don't get so involved
in spiritual matters that you neglect your body. And don't put so much
emphasis on good eating and exercising that you forget to spend time in
worship and service. Balance is the key to living a dynamic, productive life.

Lord, restore balance to my life when I'm out of control.

❖ August 12 ❖

Eat More Carbohydrate Calories   Read: Exodus 16:9-21

. . . in the morning ye shall be filled with bread; and ye
shall know that I am the Lord your God (Exod. 16:12).

Once we start reducing the fat in our diet, we've got to get our calories
somewhere. And to look at the typical American diet, we'd better start with
carbohydrates.

"I think from a disease standpoint, fat is the thing that everyone is most
concerned about," says Judith Anderson, a professor in Michigan State
University's Food Science and Human Nutrition Department. "It's related to
heart disease, cancer, and weight management."

Reducing fat means getting more calories from carbohydrates. Here are
several ways to do that:

• Eat six 1/2-cup servings of vegetables or fruit every day.

• When eating out, head for the salad bar but stay away from high-fat
dressings.

• Broil, don't fry.

• Snack on bagels instead of doughnuts, fruit instead of potato chips.

• Eat whole-grain breads. Instead of butter use a teaspoon of jelly.

• Invest in a good cookbook that can help you change the way you cook.

Lord, give me a taste for whole grains, fruit, and vegetables.

❖ August 13 ❖

You've Got to Believe!　　　　　　　　Read: Hebrews 11:1-6

Now faith is the substance of things hoped for,
the evidence of things not seen (Heb. 11:1).

Many of the benefits of a regular exercise program are not immediately evident. Eventually you should notice firmer muscles and a thinner waistline. But when you look in a mirror, you won't see an improved cardiovascular system — but it's there. You won't be able to look at your lowered cholesterol levels — but they've dropped.

An exercise program combined with good nutrition needs one key element to be successful, and that's faith. Faith will keep you on your regimen even when you don't see change. Faith will help you push to the next plateau of fitness. And remember — God always rewards those who act in faith.

Lord, increase my faith that You are at work in my
body as I exercise and eat right.

❖ August 14 ❖

Trans Fatty Acid　　　　　　　　Read: Nehemiah 9:24-27

. . . so they did eat, and were filled, and became fat . . . (Neh. 9:25).

What is trans fatty acid? Companies use partially hydrogenated oils because they stay solid at room temperature and don't go rancid as quickly as polyunsaturated oils. But when an oil is hydrogenated, some of its fats are changed from the naturally occurring cis structure to a trans structure. Cis fats have a "bend" in their chain of carbon atoms; trans fats are straight, making them solid at room temperature.

Trans fats are found in margarine, shortenings, and partially hydrogenated oils that are added to hundreds of cakes, crackers, cookies, french fries, chips, and other foods. Food companies can't even tell consumers how much trans is in any particular food. Even the FDA's new labeling doesn't require packages to disclose how much trans fats they contain.

So what should you do to get less trans fat in your diet? Eat less fat. Food labels could help by dividing fats into two groups: those that promote heart disease and those that don't. Until we know more, don't stop eating foods that contain "partially hydrogenated" oil. Just assume that fattier foods contain more trans than lower fat foods.

Lord, remind me to read labels on
foods to check for fat content.

❖ August 15 ❖

Dangers of Secondhand Smoke

Read: Ezekiel 18:1-4

*The fathers eat sour grapes, and the children's
teeth are set on edge (Ezek. 18:2;NIV).*

Secondhand smoke is dangerous. The National Cancer Institute says a nonsmoker married to a smoker has a 30 percent higher risk of contracting lung cancer than nonsmokers who live with nonsmokers. That risk increases to 70 percent if your spouse is a heavy smoker.

Nonsmokers are exposed to four thousand compounds and chemicals in tobacco smoke. Fifty of these compounds are carcinogenic — benzene, carbon monoxide, carbon dioxide, etc.

Nonsmokers can suffer eye irritation, headaches, nasal symptoms, and coughing.

The *Journal of the American Medical Association* reported the results of a recent study using volunteers in the nonsmoking sections of four airline flights. Up to three days after the flight, researchers found a by-product of nicotine in the urine of these nonsmoking volunteers. Other studies have found increased levels of deadly carbon monoxide in nonsmokers exposed to cigarette smoke.

The National Cancer Institute says children of smoking parents have a decline in lung function. Wheezy bronchitis increased 14 percent among children whose mothers smoked more than four cigarettes per day, and 49 percent if mothers smoked more than fourteen times a day.

*Lord, thank You for reminding me that my habits
— good or bad — affect those closest to me.*

❖ August 16 ❖

Fascinating Facts

Read: Proverbs 23:4-6

*Eat thou not the bread of him that hath an evil eye,
neither desire thou his dainty meats (Prov. 23:6).*

Breadsticks can be surprisingly high in fat. Most commercial brands are made with oil, and some contain high-fat sesame seeds. Typically, three sesame breadsticks (1 ounce) have 150 calories and 7 grams of fat; the fat supplies 42 percent of the calories.

*Lord, give me insight into what
foods to order when I dine out.*

❖ August 17 ❖

High-Fat Diets and Stress   Read: Matthew 13:18-23

> The one who received the seed that fell among the
> thorns is the man who hears the word, but the worries
> of this life and the deceitfulness of wealth
> choke it, making it unfruitful (Matt. 13:22;NIV).

Previous research has linked stress hormones to elevated levels of fats and sugars in the blood and also to high blood pressure, all of which raise the risk of heart disease.

Stress hormones also have been shown to suppress the body's disease-fighting immune system, possibly increasing the risk of developing cancer.

The study, presented at the Society for Neuroscience's annual meeting, indicates that the combination of a high-fat diet and stress makes the risk of heart disease and possibly cancer much worse than either factor alone.

> *Lord, Your feet are the best place*
> *for me to cast my daily cares.*

❖ August 18 ❖

Low-Cholesterol Breakfast   Read: Colossians 3:22-24

> Whatever you do, work at it with all your heart, as
> working for the Lord, not for men (Col. 3:23;NIV).

Are you a single parent, busy mom or dad, and say you don't have time to fix a good breakfast? You'll be glad to know the best breakfast for fighting and lowering cholesterol is a breakfast of ready-to-eat cereal.

One study showed that women and children who eat a cereal breakfast actually consume less cholesterol all day than those who skip breakfast or who eat some other nutritious breakfast. Why? Cereal has virtually no cholesterol in it. Second, cereal eaters do not snack later in the morning with high-cholesterol items such as doughnuts, danish, etc. Breakfast-skippers usually attack these about mid-morning. Even those in the study who did eat some of these things had much lower cholesterol by starting the day with a low-cholesterol breakfast.

So, how about a good breakfast? It will boost your nutrition and work performance. Ask the Lord to help you begin the healthy habit of eating breakfast. And get ready to have a great day!

> *Lord, remind me that a good breakfast will help me put*
> *forth my best effort for my family and employer.*

❖ August 19 ❖

Don't Skip Breakfast! Read: 1 Kings 17:2-7

> The ravens brought him bread and meat in the morning
> . . . and he drank from the brook (1 Kings 17:6;NIV).

Remember your mom's constant harping on you to eat a good breakfast? That was no "wives' tale." Breakfast is vital and determines the very course your body will take the rest of the day.

A controlled study was done on children living on meager diets. Teachers complained that these children were unable to concentrate, slow to learn, had poor retention of the material they were taught, and did not pay attention in class. But when their diets were improved (starting with a good breakfast), these conditions changed.

A good diet has positive effects on school achievement. Other studies showed that children who eat a good breakfast perform at a much higher level and have a better attitude toward school. If they don't eat breakfast, children are fidgety and troublesome by mid-morning. Those who have a good breakfast perform well until lunch.

If this is true for children, it is true for adults. Your day at work and in the home will be much better on a stomach full of a nutritious breakfast.

Lord, remind me to give my family a good start
each day with breakfast.

❖ August 20 ❖

Handling Failure Read: Joshua 7:1-10

> The Lord said to Joshua, "Stand up! What are you
> doing down on your face?" (Joshua 7:10;NIV).

What happens when you sleep in, splurge on a banana split, or miss your exercise class? All of us need to know how to bounce back from failure and the guilt that so quickly engulfs us. We usually fall back into old patterns to satisfy an emotional need.

But God's Word has everything we need to be emotionally fulfilled. He has given us all things pertaining to life and godliness. What do you feel you lack? Go to Him and find what He has for you. He orders each day of your life so that you can walk confidently with Him, without fear of failure. If you do fail, however, our merciful God awaits you with open arms. He will pick you up and help you to get started again.

Lord, allow me to see my failure as a learning experience.

❖ August 21 ❖

Breaking Bad Habits   Read: Ephesians 4:20-29

> And be renewed in the spirit of your mind; and that ye
> put on the new man . . . (Eph. 4:23-24).

How do you break a bad habit? You must not only stop the bad habit but replace it with something positive. Here's how:

1. Plan ahead. Ride out the urge — which usually lasts only three to ten minutes — to resume the old habit. Take a walk, call a friend, read a book, or pray. Learn to make these planned responses automatic to the urge.

2. Develop new habits. Find ways to get your emotional needs met that do not bring negative results. Rely on God's power to sustain and fill you emotionally.

3. Enlist help. Tell friends what you are doing. Their support and encouragement can go a long way. A little accountability will keep you on guard.

4. Avoid high-risk situations that may cause you to slip.

5. Be realistic. Set attainable goals.

6. Reward yourself! But don't treat yourself to the spoils of your old habit. The reward for losing weight should not be food, and the reward for exercising should not be to stop. Choose a new dress, a portrait, etc.

7. A lapse does not have to be a relapse. Analyze what happened. Learn from your mistake and begin again.

Lord, strengthen me so I don't succumb to old patterns.

❖ August 22 ❖

Burning Calories   Read: Isaiah 40:27-31

> . . . they will run and not grow weary, they will walk
> and not be faint (Isa. 40:31;NIV).

New research tells us that exercising after a meal ignites the food's thermic effect — the food's natural ability to boost metabolism and burn more calories.

When men take a twenty-minute walk following a meal their metabolic rate rises 29 percent. A brisk walk speeds up the calorie-burning effect of the food and burns calories from the exercise also.

Just make sure that when you exercise after eating it's something not too strenuous. A nice brisk walk can actually speed up digestion, but anything more might actually interfere with digestion of your meal.

Lord, boost my metabolism as I increase my activity.

❖ August 23 ❖

Protection from Bladder Cancer Read: Proverbs 4:7-12

I have taught thee in the way of wisdom;
I have led thee in right paths (Prov. 4:11).

We know fruits and vegetables protect us from a multitude of illnesses. New research says these foods may even lower the risk of bladder cancer.

Researchers looked at the dietary histories of 351 men with bladder cancer and compared them with 855 men without the illness. The highest consumers of fruits and vegetables had a 60 percent lower risk of developing bladder cancer.

The antioxidant beta carotene and other carotenoids found in fruits and vegetables seem to be the most likely disease fighters. "Flavenoids," other substances in fruits and veggies, may help, too. You may be lowering your intake of fats to make room for these healthier foods, which will cut down on the fat carcinogens from foods that are metabolized and end up in your bladder.

Higher total-calorie intake increased the risk. So did a higher intake of sodium. The study suggested that smokers as usual play with fire, tripling their risk of developing bladder cancer when compared with nonsmokers. Taken together, these findings suggest it's a combination of healthy habits that may protect you from bladder cancer.

Lord, give me the grace to do what is right.

❖ August 24 ❖

Butter or Margarine? Read: Psalm 55

The words of his mouth were
smoother than butter . . . (Ps. 55:21).

First the experts told us butter was loaded with saturated fat and that we'd be better off eating margarine. Now they say that margarine is full of something called trans fats, which increase the risk of heart disease.

Here's the bottom line: Don't switch back from margarine to butter. Choose fat-free or low-fat versions of cakes, cookies, crackers, chips, etc. When you sauté foods, use small amounts of olive oil. It doesn't raise cholesterol or promote tumors in animal studies. If you don't like your bread plain or with a little olive oil, drizzle on diet or whipped margarine. Both have less trans. Try olive oil for baking. The other ingredients in baked goods usually mask its strong flavor. If you need a margarine taste, use a liquid margarine. Like any liquid fat it has far less trans than a solid fat.

Lord, help me make wise
substitutions in food preparation.

❖ August 25 ❖

Cinnamon and Insulin

Read: Exodus 30:22-33

> Take the following fine spices: . . . fragrant
> cinnamon . . . (Exod. 30:23;NIV).

Cinnamon, that sweet spice, may help our bodies digest sugar. Researchers found that cinnamon gives a boost to insulin, a hormone that carries sugar into our cells.

Researchers measured insulin activity in the presence of ice cream, peanut butter, six baby formulas, nine kinds of beans, and thirty-four spices. Most substances had no effect on insulin activity. Peanut butter and ice cream increased insulin activity slightly but cinnamon, cloves, turmeric, and bay leaves tripled it.

These spices may eventually be useful in the treatment of Type II (adult onset) diabetes. People with this type of diabetes produce insulin but often not efficiently enough to meet their body's needs. Often times their bodies are somewhat resistant to the effects of insulin.

They believe if a Type II diabetic consumes cinnamon, which makes the insulin he produces more active, he might need to inject less insulin or maybe even none. They believe that a very small amount of cinnamon (1/8 tsp.) could be spread on a piece of toast and have a good effect on the insulin. Soon, they plan to test cinnamon foods on people.

Lord, unlock the beneficial effects of this spice.

❖ August 26 ❖

Calcium

Read: Exodus 3:13-22

> And I have promised to bring you up out of
> your misery in Egypt into . . . a land flowing
> with milk and honey (Exod. 3:17;NIV).

Children age six to twelve who consume nearly twice the 800 milligram daily Recommended Dietary Allowance for calcium — the equivalent of about five glasses of milk a day instead of three — develop stronger bones, according to a study published in the *New England Journal of Medicine*. The greater bone mass, if maintained over the years, could protect against future fractures.

"Be not wise in thine own eyes: fear the Lord, and depart from evil. It shall be health to thy navel, and marrow to thy bones" (Proverbs 3:7-8).

Lord, help me to provide a calcium-rich diet for
my child in his formative years.

❖ August 27 ❖

It's Within Your Reach!

Read: Philippians 3:8-14

> . . . Forgetting what is behind and straining toward what
> is ahead, I press on toward the goal . . . (Phil. 3:13-14;NIV).

Too often we think of health negatively — as the absence of sickness. We should view it positively. Good health is something we can achieve with action: sensible diet, regular exercise, sufficient sleep, and generally good habits. In many cases, getting and maintaining good health is quite economical.

A nutritious diet is often less costly than one full of rich and/or empty-calorie foods.

Kicking the tobacco habit can save you hundreds — even thousands — of dollars each year.

Stretching exercises, aerobics, and long walks don't cost a thing.

Some doctors say establishing and maintaining a conscientious wellness program is more important than having an annual physical. Good health is within your reach. Go for it!

Lord, spur me on to pursue a healthy lifestyle.

❖ August 28 ❖

Breakfast Blunders

Read: 1 Corinthians 10:23-31

> So whether you eat or drink or whatever you do,
> do it all for the glory of God (1 Cor. 10:31;NIV).

An alarm sounds in your home every morning — and it's not coming from your bedside clock radio. It's coming from the kitchen, where your child's breakfast habits may be causing an unhealthy commotion.

Groan at the latest facts: Of the 467 ten-year-old children in one study, 16 percent skipped breakfast — and they didn't bother to make up for the calories or nutrients at other meals. The 41 percent who grabbed breakfast at home didn't do much better — eating junk foods higher in sucrose than the rest of the survey kids who ate at school.

The kids who ate breakfast at home chose cakes, cookies, and desserts instead of healthier foods. Why? When both parents work, it's tougher to supply kids with healthy breakfasts. But even a busy family can start their morning with a healthy nutritional bang. Why not prepare fruit-based muffins ahead of time? Keep bagels, low-fat or nonfat yogurt, cereals, fruit, and skim milk available so children have plenty of choices that need little or no preparation.

Lord, remind me to take a few extra minutes
to nourish my family at breakfast.

❖ August 29 ❖

Benefits of Low-Fat Eating

Read: Psalm 19:7-11

The statutes of the Lord are right, rejoicing the heart (Ps. 19:8).

The rewards of following a low-fat, heart healthy diet may seem remote, especially if you're in good health now. But forgoing heavy high-fat meals yields immediate benefits. You can prevent clogging your arteries over the long haul and forming blood clots in the short term.

What produces the clot? It's a complex process involving platelets, other blood proteins, and a sudden chemical breakdown in the plaque itself. High levels of a protein called factor VII also triggers clots.

What causes it? A high-fat meal leads to high levels of fat in the bloodstream. These fats may then set up a chemical chain reaction that eventually promotes high levels of several clotting factors, including factor VII.

The experts say this effect is short-lived when you eat just one fat-rich meal, but it may become permanent with a high-fat diet. Reducing fat intake appears to lower the level of factor VII quickly. Even if a low-fat diet did not lower your blood cholesterol level right away, it would still reduce your risk of heart attack.

Lord, help me to eat well for today — and tomorrow.

❖ August 30 ❖

Faithfulness Counts

Read: Luke 19:11-27

. . . Because you have been trustworthy in a very small matter,
take charge of ten cities (Luke 19:17;NIV).

The care of our bodies may seem insignificant when so many other things in life beckon for our time and attention. But our health is one of those "little things" God has entrusted to us. We must prove ourselves faithful not only for our own well-being, but so that we may be able to carry out the more demanding tasks the Lord may give us.

*Lord, increase my faithfulness as I cultivate
a desire to exercise and eat right.*

❖ August 31 ❖

Does Exercise Protect Against Cancer?   Read: Psalm 3:1-6

But you are a shield around me, O Lord (Ps. 3:3;NIV).

Highly or moderately active persons have a 50 percent lower risk of colon cancer than those who were less active. Active men expended more than 1,000 calories per week in recreational activity—the equivalent of jogging or playing tennis two hours a week or walking 10 miles a week. A twenty-one-year study of eight thousand Japanese men in Hawaii suggested that those who were physically active at home or at work were as much as 70 percent less likely to develop colon cancer than the sedentary men.

Similarly, studies of Swedish men and women show that being sedentary may increase the risk of colon cancer more than three-fold. Physical activity and a low-fat, high-fiber diet may account for much of the reduction in the risk of colon cancer. Harvard researchers reported that exercise seemed to have a protective effect — independent of diet.

Exercise may not prevent cancer as well as it can stave off heart disease and diabetes. Still, the American Cancer Society recommends regular exercise as part of its cancer-prevention program. It might help, it can't hurt, and it has many other proven benefits.

Lord, protect my health as I practice what You've shown me.

❖ September 1 ❖

Sweets and Weight Loss   Read: Proverbs 25:16-28

Like a city whose walls are broken down is a man who
lacks self-control (Prov. 25:28;NIV).

Many people think that a sweet tooth caused them to be overweight. But overweight people deprived of sweets don't stop eating — they just overeat nonsweets, always trying to satisfy their fat craving.

Losing weight is a complex undertaking. You have to:

1. Cut back on fat.

2. Eat complex carbohydrates that are high in fiber, such as vegetables, fruits, and whole grains.

3. Increase exercise.

4. Reduce calories.

What about desserts and soft drinks sweetened with non-nutrient sweeteners like aspartame? Some participants in weight-loss programs who are allowed to have desserts sweetened with non-nutrient sweeteners feel that they are not deprived, so this helps them to lose weight.

But are non-nutrient sweeteners safe? Artificial sweeteners have been the subject of what is probably the most intensive Food and Drug Administration investigations of any food product. They have passed all the tests, so they should not jeopardize your health. You should be more concerned with fat in your diet — not moderate amounts of non-nutrient sweeteners.

Lord, instill the discipline of moderation in my life.

❖ September 2 ❖

Food Allergies in Children   Read: James 1:1-8

If any of you lacks wisdom, he should ask God,
who gives generously to all without finding fault,
and it will be given to him (James 1:5;NIV).

The most common foods that are responsible for allergic reactions in children are milk, eggs, fish, lentils, and nuts — especially peanuts. Now the *American Family Physician* suggests adding two others to the list: peaches and sunflower seeds.

The typical allergic reaction is to the skin, in the form of hives, but upset stomach can also be an allergic reaction to food. If you or your children are experiencing such reactions, check your diet for these foods.

*Lord, give me wisdom in altering my
child's diet when he reacts to food.*

❖ September 3 ❖

Kids and Calcium

Read: 1 Peter 2:1-2

> Like newborn babies, crave pure spiritual milk, so that
> by it you may grow up in your salvation (1 Pet. 2:2;NIV).

Calcium's bone-thickening power is confirmed! A landmark three-year study looked at forty-five sets of twins between the ages of six and fourteen. One child from each pair ate the Recommended Dietary Allowance of calcium (800 milligrams a day), and the other child nearly doubled that amount with supplements added to the diet. The latter preteens gained 3 percent in total bone density. That boost in calcium — if maintained — would mean a 30 percent decrease in fracture risk.

The RDA for calcium for children under eleven translates roughly into three glasses of milk. But parents shouldn't stop there. Five or six servings of calcium-rich foods from concentrated sources such as milk, yogurt, fortified juices, broccoli, and oranges should be included in their diet. Keep this in mind when your child is hovering by the refrigerator for a snack. Why not peel an orange for him?

> *Lord, help me provide my child with nutritious foods*
> *that will benefit his growth.*

❖ September 4 ❖

Overweight Children

Read: Proverbs 3:1-10

> My son, do not forget my teaching . . . they will prolong your
> life many years and bring you prosperity (Prov. 3:1-2;NIV).

Is my child overweight?" Overweight children are not only the target for emotional abuse from their peers, but these children also risk developing hypertension, orthopedic disorders, and heart and respiratory disease, not to mention high cholesterol.

Parents must take wise action. Here are some tips: 1. Get the help of a physician when dealing with diets for children. Consider your child's height, weight, and age. Most children do not thin out until age five or six. 2. Check the activity level of your child. 3. How much does the child eat? What is the child's cholesterol level? 4. Are you or your spouse overweight? If you both have a weight problem, your child has an 80 percent chance of having the same. If one of you is overweight, the chance drops to 40 percent; if neither, the chance is 10 percent. 5. Teach good dietary habits. Teach the child to know when his body is full. 6. Exercise as a family. Most of all, be positive!

> *Lord, help me prolong my child's life with*
> *good habits established in our home.*

❖ September 5 ❖

Garlic and Cancer

Read: Psalm 46:1-11

> . . . He is my refuge and my fortress, my God,
> in whom I trust (Ps. 91:2;NIV).

Cancer, a leading cause of death in the United States, is second only to heart disease. As many as 80 to 90 percent of factors contributing to cancer can be traced to environmental factors like tobacco and diet.

Researchers found people in one province of China who had a very low incidence of stomach cancer (3 in 100,000). Those in a nearby county had three times the deaths from stomach cancer. What was the difference between the two groups? Those in one county regularly ate 20 grams of garlic a day; those in the other county rarely ate it. The garlic eaters had lower concentrations of nitrites in their gastric juices.

Scientists discovered that when garlic was ingested directly into the tumors of mice with bladder cancer, the cancers were cured. Garlic compounds may function as a dietary anti-carcinogen, thus preventing the formation of certain cancers. How does it work? In order for carcinogens to cause cancer, they must first bind with DNA molecules in tissue cells. Garlic compounds do inhibit certain carcinogens from binding with DNA. So it appears garlic is beneficial, and we should include some in our diet.

> *Lord, allow me to protect myself*
> *from cancer-causing agents.*

❖ September 6 ❖

Too Much TV

Read: Proverbs 15:12-19

> The way of a sluggard is blocked with thorns, but the
> path of the upright is a highway (Prov. 15:19;NIV).

You may have heard that children who use TV as a plugged-in pacifier stand a greater chance of having higher than normal cholesterol levels. The same scary link may hold true for adults. Those who watch three to four hours of TV a day had about twice the risk for developing high cholesterol. It seems the more TV viewing you do, the worse off you may be.

The video screen doesn't send out rays of cholesterol that plug up your veins — but it might as well. TV puts you in a position (usually on a couch) that jeopardizes your health. A person who watches too much TV tends to eat while watching, and it's usually fattening stuff. You also tend to exercise less because you're in the "dozing" zone. These findings should warn us that watching too much TV may be hazardous to your health.

> *Lord, guard me from sedentary habits that endanger my health.*

❖ September 7 ❖

Does Exercise Boost Immunity?   Read: Isaiah 41:8-10

> . . . I will strengthen you and help you; I will uphold
> you with my righteous right hand (Isa. 41:10;NIV).

Many people who run, swim, or exercise in other ways, say that it makes them feel healthier — in particular, that it bolsters their resistance to colds and the flu.

Yet some experts say that the effect of exercise on immunity may be a double-edged sword: work out moderately and you may indeed boost your body's ability to fight off colds and other illnesses, but exercise long and intensely and you may unwittingly depress your immune system and leave yourself more prone to such infections.

The workings of the immune system are extremely complex, and research in this field is only just beginning. However, several recent studies have found that *moderate* exercise may have some immune-boosting effect. One study showed that brisk walking (forty-five minutes, five times a week for fifteen weeks) boosted the activity of natural killer cells, which help knock out viruses and malignancies in the body's cells.

Though the walkers got as many colds and flus as a sedentary group, they experienced only half as many days with cold or flu symptoms.

Lord, strengthen my body's defenses as I work out.

❖ September 8 ❖

The Greasy Spoon   Read: Proverbs 21:1-11

> . . . when a wise man is instructed,
> he gets knowledge (Prov. 21:11;NIV).

It's mealtime and the only restaurant nearby is a greasy spoon. Order a baked potato, cottage cheese, and a side order of vegetables. Then assemble your made-to-order dinner. Cut the potato in half, top with the cottage cheese and veggies, and sprinkle with pepper. This is about as nutritious a meal as you're likely to get at any diner. And even if the only available cottage cheese is from whole milk, the entire dish probably won't exceed 350 calories, with under 15 percent from fat.

Lord, show me a way to avoid
high-fat foods when I eat out.

❖ September 9 ❖

Benefits of Walking

Read: Genesis 13:14-18

> Go, walk through the length and breadth of the land,
> for I am giving it to you (Gen. 13:17;NIV).

A daily walk can help protect you from a stroke. The *British Medical Journal* reports that a nine-year study of eight thousand middle-aged men revealed that regular, moderate activity reduced their risk of having a stroke by 40 percent.

Aerobic exercise also reduces the frequency, severity, and duration of migraine headaches. So next time you're tempted to head for the medicine cabinet, think again. Take a brisk walk, enjoy the change of scenery, and see if it doesn't help. As Charles Dickens said, "Walk and be happy; walk and be healthy."

Lord, thank You that something as simple and
pleasurable as walking can greatly improve my health.

❖ September 10 ❖

What Causes Heartburn?

Read: Proverbs 3:21-26

> When you lie down, you will not be afraid; when you
> lie down, your sleep will be sweet (Prov. 3:24;NIV).

Heartburn results when stomach acid backs up into the esophagus and irritates its sensitive lining. Normally, a muscular gate between the esophagus and stomach pinches itself shut to prevent this backup. But several things can cause this muscle to relax.

Lying down is one of them, and lying on your right side in particular can contribute to stomach acid back up. Lying on your right side may uncrimp the esophagus where it enters the stomach, making it easier for stomach acid to enter.

What can you do if you're susceptible to heartburn?

• Wait at least three hours after eating before lying down. If that's not possible, lie on your left side.

• If heartburn persists, prop up your head or the head of your bed at least six inches. That way, gravity will help keep stomach acid where it belongs.

• Avoid fatty foods, chocolate, alcohol, and cigarettes, all of which help relax the muscles in the esophagus.

• Try an over-the-counter antacid or drink water.

• Lose weight if you are overweight.

• See a doctor if your heartburn is persistent.

Lord, thank You for showing me how to alleviate this ailment.

❖ September 11 ❖

Burning Fat

Read: Isaiah 28:9-10

*For precept must be upon precept . . . line upon line
. . . here a little, and there a little (Isa. 28:10).*

When you exercise, are you metabolizing (burning) fat or carbohydrates? Well, it depends on how you are exercising.

It takes twice as much oxygen to burn fat as it does carbohydrates. This means that aerobic exercise burns fat. During aerobic exercise in which the exerciser is experiencing oxygen debt, carbohydrates are being burned.

Research shows that to maximize the metabolism of fat, exercise should be of low-intensity for a prolonged period of time. This means that walking is an excellent way to burn fat.

A physically fit person burns more fat (even at rest) than an unfit one because he processes oxygen more efficiently. The good news is that the more physically fit you become through exercise, the better your body will be able to burn fat.

So if you're over-fat, the challenge is two-fold: a low-fat diet and a low-intensity exercise program.

*Lord, help me to progressively increase
my exercise to yield the most benefit.*

❖ September 12 ❖

Decompression Routine

Read: Isaiah 26:1-4

*You will keep in perfect peace him whose mind is steadfast,
because he trusts in you (Isa. 26:3;NIV).*

Do you find it difficult to unwind at the end of the day? Here's a simple "decompression routine:"

1. When you've finished your work for the day, take three to five minutes to just sit quietly.

2. Drive home by a different route, exploring the new scenery.

3. When you get home, don't go into the house immediately. Walk around the yard or neighborhood and "smell the roses."

4. Insist that the first fifteen minutes at home be peaceful ones; that you not be asked to deal with hassles or crises. That will give you time to change clothes, collect your thoughts, and get settled. Then you can deal with any issues in a relaxed manner.

Lord, allow me to relax even in the midst of stress.

❖ September 13 ❖

Pregnancy and Nutrition

Read: Jeremiah 1

> . . . the Lord came to me saying, "Before I formed
> you in the womb I knew you . . ." (Jer. 1:5;NIV).

Our health is first affected during the brief time we are in our mother's womb. During those nine months, in which all our organs are being created, our bodies are especially vulnerable to chemical insults.

Adequate nutrition, increased amounts of vitamins and minerals, especially iron, are required to fine tune the little person's growth. Mothers need a well-balanced diet including whole grains, beans, low-fat dairy products, fruits, varied vegetables, lean meat, poultry, and fish. High fat and sugar are "empty" calories and should be avoided.

Additional calcium is needed for bones and teeth to develop. Skim milk (two glasses) and two cups of dark green, leafy vegetables, such as cabbage, turnip greens, and kale provide the daily requirement. Spinach, beet greens, and Swiss chard should be avoided because they interfere with both calcium and iron absorption. Junk foods, processed meats, snack foods, and cola drinks are high in phosphorus, which also interferes with calcium absorption.

Get your child off to a good start in life and eat right during pregnancy.

Lord, may I consider the nutritional needs of
my unborn child throughout my pregnancy.

❖ September 14 ❖

Peanut Butter/Jelly Sandwich

Read: Lamentations 4:1-6

> . . . the young children ask bread, and no man
> breaketh it unto them (Lam. 4:4).

A peanut butter and jelly sandwich on whole-wheat bread contains just 263 calories — that is, if you use only 1 tablespoon of peanut butter and 1 tablespoon of jelly. Parents sending their children to school will want to note that peanut butter and banana sandwiches make a more nutritious alternative that many youngsters enjoy. It's not that calories should be a concern for most children, but bananas supply fiber and minerals such as potassium, whereas jelly supplies little other than sugar.

Lord, remind me that my young
children still depend on me to
provide them with nourishment.

❖ September 15 ❖

A Bright Future   Read: Proverbs 31:10-31

> She is clothed with strength and dignity; she can
> laugh at the days to come (Prov. 31:25;NIV).

Have you been gloomy lately . . . maybe down in the dumps? I want you to listen carefully to this letter:

> For some part of a year, I was suffering from mild depression, which greatly affected not only my marriage but also my family life in general. I was not happy with myself or with my life. Then one of my friends began a low-fat diet and walking program which she enjoyed so much. Her program caused her to have a steady weight loss and it lifted her spirits. I decided that maybe I would feel better with a little exercise and a few pounds off.
>
> Well, I not only feel better after starting my program . . . *I feel great!* Within two weeks I began to notice my mind's depression easing up and the inches melting off my body. After just four weeks, I had dropped ten pounds. I'm feeling great . . . looking great . . . and my future looks even brighter.

Regular exercise can change your outlook on life. Why not give it a try?

Lord, give me an indomitable
optimism that smiles at the future.

❖ September 16 ❖

Brain Food   Read: 1 Corinthians 2:10-16

> . . . But we have the mind of Christ (1 Cor. 2:16;NIV).

When it comes to keeping your brain revved at top speed, all you may need is better fuel. Researchers checked brain function in twenty-eight healthy people over sixty. Those with adequate levels of the B vitamin riboflavin had better memory while those with adequate carotene levels were more quick thinking. People with high iron had brain activity levels similar to young folks in their twenties and thirties. Those low on thiamine showed some impairment of brain activity. It may be that nutrients are as important for the brain as they are for the rest of the body. A balanced diet of lean meats, fish, fruits, vegetables, and grains can give you all the nutrition for your brain that you need.

Lord, help me to see life from Your perspective.

❖ September 17 ❖

At Any Age   Read: Acts 10:23-48

> . . . I now realize how true it is that God does not show
> favoritism but accepts men from every nation who fear
> him and do what is right (Acts 10:34-35;NIV).

Great news — aerobic improvements can occur at any age. Even though it may take a little longer to progress on your program, middle-aged and older persons adapt marvelously to aerobic exercise.

Remember that increases in your body weight and percentage of body fat and declines in your maximum oxygen uptake (that just means getting oxygen to the working muscles) are not so much age-related as they are inactivity related. If you are slowing down and getting weak as you get older, the experts say it's not age related — it's because you are not exercising enough to keep up your muscle strength and endurance.

> *Lord, thank You for allowing me to reap*
> *benefits from exercise no matter how old I am.*

❖ September 18 ❖

A Healthy Lifestyle   Read: Isaiah 46:3-4

> Even to your old age and gray hairs I am he,
> I am he who will sustain you . . . (Isa. 46:4;NIV).

A healthy lifestyle begun at age thirty might extend the average life expectancy in this country by as much as fifteen years. Better yet, these could be healthy years.

Many of the debilitating conditions we associate with aging are really just consequences of our lifestyle that can be controlled. Proper nutrition and exercise can reduce risks of cardiovascular disease or cancer.

The same healthy behaviors that can help us live longer can also help us live well. The earlier such behaviors are adopted, the better. Don't get discouraged if you start late. Benefits can be gained even well into old age.

It may be even more important to adopt healthy habits as we age because our bodies become less capable of tolerating abuse. Our bodies' systems of defense weaken with age. We shouldn't think it's too late to start just because we've entered our golden years. Our golden years may need the most care of all.

> *Lord, enable me to serve You all the days of*
> *my life with the strength You supply.*

❖ September 19 ❖

How to Love Your Liver   Read: 1 Corinthians 12:12-31

> . . . those parts of the body that seem to be
> weaker are indispensable (1 Cor. 12:22;NIV).

According to the popular song of a few years ago, there are lots of ways to "leave your lover." But have you ever pondered how many ways there are to "love your liver?" The American Liver Foundation (ALF) thinks it's not a bad idea. Why?

Your liver stores iron reserves, as well as many vitamins and minerals. Your liver makes the bile you use to digest the food you eat. Your liver detoxifies all of the poisons you put in your body, including alcohol, over-the-counter drugs, and even illegal drugs.

Your liver stores carbohydrates, glucose, and fat until you need it. Your liver manufacturers blood to circulate throughout your body, and it makes the proteins that enable your body to grow.

Your liver removes the pollutants from the air that are not removed by the respiratory system. Your liver makes the clotting factor that keeps you from bleeding to death when you nick yourself while shaving. Your liver helps the body defend itself against germs that would otherwise cause serious illnesses.

All in all, the American Liver Foundation makes a pretty good case for loving your liver. Tomorrow you'll find out how.

Lord, my body reflects Your marvelous ingenuity in creation.

❖ September 20 ❖

Just Juice?   Read: Proverbs 24:3-5

> A wise man has great power, and a man of
> knowledge increases strength (Prov. 24:5;NIV).

A juicer takes fresh fruits and vegetables and makes them drinkable. Experts make claims for drinking juice — as much as six glasses a day — which for a family of four would require 50 pounds of produce a week.

While the National Cancer Institute does recommend that we eat at least five servings of fruits and vegetables a day, scientists don't agree the juice is as good as the fruit itself. Juicers remove the pulp (fiber) from the juice, and many contend that the fiber contains important nutrients.

Lord, give me wisdom in balancing my
family's enjoyment of juice and their need
for fiber in fruit and vegetables.

❖ September 21 ❖

After You Eat

> . . . the wise heart will know the proper time
> and procedure (Eccles. 8:5;NIV).

After meals isn't the time to do vigorous exercise, but it may be just right for mild activity. "You get a calorie-burning bonus of about 15 percent right after eating," says Bryant Stamford, director of the Health Promotion Center at the University of Louisville School of Medicine. For example, a mile walk burns about 100 calories. Your body uses another 100 calories to digest an average meal. "But when done together," says Dr. Stamford, "you burn an extra 30 calories for free."

Lord, thank you for teaching me the
most beneficial time to exercise.

❖ September 22 ❖

A Healthy Liver

Read: 1 Corinthians 12:12-20

> God has arranged the parts in the body,
> every one of them, just as he wanted
> them to be (1 Cor. 12:18;NIV).

Now that you know how important your liver is, how can you maintain a healthy one? Here are some ways:

1. Don't drown your liver in alcohol. Doctors advise against more than one or two drinks a day to be on the safe side.

2. Watch those drugs. All drugs are chemicals. While medicines are sometimes necessary, taking pills when they aren't necessary is a bad habit.

3. Be careful with aerosol sprays. Since the liver has to detoxify what you inhale, it has to work overtime when fumes from bug sprays, mildew sprays, paint sprays, and other chemicals get into your lungs.

4. Watch what gets on your skin. Insecticides that you spray on your lawn and vegetables can be absorbed through your skin and actually destroy liver cells. Wear protective clothing when using pesticides to minimize contact with the skin.

5. Don't eat too many fatty foods. Your liver makes cholesterol from saturated fat. A rich diet will cause your cholesterol count to soar.

Remember, you owe your life to your liver — so be a liver lover!

Lord, help me to care for the unseen parts
of my body that perform vital functions.

❖ September 23 ❖

When You Quit Smoking

Read: 1 Thessalonians 4:1-8

It is God's will that you should
be sanctified . . . (1 Thess. 4:3;NIV).

Ever wondered what happens to your body when you quit smoking? Here are just a few benefits of breaking the nicotine habit:

Twenty minutes later your blood pressure and pulse rate will have dropped to the levels they were before you smoked.

Eight hours later your blood levels of carbon monoxide will have returned to normal.

Seventy-three hours later your lung capacity will begin to increase.

Three to five years later your risk of a heart attack will be that of a nonsmoker.

Ten years later your risk of lung cancer will be that of a nonsmoker.

Lord, I consecrate my life to You in worship
and service. Don't let any questionable
practice tarnish my witness for You.

❖ September 24 ❖

Internist or Family Practitioner?

Read: Proverbs 19:1-8

He who gets wisdom loves his own
soul; he who cherishes understanding
prospers (Prov. 19:8;NIV).

Which kind of doctor is best for you and your family: an internist or a family practitioner?

Both have three years of "basic training" after med-school . . . but the training differs.

Internists specialize in diseases of the major internal-organ systems. The majority of their clients are adults, often those over the age of sixty.

The training of family practitioners, on the other hand, is broader. They not only study adult medicine, but pediatrics, gynecology, and obstetrics as well. In addition, they can do in-office surgical procedures, such as stitching up wounds and setting minor bones.

Lord, give me wisdom in selecting
the best doctor for my situation.

❖ September 25 ❖

Married Couples Stop Exercising Read: Deuteronomy 24

> If a man has recently married, he must not
> be sent to war or have any other duty laid on him.
> For one year he is to be free to stay at home and bring
> happiness to the wife he has married (Deut. 24:5;NIV).

What happens when you get married? Couples often cut back on exercising. With women the cutback is linked to pregnancy and child-rearing. With men it is a gradual reduction in activity not related to family size.

On the other hand, after a divorce exercise picks up sharply on the part of both men and women. Working out can divert us from our personal pain when we encounter a crisis in life.

Lord, may my spouse and I find a new togetherness
in keeping fit for each other.

❖ September 26 ❖

Good Mental Health Read: Genesis 39:1-23

> . . . How then could I do such a wicked thing
> and sin against God? (Gen. 39:9;NIV).

The American Medical Association lists the following as basic signs of good mental health:

- The ability to recover quickly from the stresses of life.
- The ability to judge reality accurately.
- The ability to see the long-range effects of choices.
- The ability to love and sustain personal relationships.
- The ability to work cheerfully and productively.
- The ability to exercise one's conscience effectively.

Joseph shines as an example of good mental health. Despite being sold into slavery by his brothers, he bounced back from this trauma and made himself useful to Potiphar. Joseph's integrity kept him from sinning with his master's wife. When falsely accused and imprisoned, Joseph faithfully served the warden. His relationship with God undergirded him through the trials of life, and we can believe God to do the same for us.

Lord, develop resiliency in me through
the inevitable trials of life.

❖ September 27 ❖

Napping

Read: Daniel 8:15-18

While he was speaking to me, I was in a deep sleep,
with my face to the ground. Then he touched
me and raised me to my feet (Dan. 8:18;NIV).

Taking an afternoon nap doesn't mean you're lazy. Napping can be a great pick-me-up. Here are some tips on successful napping:

The most efficient time to nap is around 2:00 and 3:00 in the afternoon — midway between the time you wake up in the morning and go to bed in the evening.

It isn't necessary that you fall asleep. Simply lying down can be just as restful as sleeping.

Limit your nap time to less than an hour. Longer than that can result in grogginess.

You can optimize catnap time . . . by keeping it to thirty minutes or less. Studies show that a short siesta in the afternoon improves alertness. The problem with snoozing longer is that about forty to sixty-five minutes after falling asleep you enter deep sleep. Being interrupted when snoozing that hard makes you feel groggy and irritable, not refreshed.

Lord, refresh me with an occasional
nap when my body needs rest.

❖ September 28 ❖

Are You a Workaholic?

Read: Psalm 127:1-2

In vain you rise early and stay up late, toiling for food to eat —
for he grants sleep to those he loves (Ps. 127:2;NIV).

Myth: Being a workaholic is bad for your health.

Fact: The ability to put in long hours at a task you like may actually promote good health. The idea that the "workaholic," if defined as a type "A" personality, is at risk for a heart attack was formalized in 1969 by two California cardiologists, Dr. Meer Friedman and Dr. Ray Rosenman. Some early studies, including the important and large-scale Framingham Heart Study, did seem to support the idea that hard-working, competitive, tense, hostile men had a higher-than-average risk for heart disease. But later studies failed to confirm this. If any factor in this mix does dispose a person to heart disease, it seems more likely to be hostility than long hours at the job. Smoking and high blood pressure turned out to be more serious risk factors than personality or behavior.

Lord, bring balance to my daily schedule
so I don't neglect You or those closest to me.

❖ September 29 ❖

Low-Back Pain

Read: Job 33:19-22

> . . . a man may be chastened on a
> bed of pain with constant distress
> in his bones (Job 33:19;NIV).

When disks get compressed, the soft "jelly" in their center may squeeze out onto the nearby nerve root endings, causing pain. The disks themselves can bulge and compress nerve root endings. Assuming a position with hip joints and knees bent will take the pressure off the sciatic nerve (which runs from the buttocks to the feet), relieving the pain. So next time you feel the hot warning twinge of a minor back attack, lie down on your back on the floor and rest your lower legs on the seat of a chair. Flip through a copy of your favorite magazine while you relax for ten or fifteen minutes. Repeat as necessary throughout the day. Chronic or intense back pain, of course, should always be checked by a doctor.

Lord, allow me to see pain as a
warning signal that something is wrong.
Give me wisdom in alleviating the cause
and not just the symptom.

❖ September 30 ❖

Hold it Close!

Read: Isaiah 66:10-14

> For you will nurse and be carried
> on her arm and dandled on
> her knees (Isa. 66:12;NIV).

Lifting twenty pounds can be like lifting three hundred.

We're all careful when we're lifting. Right? We are careful not to get the object close to us, for fear of getting dirty.

For example, it's Monday morning . . . the day to take the garbage out, and you're dressed for the office. You carefully hold the garbage can away from you to avoid soiling your clothes. But you could be messing up your back.

If you want to protect your back, always carry a heavy weight as close to your body as you can. For example, a twenty-pound child held just one foot away from your body acts on your spine like you were lifting a three hundred-pound load.

Lord, keep me from lifting
hastily or more than I can handle.

❖ October 1 ❖

Quit While You Are Ahead

Read: Proverbs 9

*Instruct a wise man and he will
be wiser still . . . (Prov. 9:9;NIV).*

If you — or someone you love — have been smoking for a long time, you may think it's futile to quit now. You are wrong. Quitting will improve your health dramatically. In fact, from the moment you stop, the tobacco-related risks of heart disease will begin to fade.

A study was done of 807 people, over the age of fifty-four, who quit the year before the study began, and who continued to abstain for six years after. There was a substantial decrease in death rates, and fewer deaths due to heart attacks. Even the oldest people in the study who already had heart disease benefited from quitting. And they had smoked for many years.

A wise person wants to do everything they possibly can to live a long and healthy life. Learn all you can about the benefits of not smoking and eventually, you will be glad to quit!

Lord, give me the wisdom to quit smoking.

❖ October 2 ❖

Iron Deficiency

Read: Hebrews 9:11-28

*. . . without the shedding of blood there
is no forgiveness (Heb. 9:22;NIV).*

Did you know that iron deficiency is the most common nutritional deficiency in the United States? Men need 10 mg. of iron; women need 15 mg; and pregnant women need 30 mg.

Why do we need it? Iron enables your body to make hemoglobin and that is the part of blood that carries oxygen to your body's cells. If you feel tired and fatigued, this could be the result of iron deficiency.

Iron is abundantly available in many common foods. The problem is that our bodies can't readily absorb the iron. Spinach, is rich in iron but it's hard for the body to get it out. The iron from meat, however, is easier for your body to absorb. This is particularly true of organ meats.

Here are some foods high in iron: oysters, beef liver, clams, lean beef, canned tuna, shrimp, enriched chicken noodles, dry cereal, bread, oatmeal, dried apricots, bananas, raisins, strawberries, dried beans, lima beans, tomatoes, turnip greens, broccoli, and potatoes.

*Thank You, Jesus, for offering Your life and
Your blood on the cross for me.*

❖ October 3 ❖

Age and Weight Gain

Read: Galatians 6

. . . A man reaps what he sows . . . (Gal. 6:7;NIV).

Do you know when most adults gain weight? The experts tell us most weight gain occurs between the ages of twenty-five and thirty-five. Do you know when most adults lose weight? Most weight loss occurs between the ages of fifty-five and sixty-five.

The interesting fact here is that most of the weight gain in the twenty-five to thirty-five decade is likely to be in the form of fat. Why? Because of the decrease in physical activity from less involvement in sports and the increased consumption of calorie rich foods.

All of the loss in weight in the fifty-five to sixty-five decade (an average of five pounds) is likely to be in the form of muscle mass. This is also due to a decrease in physical activity.

What does this tell us? That physical activity is important at all stages of life. The younger person needs to be active to prevent the unnecessary gain of body fat. The older person needs to be active to prevent the unnecessary loss of muscle tissue.

Lord, help me to sow good health habits
early in life so I can reap the benefits later.

❖ October 4 ❖

Seasoned with Salt

Read: Colossians 4:1-6

Let your speech be alway with grace,
seasoned with salt . . . (Col. 4:6).

Have you ever tasted something that needed a little more salt and you added it and then the food tasted just right? Salt is a great seasoning when used in small amounts. Most people, however, get too much salt in their diet. Where does it come from?

Would you believe that 80 percent of the sodium you consume is put into processed foods by the manufacturer? Another 10 percent occurs naturally in foods. And only about 10 percent comes from the salt shaker.

To cut down on salt try adding a few drops of lemon juice to foods. This not only perks up flavor but also gives even a *little* salt more bounce.

Do the people you live and work with every day need a little perking up? Why not be the one to add a gracious word of encouragement to your conversations? You may be pleasantly surprised by the results.

Lord, let my words always be seasoned with grace and kindness.

❖ October 5 ❖

Sleeping Tips

Read: Jeremiah 31:23-30

. . . My sleep had been pleasant to me (Jer. 31:26;NIV).

Nearly 25 percent of all adults suffer regularly from insomnia. They have difficulty falling asleep and/or staying asleep. Insomnia itself is not a medical disorder, but it *is* a symptom of problems such as stress, jet lag, chronic pain, noise, or side effects of some medications.

In order to improve your chances of restful sleep, do something that you find relaxing for an hour before going to bed. You might read, listen to music, or take a warm bath. Be sure to sleep in a quiet, dark room that is between 60 and 65º F. Establish a regular sleeping schedule, but don't go to bed until you are sleepy. If you can't fall asleep within twenty minutes of going to bed, get out of bed and return when you are sleepy. Get up at the same time every morning.

God loves you and, if you put your trust in Him, He will give you a good night sleep.

Lord God, I put my trust in You. Help me to
rest peacefully throughout the night.

❖ October 6 ❖

What Not to Do!

Read: 1 Peter 5

Cast all your anxiety on Him because
He cares for you (1 Pet. 5:7;NIV).

Yesterday we talked about what you can do to get a good night's sleep. Today we're going to discuss the things you *shouldn't* do. First, don't drink caffeinated beverages within four hours of bedtime. Also avoid cigarettes because nicotine is a stimulant.

A nightcap will not improve your sleep. While alcohol may help you fall asleep, your sleep may be light and interrupted. Taking sleeping pills can also lead to sleep disruption and daytime fatigue. Never combine them with alcohol. Sleeping pills can become addictive and should only be used for very short periods of time — never more than three nights in a row.

Don't worry. Learn to pray and cast all your anxieties on the Lord before you go to bed. He cares about you and wants you to rest peacefully.

Lord, forgive me for using artificial
means of getting to sleep. Teach me how
to give You my worries and anxieties.

❖ October 7 ❖

Perfecting Holiness

Read: 2 Corinthians 7

Having therefore these promises, dearly
beloved, let us cleanse ourselves from all
filthiness of the flesh and spirit, perfecting
holiness in the fear of God (2 Cor. 7:1).

As we look to God, He begins a work in our lives. No, we aren't changed overnight, but little by little God shows us things in our lives that do not please Him. It's not just cigarettes, alcohol, or drugs that are displeasing to God. We can lust after food, too.

God doesn't expect instant perfection from us, but as He shows us sin in our lives, victory will come. But we must *allow* God to do the work in us. You may have already started by trying to eat right, exercise, and maybe quit smoking, because you know God wants the very best for your life.

Dear Lord, show me any area of my
life today that needs Your cleansing.

❖ October 8 ❖

Absorbing Iron

Read: Phillipians 4

My God shall supply all your
needs according to His riches in
glory by Christ Jesus (Phil. 4:19).

Let's look at some ways you can get a sufficient amount of iron into your system without overeating red meat.

One good way is to get plenty of vitamin C because it helps your body absorb iron. A glass of orange or tomato juice or a half grapefruit eaten along with your fortified cereal at breakfast will help you get more iron into your system. Tea and coffee, however, reduce absorption of iron — so don't have them with your meals.

When you are cooking, use as little water as possible and reuse that water in soups and sauces. Cooking with iron skillets is another good way to get iron in our diets. Now that most people use stainless steel and other non-stick pans, Americans are just getting less iron than we once did. The nutrition experts tell us to still cook in iron pots and skillets whenever possible.

Thank You, Lord, for supplying all my
needs — both physically and spiritually.

❖ October 9 ❖

Stair Climbing Machines

Read: Job 14

Surely then you will count my steps but not
keep track of my sin (Job 14:16;NIV).

If you go to a spa these days, you have probably discovered that the most popular piece of equipment there is the stair climbing machine. People will actually wait in line to use them. Do they offer a better aerobic workout than a treadmill or a stationary bike?

The experts say "aerobically speaking" there's no difference. If you do other things at the same frequency, intensity, and duration, you get the same result. Climbing stairs uses the derriere, lower back, and lower legs more than either cycling or jogging. Climbing, however, puts greater stress on the knees.

Do remember that stair climbing can be quite exhausting, so take it easy at first and work up slowly to a longer program. Remember, too, if you are overweight, you would be wise to get most of your aerobic exercise through walking or using the stationary bike.

Isn't it wonderful to know that God knows every step you take, but that He doesn't keep track of your sin!

Heavenly Father, thank You for sending
Your Son Jesus so I could know forgiveness of my sin.

❖ October 10 ❖

Three to Five

Read: 2 Chronicles 15

. . . be strong and do not give up, for your work
will be rewarded (2 Chron. 15:7;NIV).

Yesterday we talked about stair climbing, but whatever aerobic exercise you choose — including walking — should be done continuously for anywhere from twenty minutes to an hour. If your primary goal is to lose weight, exercise more often and longer at a lower intensity.

You need to exercise three to five days a week. One or two days a week does not improve fitness levels very much. More than five days a week does not add significantly to the fitness benefits, but it might help you to keep your weight under control by exercising every day.

Be consistent. Missing an occasional workout won't hurt you, but after two weeks of not exercising your cardiovascular fitness begins to decline. After ten weeks most of the fitness benefits will have disappeared.

Lord, help me to be strong and not give up
so I can reap the rewards of my efforts.

❖ October 11 ❖

Longevity   Read: Ecclesiastes 11

However many years a man may live, let him
enjoy them all (Eccles. 11:8;NIV).

Did you know that the life expectancy of a male child born in 1988 is 71.4 years, and that of a female is 78.3 years — which is almost seven years longer?

Longevity is still in the hands of the individual men and women — and the choices they make — like watching their diet, stop smoking, exercising, and making lifestyle changes. While behavioral changes aren't easy, they offer the only practical way to live longer. Men, however, are less likely to make the changes.

A recent survey found that men play down good health advice and are less likely to limit salt, fat, or cholesterol, to eat enough fiber, to obey the speed limit, to wear seat belts, or to be careful about avoiding home accidents. Maybe they think that's the way to enjoy life. Too bad they don't realize that healthy habits make life a lot more fun!

Lord, help me to enjoy life without
abusing the body You have given me.

❖ October 12 ❖

High on Caffeine   Read: Isaiah 26

Trust ye in the Lord for ever: for in the Lord Jehovah
is everlasting strength (Isa. 26:4).

If you are like a lot of people, you probably use caffeine to help keep you going. But did you know that the amount of caffeine in one cup of coffee, if injected directly into bloodstream, would kill you? Then how can a person drink coffee and get an energy lift if this stuff is poisonous to your body?

When caffeine hits your stomach, the body senses it is being poisoned. The body immediately sounds the defense signal to your adrenal glands — which are our backup emergency glands — telling them to get some adrenaline flowing to the body. The adrenaline stimulates the liver to begin pumping its stored glucose into the bloodstream.

The blood cells must have this quick shot of energy in order to get rid of the caffeine as soon as it enters the bloodstream. Why? To keep you from dropping dead from caffeine poisoning! As a result, you feel an extra surge of energy from the added glucose in the bloodstream. That's the high you get!

Lord, help me to trust in You for my strength
and not in harmful stimulants like caffeine.

❖ October 13 ❖

A High Price   Read: Hebrews 12:1-13

*Therefore, strengthen your feeble arms
and weak knees (Heb. 12:12;NIV).*

Yesterday we talked about how caffeine gives us a temporary jolt of energy. But that initial surge comes with a high price. Put simply, you rob your body's tissues to feel good for the moment in order to fight fatigue.

Remember we learned that your body's cells change glucose to usable energy so they can metabolize the caffeine. But to do that, the cells burn vitamins and minerals. These are needed to cleanse the body of the poison, but these precious nutrients come from your body's own reserves. That's a high price to pay for a short burst of energy!

What makes it worse is that this year, one cup of coffee will make us feel good. Next year, it will take two cups to get that same good feeling. Then one day we will find we have developed osteoporosis because of the continued depletion of calcium from our body's reserves. Believe me, God doesn't want you to grow old and feeble with no strength left to enjoy life!

*Lord, show me natural ways to get energy
without harming my body.*

❖ October 14 ❖

Alcohol and Pregnancy   Read: Luke 1:26-56

*When Elizabeth heard Mary's greeting, the baby
leaped in her womb, and Elizabeth was filled
with the Holy Spirit (Luke 1:41;NIV).*

Did you know that alcohol is the greatest health threat to the unborn child? Drinking by mothers-to-be resulted in fifty thousand babies with permanent damage last year, with such terrible effects as brain damage with varied degrees of learning disability, poor coordination, and hyperactivity. In addition, pregnant women who drink are at risk of having a child whose growth is slowed down or who has heart and/or kidney defects.

Throughout pregnancy, and especially during the first three months, all drugs should be avoided unless prescribed by the attending physician. "All drugs" includes over-the-counter pain relievers and cold medicines.

Children are both the most important gift we receive, and our most important gift for the future. Do what you can to nurture and protect that gift.

*Lord, protect those babies who are growing
in their mother's womb. Fill those
mothers with Your Holy Spirit.*

❖ October 15 ❖

Ten Commandments of Exercise   Read: Psalm 119:97-101

Your commands make me wiser than my enemies,
for they are ever with me (Ps. 119:98;NIV).

Let me share with you this list of ten commandments that someone gave me concerning exercise:

(1) Find some form of exercise you love to do — biking, walking, swimming, jogging, etc. If you don't enjoy it, you won't do it. (2) Schedule a time for exercise every day. A regular structured time assures continuity and builds a confidence in yourself. (3) Keep your exercise simple. (4) Wear comfortable clothes and proper shoes. (5) Take the time while you are exercising to appreciate yourself and nature. (6) Become nutrition conscious and eat wisely. (7) Read widely from uplifting articles on exercise and nutrition to keep inspired. (8) Don't let your mind be stressed while you are exercising. Let your exercise time be your special time to be creative in your thoughts. (9) Get proper rest and relish the good sleep that exercise brings. (10) Associate with positive people who are alive with interest and activity.

Lord, help me to obey Your commands so I can become
wiser than the enemies of my soul and body.

❖ October 16 ❖

Diabetes and Weight Training   Read: Ecclesiastes 7

. . . the advantage of knowledge is this: that wisdom
preserves the life of its possessor (Eccles. 7:12;NIV).

Most people who have Type I diabetes (insulin dependent) have been told not to weight train. New evidence, however, indicates it may be safe and beneficial after all. In one study, eight men with Type I diabetes volunteered to perform a full body weight-training program for one hour, three evenings a week, for ten weeks.

The participants tested their own blood-glucose levels before and after each exercise session. At the end of the ten weeks, the results showed that the volunteers' glucose was reduced to healthier levels. Total cholesterol levels had dropped, and overall strength and bench-press endurance had improved significantly. The researchers also noted a trend toward a decrease in body fat.

So, if you have diabetes, check with your doctor and see if he will let you start lifting some weights. It's very important to check with your doctor before beginning any new form of exercise.

Lord, please use the new wisdom I am learning to preserve
my life from the effects of sickness and disease.

❖ October 17 ❖

Ripe Fruits

. . . No branch can bear fruit by itself; it must remain in the vine. Neither can you bear fruit unless you remain in me (John 15:4;NIV).

The next time you buy fresh produce, remember these facts about fruit. Fruits are tastier when they are ripe. Unripe fruit contains high concentrations of bitter substances and astringent compounds. During the ripening process, these are broken down by enzymes and starches are converted to sugars. As a result, ripe fruits are usually sweeter and softer.

Fruits taste best when they are allowed to ripen on the vine or tree. Some fruits, such as bananas and tomatoes, are picked green and allowed to ripen while they are being shipped to stores. Other fruits will not continue to ripen after picked. Melons, oranges, and pineapple will only become softer after being picked but not sweeter. Why? Because they don't store any starch in themselves; all their sugar comes from the plant.

That's the way it is with us. Our sweetness and righteousness only comes as we let Jesus produce it in us.

Jesus, keep me abiding in You so I can bear fruit in my life.

❖ October 18 ❖

Vitamin D
Read: Psalm 84

For the Lord God is a sun and shield . . . (Ps. 84:11;NIV).

Every adult needs 200 International Units of vitamin D daily. But after menopause, women may need more. Why? Because vitamin D helps your body absorb the calcium that is essential in preventing osteoporosis. Researchers say women need at least 220 IU per day after menopause.

Where do you get vitamin D? The primary food source is milk. A cup of skim milk contains 100 IU of vitamin D. Fatty fish also has vitamin D. Sunlight is another good source. The skin changes ultraviolet radiation into vitamin D. As your skin ages, however, it's not able to change sunlight into vitamin D as easily. Keep in mind, also, that elderly people tend to get out in the sunlight less often than younger individuals.

How much sunlight do you need for vitamin D? An older person can get a sufficient amount by exposing hands, arms, and face to the midday sun for ten to fifteen minutes twice a week. If you feel you don't get enough vitamin D from natural sources, ask you doctor if you should be taking a supplement.

Thank You, Lord, for providing the sun to keep me
healthy and Your protection to keep me safe.

❖ October 19 ❖

On Your Level   Read: Proverbs 16:1-15

> In his heart a man plans his course, but the Lord
> determines his steps (Prov. 16:9;NIV).

Your aerobic training can take any form you enjoy. It might be walking, jogging, hiking, swimming, cycling, rowing, cross-country skiing, or skating, as well as game activities like basketball, tennis, racquetball, volleyball, etc. The important thing is to engage in activity that uses the large muscles. But you should also choose activities you enjoy and are suited to your level of fitness. You don't want to be gasping for your breath. If you are, then you have chosen an activity that is too strenuous for you.

If you work at too high a level, you will tire of the activity and give it up. You are even more likely to injure yourself if the program is too hard. Remember to take it easy at first and gradually build up as your fitness level improves. The experts say moderate intensity exercise like walking is best for most adults.

Sometimes our plans may be on the right track, but they just need the Lord's direction.

Lord, show me which form of exercise is best for me.

❖ October 20 ❖

Fast Food — Bad Words   Read: Psalm 25

> He guides the humble in what is right and
> teaches them his way (Ps. 25:9;NIV).

What's the biggest nutrition concern for Americans? The fat content in foods. In a recent survey, 46 percent rank it number one and considered it more important than cholesterol or salt in food. And that is the way it should be. Whenever you read a label, the most important item to look for is grams of fat. We need to keep the fat content low in our diets.

One way to do that is to be on the look-out for certain "bad" words when you find yourself in a fast food restaurant. Food that is described as "double," "deluxe," "classic," or "big" is likely to be high in fat. Just get the plain food without big names.

If you don't believe me, ask to see a chart showing the nutritional content of the products sold by your favorite fast food chain. You'll probably find that even the regular size items are high in fat and salt. Don't ever be too proud to ask for the facts when your health is concerned!

Lord, help me to keep my heart humble so
You can teach me the right way to eat and how to live.

❖ October 21 ❖

Caffeine and Fatigue

Read: 1 Corinthians 15:1-34

Awake to righteousness, and sin not . . . (1 Cor. 15:34).

Each night as we sleep, our body cells are manufacturing energy for the next day's activities. When we wake, healthy cells have 100 percent of the energy they need for that day, both physically and mentally. By the end of the day our energy supply is spent and we are drowsy (not fatigued), and it is time to sleep and replenish.

But did you know that the everyday habit of drinking coffee, can weaken your body's cells to 50 percent of their normal energy output? When that happens, what do you do? Cut back on your daily energy demands the next day? No. You drink more coffee. It's a vicious cycle. The very thing that is making you feel good is slowly robbing you of the natural ability to fight fatigue.

Eventually, the time will come when ten cups of coffee will not do the trick. Then you go to bed beat and wake up tired. You need four cups of coffee to get going, but that only lasts a short while. You can't even think clearly anymore, and you're irritated and moody.

Lord, help me stop sinning against my own body.

❖ October 22 ❖

Conquering Caffeine

Read: Romans 8:28-39

. . . in all these things we are more than conquerors
through him who loved us (Rom. 8:37;NIV).

Your body was not designed to be jolted by caffeine and then flooded with glucose. If you treat it right by providing it with proper fuel that it was designed to run on, rather than low quality imitation fuel, your body will run efficiently. What should you do?

Don't quit cold turkey. Your body has become more dependent on stimulants than you think. Make a gradual change to a healthy lifestyle and slowly reduce your use of stimulants. As the body chemistry improves, the cells will become more efficient at using real nutrients and less dependent on stimulants. Soon you can eliminate stimulants altogether.

Begin by mixing decaffeinated coffee or tea with caffeinated. Then switch to decaffeinated only. Finally, go off altogether, replacing it with other hot beverages like herbal teas. In a few weeks, you'll begin to sense a new calmness, as your body begins to perform its functions without the ups and downs of a caffeine high.

Lord, I claim Your conquering power
over my addiction to caffeine.

❖ October 23 ❖

Let Go!   Read: John 14

> . . . my peace I give unto you . . . .
> Let not your heart be troubled, neither
> let it be afraid (John 14:27;NIV).

What's the secret to reducing stress? It's learning to just be aware of things without feeling the need to try to change them. So often we look at something — or someone (even ourselves) — with the feeling that we need to change the situation or the person. Life will be less stressful if we simply look at things and people as they are — without trying to change them.

Most of us want to "control" things rather than simply be aware of them. We make judgments as to whether something is good or bad. We relax when we learn to just observe without passing judgment.

It's like falling asleep. You create the "right conditions," and then you "let go." Trying to force yourself to fall asleep usually makes you more awake.

> *Lord, help me to change the things I can*
> *and accept the things I can't change.*

❖ October 24 ❖

Too Empty   Read: Isaiah 30:1-18

> . . . In returning and rest shall ye be saved;
> in quietness and in confidence shall
> be your strength . . . (Isa. 30:15).

Have you ever noticed that when you are tired or very irritated, that is the time all your good intentions concerning eating healthy go right out the window?

Guard against these weak moments. Don't ever let your stomach get too empty. A little complex carbohydrate snack like fruit or pita bread or a bagel can help keep you from feeling shaky or at loose ends. Learn to listen to your body and keep an eye on your moods. With a little discernment, you can ward off any "fat attacks!"

Also, if you are too tired to make wise choices, take time out to be quiet and rest. While you are resting, renew your confidence in the Lord to help you maintain your resolve.

> *Lord, thank You for not only the gift of*
> *salvation but for the confidence and*
> *strength of Your presence in my life.*

❖ October 25 ❖

Just one?   Read: Psalm 119:102-120

How sweet are thy words unto my taste! . . . (Ps. 119:103).

Why can't anyone eat only one potato chip? Because it's not a serving size. While there's no such thing as a one-size-fits-all serving, a single chip is unlikely to meet anyone's idea of satisfaction!

To make matters worse, salt is one of those flavors that jolts the taste buds and sets them clamoring for more. Your taste buds say: "I like that. Do it again!" This also happens with any food that is sweet, bitter, or sour or has are other taste-receptor enhancers that can overexcite the mouth. That's why you need to snack on foods that are low in fat, sodium, and sugar — and high in fiber, such as fruit or air-popped popcorn.

Salt in cooked food can also make you want more of it. That's because salt added to cooked food has a stronger taste. So, if you are trying to wean yourself away from salt, but the flavor is hard to give up, ask that salt *not* be added during cooking. Then when you sprinkle it on to taste, you'll be cutting back by 80 percent!

Lord, let me find my satisfaction in Your Word
and not in spicy foods.

❖ October 26 ❖

Early Detection   Read: Hebrews 6

We have this hope as an anchor for the soul,
firm and secure . . . (Heb. 6:19;NIV).

Breast cancer is the number one malignancy among women in this country and, after lung cancer, it's the second leading cause of death by cancer. A staggering one out of every ten women will develop the disease, with two-thirds of them having passed menopause when they get cancer. When the cancer is detected early, however — as it is in 75 to 80 percent of cases — the chances for survival are excellent.

The best way to detect breast cancer in its less advanced stages is with a mammogram. A woman should have her first mammogram at the age of thirty-five. It will show what the normal tissue looks like and is used for comparison from year to year. The next mammogram should be scheduled three years later. Because the incidence of breast cancer skyrockets as we get older, women between the ages of forty and fifty should be tested every two years. Post menopausal women should have a mammogram annually.

Lord, You are the anchor for my soul. I trust in You.

❖ October 27 ❖

Tips to Prevent Arthritis Read Psalm 6

Have mercy upon me, O Lord; for I am weak: O Lord,
heal me; for my bones are vexed (Ps. 6:2).

Did you know there are several things you can do to lower the possibility of your arthritis? First, maintain a normal body weight because obese people have a greater risk of developing osteoarthritis. Also, try to protect your joints from degeneration by maintaining good posture.

A consistent exercise program can help you develop strong bones, ligaments, and healthy cartilage. Resting when tired or injured is very important because fatigued or weak muscles have less ability to absorb shock and may transmit more impact to bones. Do not exercise on acutely injured or inflamed joints unless cleared by your physician. If you do notice any form of arthritis developing, seek medical care early. The sooner you get treatment, the less joint damage will occur. Also, you can pray as the Psalmist did and ask the Lord to heal you.

O Lord, have mercy on me and heal this pain and stiffness in my
joints. Help me to do my part to bring healing to my body.

❖ October 28 ❖

A Great Diet Drink Read: Revelation 22:1-6

. . . the river of the water of life . . . flowing . . . . On
each side . . . stood the tree of life . . . yielding its
fruit every month . . . (Rev. 22:1-2;NIV).

Most people underestimate the health-producing qualities of water. In fact, as Americans, we take this sparkling beverage for granted and often consider it to be a second-class drink. Today, let's look at some of the wonderful things water can do for us.

First, water is a great diet drink. It suppresses the appetite naturally and helps the body metabolize stored fat. In fact, a decrease in water intake will cause fat deposits to increase, while an increase can reduce fat deposits. That's why the overweight person needs more water than the thin person.

Water helps rid the body of waste. During weight loss the body has a lot more waste to get rid of because all that metabolized fat must be shed. Adequate water helps flush out the waste. When fluid balance is right, there is a loss of hunger almost overnight.

In Bible times, water was considered a precious commodity, and anyone who had plenty of it was truly blessed, as today's verse shows.

Lord, make my life like a well-watered tree.

❖ October 29 ❖

Getting Enough   Read: Isaiah 12

> With joy you will draw water from the
> wells of salvation (Isa. 12:3;NIV).

Contrary to what many people think, drinking water is the best treatment for fluid retention. When the body doesn't get enough, it holds on to the water it has. This shows up as swollen feet, legs, and hands. Only when the body gets enough water will stored water be released.

If you eat a lot of salty snacks, your system will retain more water in order to dilute the salt. You must drink more water to get rid of the salt. If you drink enough water, your system will work more smoothly and you'll avoid constipation.

How much is enough? Most people need at least six to eight glasses a day to keep their bodies functioning properly. Drink no more than ten glasses a day, unless you are losing a lot of water from perspiration or are on a rapid weight loss program. If you drink too much, you could literally wash important electrolytes out of your system.

In the Scriptures, water often symbolizes salvation because it is the only life-saving liquid.

Thank You, Lord, that I have known the joy of Your salvation.

❖ October 30 ❖

Food Is Not Love   Read: Psalm 37:1-15

> Trust in the Lord and do good; dwell in the
> land and enjoy safe pasture (Ps. 37:3;NIV).

Parents need to remember that "food is not love." Too many parents use food as a reward or they withhold food as punishment for a child. It would be better to take away a toy or turn off the TV instead of withholding a favorite dessert or making a child go to his room without supper. Food should not be used as a reward either. When a child needs to be praised give him a hug and not a cookie or a piece of candy. If you don't use food as a reward or as punishment, you will enable the child (and later, the adult) to deal with life's ups and downs without resorting to food for gratification.

God allows testing times to come into all our lives in order to build character. So often we reach for food to console us or to avoid dealing with the issue at hand. We need to trust in the Lord and to do good, even when we are going through rough times of our own.

Lord, I put my trust in You and not in food,
knowing You will always take care of me.

❖ October 31 ❖

Alzheimer's and You

Read: Psalm 40

Many, O Lord my God, are thy wonderful works which
thou hast done, and thy thoughts which are to us-ward . . .
they are more than can be numbered (Ps. 40:5).

By now I hope you are convinced that regular exercise and a low-fat diet
are essential to your health. We already know that by making these part of your
lifestyle you can roll back your risk for a heart attack. Now we know that you
may be getting a extra bonus — protection against illnesses like Alzheimer's.

For ten years researchers monitored 448 men and women between the
ages of seventy-five and eighty-five. The women who had a history of heart
attacks were five times more likely to develop Alzheimer's. There was no such
link in the men. The researchers believe there is a substance released in the
women after a heart attack that damages brain cells. Preventing a heart attack
would keep this from happening. So, remember, exercise and a low-fat diet
help to prevent heart attacks, and this could possibly give you protection from
Alzheimer's.

We take for granted the many, many blessings of God. Let's stop and
count our blessings. They are more than can be numbered.

Thank You, Lord, for the many wonderful things
You have done for me. I am eternally grateful.

❖ November 1 ❖

It's What's Up Front

Read: Judges 3:12-30

> Ehud reached with his left hand, drew the sword from his right thigh and plunged it into the king's belly. . . . Ehud did not pull the sword out, and the fat closed in over it (Judg. 3:21-22;NIV).

Carrying your weight in your hips and thighs may distress you, but experts don't consider it a health hazard. A big belly, on the other hand, well, that's a different matter.

Studies in Sweden suggest that fat in the abdominal area is as bad for the heart as smoking.

According to researchers reporting their findings at a recent meeting of the American Heart Association, a fat stomach produces a five- to ten-fold increase in the risk of heart disease, stroke, diabetes, and premature death.

The study indicates that the belly is the worst place for fat storage. (Interestingly, men tend to have big bellies more than women — at least until after menopause.)

The reason is that fat stored in the abdominal area is very prone to getting into the bloodstream where it raises blood fat and insulin levels.

So, if your fat is up front, it's in a dangerous place.

Lord, help me avoid putting weight on in the wrong places.

❖ November 2 ❖

Breathing Stress Away

Read: Romans 8:1-8

> . . . The mind controlled by the Spirit is life and peace (Rom. 8:6;NIV).

If you've ever looked at books on stress, you've noticed that most of them have a chapter on deep breathing exercises. That's because deep breathing has long been regarded as having a calming effect on the body. Scientists aren't sure how it works. Some suggest that it may be due to the increased oxygen level in the bloodstream that results from concentrating on breathing. Others say that respiratory nerve centers in the brain release chemicals that help relax the body.

Begin by finding a comfortable position. You may want to sit with your legs crossed or lie on your back with your knees bent. Whatever position you choose, make sure it's one that you can easily maintain for awhile.

Inhale slowly through your nose. Your stomach and lungs should expand fully as you inhale. Then slowly exhale through your mouth. When you completely exhale, your lungs and stomach should be contracted.

Focus your mind on the breathing process.

Lord, may my anxieties dissipate with each deep breath I take.

❖ November 3 ❖

Low-Fat Diets for Kids?   Read: Isaiah 7:10-17

> . . . The virgin will be with child and will give birth
> to a son, and will call him Immanuel. He will eat
> curds and honey when he knows enough to reject
> the wrong and choose the right (Isa. 7:14-15;NIV).

Should children be on a low-fat diet? According to the American Academy of Pediatrics, children under the age of two should not have any restrictions in their fat or cholesterol intake because of the rapid growth rate during that period.

After the age of two, the AAP recommends that 30 percent of their calories come from fat. (The average American gets 40 percent of calories from fat.) The organization recommends that parents begin at an early age to encourage children to eat low-fat dairy products — such as skim milk and low-fat yogurt — and lean meats.

Lord, help me not to be too concerned with my
child's baby fat during his first two years.

❖ November 4 ❖

Cellulite   Read: Exodus 34:1-9

> The Lord (visits) . . . the iniquity of the fathers
> upon the children, and upon the children's children,
> unto the third and fourth generation (Exod. 34:6-7).

I've never had a speaking engagement without someone asking, "What is cellulite and how can I get rid of it?"

Cellulite — that dimpled, orange-peel look of skin around the hips, buttocks, and thighs — is nothing more than a buildup of fat cells. Women have more cellulite than men because they are genetically determined to carry more fat in these areas. Men also have a thicker network of fibrous connective tissue in the skin, which helps it maintain a more uniform tone.

Genetics play a big part in cellulite. If your mother, sister, or aunts have it, the chances are greater that you will have it, too. Weight gain or lack of physical fitness can cause cellulite to develop. Dropping excess pounds and increasing aerobic activity is the best solution for those who are overweight. Even normal-weight women with cellulite will find that regular exercise, both aerobic and resistance training, will help by reducing their overall body fat and improving muscle tone.

Lord, don't let me succumb to gimmicks when
only exercise and low-fat eating will bring results.

❖ November 5 ❖

Ten No-No's   Read: Exodus 20:1-17

I am the Lord your God . . . (Exod. 20:2;NIV).

We hear so much about all that is bad for you: sugar, fat, additives, and calories. But today let's look at what the nutrition experts say are the top ten nutritional No No's.

1. Eating without a plan or a goal.
2. Exceeding the speed limit.
3. Going longer than five hours without eating.
4. Eating excess fat.
5. Skipping produce and grains.
6. Cleaning your plate.
7. Trying to be too thin.
8. Trying to lose weight without an exercise program.
9. Skimping on water.
10. Calling food good or evil.

Lord, give me the grace to avoid these nutritional pitfalls.

❖ November 6 ❖

Potassium and Blood Pressure   Read: Leviticus 17:1-16

For the life of the flesh is in the blood . . . (Lev. 17:11).

Just how important is potassium to your body, what does it do for your health, and where can you find it?

High blood pressure is the most important risk factor in the development of a stroke. You've probably heard that sodium adversely affects blood pressure, but do you know how important potassium is in neutralizing the affects of sodium? Potassium has a protective influence all its own. People with a positive potassium-sodium ratio have a reduced chance of having high blood pressure. These studies show that some people eat roughly half of the necessary potassium they need in their diets.

But take heart — the best source of potassium is fresh fruit. Cantaloupe, tomatoes, oranges, bananas, and peaches are good sources. Fresh fruit should be eaten with every meal as a good protection against a stroke.

A low-sodium, high-potassium diet will usually help lower blood pressure. So will moderate exercise. Tests show that the best way to tackle high blood pressure is a low-sodium, high-potassium diet coupled with moderate exercise.

Lord, show me what to do to prevent silent
killers like stroke and heart disease.

❖ **November 7** ❖

Are You a Type A Personality?   Read: Proverbs 22:15-29

> Do not make friends with a hot-tempered man, do not
> associate with one easily angered, or you may learn his
> ways and get yourself ensnared (Prov. 22:24-25;NIV).

We have heard that type A personalities have a higher risk for serious health problems. What's a type A personality anyway? It is characterized as hard-driving, aggressive, and hostile. A type B personality is calm, laid-back, and easy-going. Will anything minimize the health risks of a type A personality? Exercise can change the blood readings of one with a type A personality into those of a type B personality.

Type As have a very high level of a chemical in their blood which causes the blood to clot by promoting platelet stickiness. This condition, which increases the risk of heart disease, has been called "angry blood chemistry."

The striving, competitive type A personality releases hormones and neurochemicals in response to stress in his life. But exercise reduces the levels of this stressful chemical in the blood. Studies indicate that physically fit type As have the same levels of this stress substance as type Bs. Scientists say exercise may block the chemical, which prevents these individuals from having heart attacks. So, when we include regular exercise in our lifestyle, it even makes our blood chemistry happy!

> *Lord, help me to avoid the*
> *pitfalls of a driven personality.*

❖ **November 8** ❖

Fascinating Facts   Read: Jeremiah 33:1-3

> Call to me and I will answer you and
> tell you great and unsearchable things
> you do not know (Jer. 33:3;NIV).

You would have to eat nearly 2 quarts of plain, unbuttered popcorn to get the calories in one ounce of potato chips (about fifteen chips). By substituting 1 cup of plain, unbuttered popcorn for a 1-ounce bag of potato chips you save 135 calories and 10 grams of fat. Think about that next time you're tempted to snack after dinner!

> *Lord, I have so much to learn about nutrition!*
> *Teach me truths that I can quickly*
> *apply to my own eating habits.*

❖ November 9 ❖

Sleepy Cells

Read: Genesis 2:18-25

So the Lord God caused the man to fall into a
deep sleep . . . (Gen. 2:21;NIV).

Cancer cells "get sleepy" in the company of carotenes (which is the substance that your body converts to vitamin A). Three hours after scientists treated human tumor cells with alpha carotene, the activity of the cells' growth-promoting gene had slowed by 24 percent, and after eighteen hours by 82 percent. Researchers believe alpha carotene may slow developing tumors by locking them into the rest phase of their growth cycle. Alpha carotene and beta carotene are abundant in red, yellow, and leafy green vegetables. So, it's important to get your vegetables. It looks as if a diet high in red, yellow, and leafy green vegetables can even slow down cancer growth.

Lord, help me to eat foods that will prevent
or resist the growth of cancer in my body.

❖ November 10 ❖

Top Weight-Loss Strategies

Read: Romans 13:11-14

Clothe yourselves with the Lord Jesus Christ,
and do not think about how to gratify the desires
of the sinful nature (Rom. 13:14;NIV).

What are the best strategies for lowering weight? Choose the ones that you think would be helpful in your own efforts to shed excess pounds:

- Reducing fat intake
- Reducing total calories
- Eating fewer sweets
- No problem foods in the house
- Reading food labels for content
- Eating low-fat and nonfat foods
- Enjoying exercise
- Planning what you'll eat
- Eating smaller, more frequent meals
- Exercising regularly
- Drinking more water
- Walking
- Increasing high-fiber foods
- Keeping a food diary
- Cutting back on meat intake
- Increasing your self-esteem
- Having a support group
- Doing aerobics
- Becoming more conscious of why you eat at certain times
- Eliminating or reducing between-meal snacks

Lord, give me a plan to lose weight
slowly and consistently.

❖ November 11 ❖

Building Resistance

Read: Judges 16:4-22

... tell me the secret of your great strength ... (Judg. 16:6;NIV).

When "aerobics" became the exercise craze thirty years ago, exercise for specific muscles like arms, shoulders, chest, back trunk, hips, and legs took a back seat. Now scientists say these areas of the body need to be exercised just as much as the heart does through aerobics. This kind of exercise is called "resistance exercise" or "weightlifting." That's why I encourage all who exercise with me on television and with tapes to use ankle and wrist weights as soon as they are strong enough.

Why exercise? Because muscles waste away when they are not used. When they are exercised, especially with weights, they grow stronger and develop endurance.

The experts tell us we can being with a weight that we can lift comfortably eight times. As it gets easier to life this weight, you might want to do more lifts. As you get stronger you can use a heavier weight and then increase your repetitions as you get even stronger.

Always remember that a good exercise program should include a warm-up, stretching, resistance exercise (like lifting weights), aerobic conditioning (like walking briskly), and then a cool-down period.

Lord, increase my strength as I faithfully exercise.

❖ November 12 ❖

Workaholic Myth

Read: Ecclesiastes 5:13-20

Then I realized that it is good and proper for a
man to eat and drink, and to find satisfaction
in his toilsome labor ... (Eccles. 5:18;NIV).

Being a "workaholic" is not always the same as being hard-driven and competitive. A study presented at a meeting of the American Psychological Association found no relation between long work hours and symptoms of ill health among nine hundred Canadian workers surveyed. Indeed, the healthiest were those who worked long hours because they were absorbed in their work and enjoyed it. Most researchers in this field are coming around to the view that it's not devotion to work that harms your health, but a job that makes you feel powerless and insecure. One expert wrote, "It is our attitude toward work and toward others that is important ... Dissatisfaction with work lowers resistance to disease, while job satisfaction seems to have fortifying properties."

Lord, strengthen me to work heartily today, pleasing
You with the talents and abilities You've placed at my disposal.

❖ November 13 ❖

Side Stitch   Read: 2 Corinthians 4:16-18

For our light and momentary troubles are
achieving for us an eternal glory that far
outweighs them all (2 Cor. 4:17;NIV).

Why do you sometimes get that pain in the side when you're exercising? Nobody knows for sure, nor do they know for certain what it really is. It usually affects those who are just beginning a conditioning program rather than those who are already in good shape. One theory suggests it is due to insufficient oxygen getting to the diaphragm.

Whatever the case, the pain will go away if you slow down a bit and take a few deep breaths.

*Lord, help me to push beyond the minor aches
and pains that often accompany an exercise program.*

❖ November 14 ❖

Widow Regains Health   Read: Acts 3:17-23

Repent, then, and turn to God, so that your sins
may be wiped out,that times of refreshing may
come from the Lord (Acts 3:19;NIV).

Dear Abby: This is in reply to 'Enjoying Life in Florida,' who felt comfortable about being overweight. When I was a bride, I was 5 feet tall and weighted 105 pounds. After thirty-two years of marriage, I was widowed. Within a year, my weight had doubled.

"On my eightieth birthday, I was a cripple. Today, I'm eighty-five; I wear a size 10 dress, and I am free of pain. I walk a mile in twenty minutes.

"Remember, you didn't get fat overnight. Ease into your new habits. Cut down the size of your servings; then limit your meals to healthful foods such as fruits, vegetables, cereals, lean meat, and non-fat milk. Drink at least 10 glasses of liquids a day (mostly water).

"Start exercising. Begin slowly, then gradually increase the time, but do it so regularly that it becomes a habit. — Happy At Last In Oklahoma"

"Dear Happy: Too bad we'll never know how many people over fifty got off their duffs and followed your lead. Thanks for the wake-up call."

If this eighty-five-year-old widow can regain her health, so can you!

*Lord, thank You for giving me the ability to
change my behavior at any age.*

❖ November 15 ❖

The Perfect Diet   Read: Psalm 119:89-96

To all perfection I see a limit; but your commands
are boundless (Ps. 119:96;NIV).

Your basal metabolic rate (the amount of energy used while at rest) is
determined by the amount of lean muscle you have.

An unsupervised or very low-calorie fad diet causes you to lose lean
muscle mass, and this lowers your basal metabolic rate so your body requires
fewer calories at rest and during exercise. Over a period of time the body
requires fewer calories to function. This causes weight gain even if you are
eating fewer calories.

Fat-trapping dieting causes your body to lose its ability to shed fat and
leads to a very dangerous increase in body fat percentage. As you continue with
a low-calorie diet and no exercise, you lose lean muscle mass and slowly build
up fat all over your body.

All diets can produce weight loss, but all weight loss is not equal.
Remember, the perfect diet results in maximum fat loss and minimum lean
muscle loss.

Lord, give me a taste for sensible eating.

❖ November 16 ❖

Potassium Supplements?   Read: Genesis 2:15-17

And the Lord God commanded the man, "You are free to
eat from any tree in the garden" (Gen. 2:16;NIV).

You can get too much of a good thing. Potassium is an example. This
mineral, which is essential to good health, helps with the maintenance of a
proper water balance, transmission of nerve impulses and contraction of
muscles, including the heart muscle.

According to one nutritionist, it's hard to get too little of this mineral. It
is abundant in a balanced diet — one cup of orange juice or one banana provide
one-third of the body's daily needs. Other sources include milk, meat, cantaloupe, tomatoes, potatoes, and dark green, leafy vegetables.

Contrary to popular belief, the average athlete does not require potassium
supplements, unless sweat loss exceeds 4 liters per day.

Too much potassium can result in an abnormal heart rate. One source is
salt substitutes which replace sodium with potassium. Persons with heart
failure or kidney disease should check with their physician before using them.

*Lord, remind me that I can get all the nutrients
I need by eating fruits and vegetables.*

❖ November 17 ❖

Stress Signals   Read: James 1:5-8

> That man should not think he will receive anything
> from the Lord; he is a double-minded man,
> unstable in all he does (James 1:7-8;NIV).

Recognizing the signals of stress can help you slow down and begin to take care of yourself. Here are four signals of stress to look out for:

• **Disorganization.** Losing things, forgetting where you put things, making dumb mistakes. Starting to go somewhere and forgetting why.

• **Escape fantasies.** Dreaming about escaping to a faraway place where you don't have to do anything or take care of anyone.

• **Indecision.** Finding it difficult to make everyday decisions — what to wear, what to eat, where to go, what to do.

• **Introversion/Depression.** Wanting to lock the door, curl up in bed, and pull the covers over your head.

If you are experiencing any of these signals, it may be time for a vacation or a change or even seeking professional help.

Lord, alert me to the pressures of life,
and help me to leave them with You in prayer.

❖ November 18 ❖

God's Amazing Results   Read: Galatians 6:6-10

> . . . A man reaps what he sows (Gal. 6:7;NIV).

I can't believe how great you look!" Those words boost the confidence of the person who has been slowly but surely trimming her weight through healthy eating and exercise. I've seen such wonderful, amazing changes in people that sometimes I have thought all heaven was standing in applause.

You may be saying, "Not me. It will never happen for me." But it can. With God's help and the support of a caring family and professionals like me, you certainly can amaze everyone someday with the new you.

If you have prayed, "Lord, let me glorify You in my body," and are committed to healthy eating and regular exercise, you can look forward to amazing results. People are watching you, and one day they will say, "How did you do it? You look great!"

God knows when we mean business about our spiritual and physical condition. And when He sees commitment and faith in us, He will supply grace and strength for victory.

Lord, thank You allowing me to enjoy the results
of good nutrition and regular exercise!

❖ November 19 ❖

Exercise Means Better Sleep
Read: Ecclesiastes 12:1-5

> Remember your Creator in the days of your youth,
> before the days of trouble come . . . when men rise up at
> the sound of birds . . . (Eccles. 12:1,4;NIV).

The older you get, the "lighter" you tend to sleep. And light sleep is not as satisfactory as deep sleep.

In a recent study of two dozen men ages sixty to seventy-two, researchers found that those who exercised vigorously three times a week fell asleep twice as fast and enjoyed deeper sleep.

Activities that help are jogging, aerobic walking, swimming, bicycling, and tennis.

Lord, give me vigor for each day and sound sleep each night.

❖ November 20 ❖

You Be the Boss
Read: Jeremiah 17:5-8

> He will be like a tree planted by the water . . . .
> It does not fear when heat comes. . . . It has
> no worries in a year of drought . . . (Jer. 17:8;NIV).

When anxiety hinders your daily life, it's time to reassert your control. First, determine what you're anxious about. Some circumstances, of course, are beyond your control. But what can you do about situation you can change?

- **Talk about the problem with a friend or relative.** Sharing your burden may lighten your load. Acknowledge your limitations.
- **Do something you enjoy.** Gardening or watching a funny movie will distract your mind and help you relax.
- **Get enough rest.** A good night's sleep will restore you and leave you better able to cope.
- **Exercise regularly.** Physical activity can relax you and help you fall asleep more promptly.
- **Eat properly.** Good nutrition can be a buffer against anxiety. Caffeine, chocolate, and alcohol may worsen anxiety.
- **Plan your time.** A day with too much or too little to do may aggravate anxiety. Have a step-by-step plan for your day.
- **Accept reality.** It can help liberate you from worry.
- **Get involved.** Help yourself by helping others. Isolation can magnify your worries. Get involved with other people and worthwhile endeavors.

Lord, allow me to act with confidence and quiet trust in You.

❖ November 21 ❖

Pre-empting Middle-Age Spread Read: 1 Corinthians 4:14-17

I am not writing this to shame you,
but to warn you . . . (1 Cor. 4:14;NIV).

In a ten-year study, researchers monitored the weights of ten thousand men and women between the ages of twenty-five and seventy-four. They found not only that weight gain was highest for both men and women between twenty-five and thirty-four, but that women were twice as likely as men to experience major weight gain (30 pounds or more). Women younger than forty-five who were overweight to begin with had an even greater chance of major weight gain during the ten years of the study. Interestingly, after men and women reached the age of fifty-five, their weight began to drop slightly.

Many middle-aged people have weight problems, but these problems develop early on. A weight gain of 30 pounds or more over a short period of time is dangerous. But, so is simply being overweight — especially for women. It's proven that excess weight increases your risk for high blood pressure, heart disease, and diabetes.

What can you do? Adopt healthy habits early to head off potential weight gain later in life. Weight control shouldn't start when you are fifty-five. Consider exercise like walking, which if done regularly will help prevent the accumulation of excess fat.

*Lord, may I take precautions to avoid
gaining weight in middle age.*

❖ November 22 ❖

Walk and Burn Read: James 1:22-25

Do not merely listen to the word . . . .
Do what it says (James 1:22;NIV).

Listen to this. A 130-pound woman will burn the following number of calories in a half hour . . .

If she jogged: 342 (at a rate of a mile in nine minutes).

If she walked: 144 (at a moderate pace).

Now if this same 130-pound woman just sits, she burns 39 calories. Doesn't that inspire you to take a brisk thirty-minute walk and burn 144 calories instead of just sitting and burning 39?

*Lord, remind me that knowing truth is not the same as
experiencing truth. Help me to be a doer when
it comes to healthy nutrition and regular exercise.*

❖ November 23 ❖

Coping with Stress

Read: 1 Samuel 1:1-20

And because the Lord had closed her womb,
her rival kept provoking her . . . . In bitterness
of soul Hannah wept much and prayed
to the Lord (1 Sam. 1:6,10;NIV).

Webster defines "coping" as striking back with success. Doctors say that coping is the best way to deal with stress.

Stress has been defined as the "disruption of one's internal environment." Exposure to heat or cold is, for example, stressful. External temperatures can affect the body's internal temperature. And so to cope with the stress of heat or cold, you adjust the thermostat, move into the shade or into the sun, or take off or put on your coat.

Coping, therefore, does not rid you of the stress, but it does alleviate the discomfort caused by it, or puts it within the limits the body is able to adapt to. Scientists say that the key to dealing with stress is not to eliminate it, but to cope with it — to fight back, to take control.

Stress is not necessarily bad. While your boss may place new demands on you, the added stress can result in accomplishment and in greater capacity. A positive attitude toward stress regards it as an opportunity to grow and helps you meet the challenge.

Lord, may I turn to You first in times of stress and not to food.

❖ November 24 ❖

Smoking and Your Teeth

Read: 1 Corinthians 3:16-17

Don't you know that you yourselves
are God's temple and that God's Spirit
lives in you? (1 Cor. 3:16;NIV).

You know that smoking stains your teeth. Now there's evidence that what it does is even worse than that.

Smokers have more cavities, greater plaque formation, and more gum disease than nonsmokers. Dentists believe it's because smoking reduces the pH of the saliva in the mouth, making it more acidic and less resistant to tooth destroying bacteria.

*Lord, convict me of any behavior
that would defile my body.*

How Many Calories a Day?   Read: 2 Samuel 18:19-33

> Now Ahimaaz son of Zadok said, "Let
> me run and take the news to the king that
> the Lord has delivered him from the hand
> of his enemies" (2 Sam. 18:19;NIV).

How many calories do you need a day to maintain your normal weight? You can figure your caloric needs by multiplying your weight by a given number of calories per pound, based on your activity level. Here's their recommendation:

Your Activity Level	Calories/Pound
Inactive	12
Lightly active	15
Moderately active	16-20
Very active	21-25

You can see that someone in good health like the runner who brought news of the battle needs more calories to maintain his weight. The opposite is also true. If you lead a sedentary life, you need fewer calories.

Lord, remind me that the more active
I am, the more calories I need.

❖ **November 26** ❖

Aluminum from Drink Cans   Read: Judges 2:1-5

> . . . Yet you have disobeyed me . . . . they
> will be thorns in your sides and . . . a snare
> to you (Judg. 2:2-3;NIV).

The accumulation of aluminum in the brain is thought to be associated with the development of senile dementia. Cola drinks from aluminum cans contain three times as much aluminum as those from bottles or plastic containers. Beer from cans contained six times as much aluminum.

Lord, may the consequences of
disobedience keep me from
breaking Your laws of good
health and nutrition.

❖ November 27 ❖

Low Back Pain   Read: Psalm 1:1-6

> Blessed is the man who does not . . . sit in the
> seat of mockers (Ps. 1:1;NIV).

Do you suffer from backache? Eight out of ten people suffer from what is called "low-back pain" at some time in their lives. Doctors can pinpoint the cause of this back pain in only 12 percent of the cases.

Did you know that sitting places 40 to 60 percent more strain on the back than standing? If you want to avoid back pain, make sure your chair supports your spine.

Listen to these facts . . . Every pound you are overweight adds ten pounds of stress to your back. This is what health experts tell us. If your back is hurting, remember that just losing weight really helps. For every pound you lose, you will be reducing the stress to your back by ten pounds. Probably the very best exercise for losing weight is developing a daily program where you walk briskly for thirty to forty-five minutes at a time.

Lord, help me alleviate pressure on my spine by standing,
walking, and maintaining good posture throughout the day.

❖ November 28 ❖

Lifestyle-Trap   Read: Isaiah 30:15-21

> . . . In repentance and rest is your salvation, in quietness
> and trust is your strength . . . (Isa. 30:15;NIV).

During the week there are jobs to get done, quotas to attain, deadlines to meet. That's to be expected in the work-a-day world.

But are your weekends like that, too? Do you dash into the weekend with a to do list? Of course, the gutters need to be cleaned and the yard needs to be raked. But are your weekends becoming more and more like your weeks? Do you go back on Monday more stressed out than you were on Friday?

It's called the "lifestyle-trap" — a set of obligations, roles, and duties that keeps us in a mental performance zone even when we aren't "working."

Saturday can be so crammed full of activities: neighborhood tennis match, soccer practice for the kids, grocery shopping, clean the garage, dinner party. You feel like a failure if you haven't accomplished them all.

What's the answer to cramming more and more into our week and our weekend? While there'll always be things to "do" in leisure time, the doing should be part of the enjoyment, and the satisfaction should come from more than achieving.

Lord, help me to slow down and not frazzle myself on weekends.

❖ November 29 ❖

Baby and the Bath Water   Read: 1 Thessalonians 5:16-22

Test everything. Hold on to the good.
Avoid every kind of evil (1 Thess. 5:21-22;NIV).

Lowering cholesterol can be like "throwing the baby out with the bath water." When you lower cholesterol, you can also lower the good kind of cholesterol at the same time.

Good cholesterol — high-density lipoprotein cholesterol (HDL) — carries excess cholesterol out of the bloodstream into the liver for removal from the body. According to the National Institute for Health, a low-fat diet does reduce total cholesterol, but it can also lower the level of good cholesterol.

Americans who feel secure in the knowledge that their total cholesterol has gone down may be developing heart disease without knowing it because their good cholesterol is also down.

But a regular exercise program of walking or jogging an average of ten miles a week offsets the HDL-lowering effects of low-fat diets.

Men who followed a regimen of a low-fat diet and regular exercise lowered their total cholesterol levels while significantly raising their HDL levels. Women, on the other hand, lowered their total cholesterol while maintaining their HDL levels.

Lord, keep my good cholesterol levels up
as I eat right and exercise.

❖ November 30 ❖

Lower Sodium Intake   Read: 2 Corinthians 6:16-18; 7:1

Since we have these promises, dear friends, let us purify ourselves
from everything that contaminates body and spirit, perfecting
holiness out of reverence for God (2 Cor. 7:1;NIV).

We know that sodium can help cause high blood pressure in sodium sensitive people. Now scientists are investigating the possibility that sodium might also cause artery damage, cholesterol buildup, and eventually strokes and heart attacks.

How can we protect ourselves against these diseases? Cut sodium intake and eat plenty of potassium-rich foods like bananas. Other potassium-rich foods are apricots, avocados, potatoes, lima beans, spinach, yogurt, dates, orange and grapefruit juice, chicken, brussels sprouts, skim milk, carrots, tomatoes, and prunes.

Lord, open my eyes to the many ways salt has entered my diet.

❖ December 1 ❖

Leg Cramps

Discretion shall preserve thee, understanding
shall keep thee (Prov. 2:11).

Do you suffer from painful nighttime leg cramps that come on without warning? What causes them? Deficiencies in certain minerals — like sodium, potassium, and calcium — may contribute to cramping. If you're working out regularly and sweating, it's a good idea to include some salty foods in your diet. Low potassium reserves can also contribute to muscle cramps. Foods rich in this mineral include tomatoes, broccoli, potatoes, oranges, and bananas. Calcium helps regulate muscle contraction. Good sources include: skim milk and low-fat dairy products, such as yogurt.

Dehydration due to high intensity exercise can also deplete the body of fluids. The best way to avoid muscle cramps is to drink plenty of water during hard exercise. If you use discretion in how much you exercise and if you eat the right foods, you can keep from having painful leg cramps.

Lord, give me discretion and
understanding in everything I do.

❖ December 2 ❖

Sight Protection

Read: Psalm 119:17-40

Open my eyes that I may see wonderful
things in your law (Ps. 119:18;NIV).

You can find eye protection in the fresh produce section of your grocery store. Researchers have found that eating vitamin-rich fruits and vegetables is linked to lower risk of cataracts.

As you grow older, your risk for developing cataracts grows greater. Right now studies tell us that cataracts cloud the vision of up to half of all Americans over the age of seventy-five. Eating a healthy diet may delay the usual aging of the lens. Why? Doctors thinks it may be due to nutrient combination abundant in fruits and vegetables.

There is also a link between the development of cataracts and cigarettes. Researchers at Johns Hopkins University have found cataracts to be more common in cigarette smokers. They say that toxic substances from cigarette smoke damages the lens of the eye, causing clouding.

Lord, please help me keep my eyes healthy
so I can always read Your Word.

❖ December 3 ❖

The Top 15   Read: Daniel 2:1-23

. . . He gives wisdom to the wise and
knowledge to the discerning (Dan. 2:21;NIV).

*P*revention Magazine recently polled over 2,000 leading cancer experts
to find out the most important things a person can do to prevent cancer. Here
are the magazine's top 15 cancer-prevention measures, in order of priority:

(1) Don't smoke or chew tobacco. (2) Get regular cancer screening tests.
(3) Perform self examinations. (4) Limit exposure to sunlight. (5) Avoid
passive smoking (that's inhaling other people's smoke). (6) Avoid alcohol
intake. (7) Reduce overall dietary fat. (8) Eat more food with fiber. (9) Eat more
fruits and vegetables. (10) Eat more whole grain, high fiber cereals. (11)
Maintain normal weight. (12) Avoid household toxins. (13) Get regular
exercise. (14) Limit exposure to nitrites. (15) Eat more cruciferous vegetables
(cabbage, broccoli, Brussels sprouts).

It's up to you to change your lifestyle. No one else can do it for you.

Lord, teach me to be wise for my own sake.

❖ December 4 ❖

Poison by the Cupful   Read: Proverbs 12

The way of a fool seems right to him, but a
wise man listens to advice (Prov. 12:15;NIV).

Have you ever wondered who discovered coffee? Well, about A.D. 850
an Arabian goat-herder noticed that his goats, usually quiet animals, were
jumping and running more than usual. He realized they had been eating some
bush berry and decided to try the berry himself. He experienced an unusual
exhilaration and told his fellow goat-herders. They informed the villagers, and,
by the seventeenth century, coffee drinking had spread throughout the Arab
countries and Europe.

Coffee drinkers at that time had no way of knowing what gave them such
satisfaction and exhilaration. Now the unique flavor and stimulating action of
coffee and tea have made these beverages common all over the world. But the
caffeine that lifts you also dumps you down.

Caffeine induces mild euphoria, increased alertness, and apparently a
decrease in fatigue. It appears to lessen headaches, irritability, and nervousness, but most of these effects are illusions. Caffeine, however, has no effect
on the fatigue mechanism of the body.

*Lord, help me to listen to the advice I am
learning and apply it to my life.*

❖ December 5 ❖

Caffeine — A Drug   Read: 1 Corinthians 6:1-11

. . . Do not be deceived . . . (1 Cor. 6:9;NIV).

Many people have been deceived into thinking that caffeine is not harmful. It gives us no calories, no nutrition, no vitamins, and can even be a deadly drug. Caffeine deceives your nervous system by acting as a stimulant. If first mobilizes our reserve stress mechanism by increasing our blood sugar, our heart output, and blood pressure. It causes our kidneys to put out more urine, and increases our respiratory rate.

Caffeine forces our bodies to borrow from our energy reserves. And those reserves are not easy to replace. Some might be impossible to replace. So why do millions of people continue to drink coffee and tea? Because — like so many of us who were deceived — they don't know the facts. Now that you have been informed about the dangers of caffeine, what will you do about it?

Lord, I don't want to be deceived any
longer. Deliver me from the desire for
caffeine and it's harmful effects.

❖ December 6 ❖

A True Villain   Read: Psalm 107:1-22

Fools because of their transgression, and because
of their iniquities, are afflicted (Ps. 107:17).

Caffeine is like an actor. It only brings about an *illusion* of well being and health. If we keep living an illusion of energy and alertness, we will one day pay the price. Continual tiredness and weakness of nerves and organs will finally catch up with us.

Statistics show that heavy tea and coffee drinkers are more susceptible to all types of disease. Caffeine causes your stomach to produce more acid, often creating heart burn. In fact, the Mayo Clinic refuses to treat any ulcer patient who is unwilling to quit drinking tea or coffee. Caffeine also produces a stress effect, which can elevate blood pressure in coffee drinkers. High blood pressure is one of the main risk factors in heart attacks.

The caffeine stress effect also partially paralyzes the intestinal tract. Digestion and absorption of food take longer. What you eat stays longer in your intestines. This produces gas, indigestion, and increases the chance of colon cancer. Caffeine is a villain.

Lord, forgive me for being foolish and
harming my body by drinking caffeine.

❖ December 7 ❖

How's Your Midriff?

Read: Psalm 108

With God we will gain the victory, and he will
trample down our enemies (Ps. 108:13;NIV).

What do you see when you look in the mirror? Is your midriff sleek and firm or fat and flabby? What are the main causes of the potbelly syndrome? In a study involving 2,000 men and women, those who consumed two drinks of an alcoholic beverage a day were found to have the largest mid-sections. Those who smoke had two times as many potbellies as non-smokers.

So how can you "deflate" your midriff "spare tire"? Cut out alcohol; if you smoke, stop; take a brisk daily walk; and load up on complex carbohydrates instead of saturated fat. The benefits from doing this will be more than just making you look good. You see, the potbelly has been known to boost your risk for heart disease, diabetes, and hypertension.

So get working on deflating that midriff! God will give you the victory and trample down those enemies that are waging war against your body. But, like King David, you still have to go out and fight!

*Lord, give me courage for the battle and faith to know that You
will help me defeat the enemies of my body, soul, and spirit.*

❖ December 8 ❖

Melt That Potbelly

Read: John 4:27-38

My food . . . is to do the will of him who sent me . . . (John 4:34;NIV).

You probably think I'm going to tell you to do sit-ups, don't you? Well, I'm not — because even if you do one hundred sit-ups a day, they have *never* been found to melt a potbelly. They can tone the underlying muscles, but the fat itself does not burn even when your stomach muscles feel like burning coals.

The reason? The few minutes it takes to grind out one hundred sit-ups isn't nearly enough to torch the fat-burning process. What you need is bouts of brisk aerobic exercise like walking, biking, or rowing that get those big muscles — like the thighs — working. Do this for at least thirty minutes or more. That is what it takes to burn fat. Another helpful tip is to stay away from the saturated fat found in cheese-cakes, burgers, and cream sauce. It seems these have a preference for being stored on the midsection! Carbohydrates found in vege-tables, fruits and grains, however, lead to a better shape all around.

More important then being in shape physically is the spiritual condition of our hearts. Our main goal in life should be to do God's will.

*Lord, I delight to do Your will because it is
always a joy to please You.*

❖ December 9 ❖

Boost Your Creativity

Read: Romans 12

> . . . be transformed by the renewing
> of your mind . . . (Rom. 12:2;NIV).

Does your mind need renewing? Then you need to read God's Word and do His will. You can also help get those creative juices flowing by taking your body out for some exercise. Physical activity has been proven to boost the brain and lift the mood. Researchers have also learned that physical activity can stimulate creativity.

A test was done with forty-two college students in which twice a week they did a thirty-minute jog. Their creativity levels were studied before they were placed on this exercise program, and it was found that after several weeks of jogging, they were much more creative. In yet another test, just one twenty-minute aerobic class was found to spur creative thinking.

Repetitive activities like running and aerobics may shut down the analytical left side of our brain and give free rein to the artistic right side. Also, we feel less stressful and drop inhibitions that interfere with creativity.

So, don't just sit there. Stimulate your own mind today by engaging in a 30-minute exercise program. Go out and take a brisk walk.

Lord, renew my mind through the power of Your Word.

❖ December 10 ❖

Two Sides

Read: Proverbs 19:15-29

> The fear of the Lord leads to life: Then one rests content,
> untouched by trouble (Prov. 19:23;NIV).

Some people think they can eat anything if they have a regular exercise program. The famous runner Jim Fix who wrote *The Complete Book Of Running* thought he could. In an interview with a newspaper he said that he was not very concerned about his diet because a running program of 10 miles a day would sufficiently burn up whatever he ate. He said for breakfast he had fried eggs, sausage, fried potatoes, butter and cream — talk about a cardiac disaster! As you may recall, Jim Fixx died suddenly while on a daily run.

On the other hand, some folks watch their diet religiously but are rarely physically active. They eat grains, fruits and vegetables and know the latest nutrition facts, but they don't move their bodies. This approach doesn't work either. What does work is the balance of a healthy lifestyle that includes a low-fat way of eating and regular exercise. Balance is the key.

Lord, teach me to fear You in a healthy
way that will help me avoid trouble.

❖ December 11 ❖

Strength Training   Read: Proverbs 14:16-35

A sound heart is the life of the flesh (Prov. 14:30).

We know strength training builds and pumps up muscles, but how about the most vital and vigorous one — the one that pumps on its own — your heart? Recent studies show powerful evidence that strength training may take a healthy whack at heart-disease risk and at the same time give your heart muscle mass.

Strength training (like lifting weights or using machines) was shown to be safe for people with mild to moderate high blood pressure. In fact, it helped lower blood pressure and the bad cholesterol and boost the good cholesterol as successfully as taking heart medication.

Strength training may help offset a problem called cardiac atrophy, which occurs when heart-muscle tissue is lost due to dieting. As you lose weight, you reduce the heart's workload because there's less body mass to pump blood to. The heart is like any muscle — when there isn't work to do, it shrinks. When you increase the heart's workload through strength and aerobic training, this helps maintain and even boost your heart muscle mass.

Lord, help me to keep my physical and spiritual heart
sound and healthy so I can live for You.

❖ December 12 ❖

What I Do   Read: Colossians 1

We give thanks to the God and Father of our Lord Jesus Christ,
praying always for you (Col. 1:3).

People often ask me, "What kind of exercise do you do?" I walk briskly for thirty minutes every day on my treadmill and do at least one-half hour of floor exercises using wrist and ankle weights. Walking burns calories and provides aerobic conditioning. The floor exercises increase flexibility, and the weights firm muscles.

I began doing strength training when I learned it provides a definite increase in bone. How? Our bones respond to pressure, and strength training provides the pressure — more so than aerobic training.

I also pray for my television viewers, my radio listeners, and my devotional readers every day, thanking God for you and asking Him to bless your efforts toward a healthier lifestyle.

Thank You, heavenly Father, for these dear friends.
Bless them as they seek to please You in everything they do.

❖ December 13 ❖

Who Needs A Cane?

Read: Matthew 11:1-19

> . . . Go back and report to John what you hear and
> see . . . the lame walk (Matt. 11:4-5;NIV).

Falls are very dangerous as you get older. Can you prevent them? Yes, strength training helps you regain your balance after having been slightly knocked off center. Building stronger leg and stronger hips through strength training can postpone and possibly even prevent these highly destructive falls. Strength training gives you more confidence, more control over your own body. With that, you have less chance for injury, and less chance for falls.

In one experiment that was done they took 10 people (average age 90) and had them do simple leg exercises three times a week over eight weeks. They not only built up their strength but saw improvement in their lives from this moderate muscle pumping. They became more mobile, more flexible, and their walking speed noticeably improved. They had a doubling, even a tripling of the muscle strength in their legs. Two of them threw away their canes!

If 90 year olds were able to do strength training and benefit from it — surely it will help you!

Lord, may I be able to report that You have healed me.

❖ December 14 ❖

Food Headaches

Read: Matthew 7

> Ask and it will be given to you; seek and you will find . . . (Matt. 7:7;NIV).

Researchers believe that what you eat and drink may contribute to certain kinds of headaches — especially migraines. But proving a definite link between diet and headaches is often difficult, and no single food affects all sensitive people. The following have been most commonly involved: Aged cheeses, alcoholic beverages (especially red wine), nuts and peanut butter, yogurt, sour cream, cured or processed meats, caffeine-rich drinks, freshly baked yeast products, chocolate, MSG, hydrolyzed vegetable protein, and aspartame (artificial sweetener).

Most of the suspect foods and beverages contain substances that may constrict or dilate blood vessels of the brain. One major culprit is tyramine, a chemical that occurs naturally in many foods. Nitrites, used in cold cuts and frankfurters, can also dilate blood vessels. For some people, not eating for many hours, or suddenly abstaining from certain foods — such as coffee — may bring on headaches.

Lord, I ask You to show me what is causing
my headaches and help me to find the answer.

❖ December 15 ❖

Starving to Gorge?   Read: Hebrews 11:23-31

By faith Moses . . . chose to be mistreated . . . rather than
enjoy the pleasures of sin for a short time (Heb. 11:24-25;NIV).

It's that time of the year again — time for feasting and celebrating. Just before a major holiday, some people like to save up their calories so they can enjoy a huge a feast without worrying about gaining weight. When we come to the dinner table half-starved, we tend to overeat, selecting high-fat, high calorie treats instead of nutritious foods.

Is it healthy to skip meals so you can eat more later? I admit, it's a pleasure to sit down to a delicious meal with a hearty appetite, but there are risks involved whenever you habitually starve yourself so you can "pig out" later.

This may be okay once in a while, but too often it gets out of hand and can lead to the "starve-gorge syndrome." Over time, this habit can throw off your metabolism and eventually destroy your health.

*Lord, during this holiday season, help me to behave decently
and not think about how to gratify my fleshly desires.*

❖ December 16 ❖

Banking Calories   Read: 1 Corinthians 11:17-34

. . . when you come together to eat, wait for each
other. If anyone is hungry, he should
eat at home . . . (1 Cor. 11:33-34;NIV).

What's the right way to "cut back" on your food so you can enjoy a guilt-free holiday dinner or a special restaurant meal? The experts tell us that moderate restraint is okay, even encouraged — if it's done wisely.

On the day of a dinner party, don't skip meals or eat so little that you are starved. Instead, make low-fat, high-fiber, carbohydrate-rich choices at breakfast and lunch and have a small snack an hour before the meal if you are hungry.

The week before the special event, cut back 100 to 200 calories a day. You can do this by substituting jam for butter on your morning toast, using lemon on your salad instead of an oil-based dressing, or skipping dessert. This way you won't feel deprived or starved.

In the early Corinthian church, some people were gobbling up all the food at their "love feasts." The apostle Paul suggested they eat at home before the feast so they wouldn't be so hungry.

*Lord, forgive me for only thinking about how to please
myself with food. Help me to consider the needs of others.*

❖ December 17 ❖

More Holiday Tips   Read: Ecclesiastes 6

> All man's efforts are for his mouth, yet his appetite
> is never satisfied (Eccles. 6:7;NIV).

Let me give you a few tips concerning controlling your eating during the holiday season. One way you can help regulate your appetite is with exercise. Exercise causes increased blood flow, and this raises blood-glucose levels, which seem to squelch hunger. If you are going out for a nice dinner, take time for a brisk walk. But don't overdo it by trying to burn up extra calories so you can eat more later.

Keep a healthy attitude about food. It isn't normal to think about food all the time. This only adds to your fear of losing control. Stuffing yourself, feeling self-hatred, and then planning to restrict your food indicates an unhealthy relationship to food. If you do this often, you need to see a counselor who specializes in eating disorders.

If you gain a few pounds over the holidays, so what? With sensible eating and regular, moderate exercise, it's unlikely your splurge will result in permanent weight gain.

> *Lord, forgive me for thinking too much about*
> *food and how to satisfy my appetite. Help me*
> *to have the proper attitude toward eating.*

❖ December 18 ❖

Drinking Poison   Read: 1 Corinthians 5

> . . . you must not associate with anyone who calls himself
> a brother but is . . . a drunkard . . . (1 Cor. 5:11;NIV).

Did you know that the body regards alcohol as a poison? Unlike food and non-alcoholic drinks — which are digested in the mouth, stomach, and intestines — alcohol is processed in the liver. It is the liver's function to detoxify poisonous substances introduced into the body.

What does alcohol do to the body? Moderate drinking over extended periods of time causes fat to accumulate in the liver. Heavy drinking can cause inflammation of the liver, known as hepatitis. When heavy drinking continues, liver cells are damaged and leads to a condition called cirrhosis. This disease can be fatal.

> *Lord, help me to choose my friends*
> *wisely and stay away from those*
> *who drink too much alcohol.*

❖ December 19 ❖

Water in the Winter   Read: Psalm 74

It was you who . . . made both summer and winter (Ps. 74:17;NIV).

Although water is neither digested nor burned for energy, it is an essential nutrient and has many benefits. Water is the lubricant that permits joints to move, eyeballs to swivel, and nasal passages to drain. Water helps maintain proper muscle tone by giving muscles their natural ability to contract and by preventing dehydration.

Water not only helps the body cool itself through the evaporation of perspiration in summer's heat, it also helps us to stay warm in the winter. Dehydration from dry winter air can bring skin temperatures down by as much as 20 percent. If you exercise, do winter sports, or are overweight, you need to increase your water intake.

How can you be sure you are getting enough water? Drink water when you're thirsty, and drink it when you're not. You can't skip water one day and try to make up for it the next. The balance must be right. If you drink cold water, it will be absorbed more quickly.

Lord, thank Your for making both summer and winter.

❖ December 20 ❖

Getting Enough Sleep?   Read: Psalm 116

Be at rest once more, O my soul, for the Lord
has been good to you (Ps. 116:7;NIV).

Do you get enough sleep at night? Do you wake up refreshed? Many of us could benefit from receiving additional sleep each night.

During a research study, individuals had to perform a variety of different tasks. After doing these tasks, the individuals then spent ten hours in bed. They did this for six nights in a row. When rested, every one of them scored higher on the tests they were given.

You can experiment with your own sleep patterns. Go to bed a half hour earlier than you normally do for one week. Do you feel more alert and rested? Next, try going to bed one hour earlier for the second week. See how you feel.

Remember, it is important to extend your time by going to bed earlier rather than by getting up later. If you rise later, your body's internal clock may not be in sync with your getting-up time, and you may wake up feeling groggy. If you have received the right amount of sleep you should wake up without an alarm clock and feel refreshed all day.

Lord, help me to get the rest I need to perform my daily tasks well.

❖ December 21 ❖

Stuff Your Stockings   Read: 2 Peter 3

. . . You ought to live holy and godly lives (2 Pet. 3:11;NIV).

Stuffing stockings during the holiday season is a tradition you will want to continue. But stuffing yourself is one some of us are trying to do away with, especially since the average American reports a seven pound weight gain between Thanksgiving and New Year's! Here are a few tips that may help keep your weight down.

At a buffet or dinner, fill your plate with fruits and vegetables. Then add very small portions of other foods. Be the last one in line to get your food, and then eat slowly. This way you won't finish eating before others and be tempted to go back for seconds.

First, put your food on your own plate and eat from that only. Don't hang around the food table. Get involved in conversation and activities. Sip on a low-calorie drink with lots of ice all evening. Nibble on vegetables and not chips. Don't drink. Alcohol is high in calories.

Lord, during this holiday season, help me to control my
body in a way that is holy and honorable.

❖ December 22 ❖

Stress Effects   Read: Isaiah 53

. . . he was bruised for our iniquities: the chastisement of our peace
was upon him; and with his stripes we are healed (Is. 53:5).

This time of the year, it's easy to become stressed out with all the holiday preparations. Stress is one thing you don't need, especially as we think about celebrating our Saviour's birth. Stress takes a toll on almost every part of your body. We've all experienced the sweaty palms and tremors that stressful situations bring.

Stress on the brain contributes to depression, agitation, anxiety, and insomnia. It affects your face. You might get dry mouth, clenched jaw, or skin disorders. Stress causes excessive hair loss and some forms of baldness.

Stress can cause or aggravate gastritis, stomach ulcers, colitis, and irritable colon. It leads to heartburn and nausea. Stress is also considered a major contributor to cardiovascular disease. In addition, stress releases a chemical that speeds muscle deterioration. It aggravates nervous tics and causes muscle pain. Remember that daily exercise will help you deal much better with the stress in your life.

Jesus, I know You died to take away my sin. Let me
find Your peace in my heart and mind today.

❖ December 23 ❖

Doing Good is Good for You   Read: Galatians 6:10-18

> . . . as we have opportunity, let us do
> good to all people (Gal. 6:10;NIV).

You already know that regular exercise and a balanced diet keep you in shape. Studies now show what God's Word has been telling us for centuries — that opening your heart to others has emotional and physical benefits.

It's called "helper's calm," a feeling of well-being that relieves headaches and other stress-related disorders and also enhances self-esteem. The highs, warmth, and increased energy that arise during social contract with others may result from the release of endorphins, the body's natural pain-reducing chemicals.

That may be why those who are involved in helping others are unusually physically healthy and emotionally secure. You don't have to be a Mother Teresa to qualify, however. Even small acts of generosity and caring for family, friends, and community are expressions of love. How can you nourish your soul and thus good health? By paying attention to all the little opportunities you're given to help others, and act on them.

> *Lord, show me how to make the*
> *most good out the opportunities*
> *You give me to help others.*

❖ December 24 ❖

The Big Banquet   Read: Song of Solomon 2:1-13

> He brought me to the banqueting house, and his
> banner over me was love (Song of Sol. 2:4).

The next time you have to attend a banquet or go out for dinner, quote today's verse. If you are afraid you may go off your diet or overeat, call on the Lord. He loves you and will go with you. You don't have to go along with the crowd and stuff yourself! Thank God for the love and wisdom he gives when it would be impossible to handle the situation on your own.

God is calling you to come and feast at His table. In fact, He is already preparing the "marriage supper of the Lamb" for you in heaven. (Read Revelation chapters 20-22.) If your name is written in the Lamb's book of life, you will be among those who will spend eternity with God and Jesus forever. Believe me, this is one banquet you don't want to miss!

> *Lord, I thank You that my name is written*
> *in the Lamb's Book of Life.*

❖ December 25 ❖

What's Impossible?

Blessed is she that believed: for there shall
be a performance of those things which were
told her from the Lord (Luke 1:45).

Mary believed that God could do the impossible. Do you? As you meditate on God's promises, you will be able to overcome all the harmful habits in
your life that "seem impossible" — maybe smoking or overeating or not
exercising. God promises to show you a new way through Jesus Christ. Things
that were impossible yesterday you can do today.

Hide this verse in your heart as you look to the Lord for His help to break
bad habits and form new, healthy ones: "I can do all things through Christ
which strengtheneth me" (Phil. 4:13).

*Heavenly Father, thank You for
sending Your only Son Jesus
to this earth to be my Saviour.*

❖ December 26 ❖

Good Substitutes
Read: Isaiah 1:18-31

If you are willing and obedient, you will eat
the best from the land (Isa. 1:19;NIV).

Instead of diet classes, go to cooking classes. Learn to substitute good
ingredients for bad. Go through your favorite recipes and replace ingredients
to make them low in fat. Substitute soft diet margarine for butter, skim milk for
whole milk, egg whites for whole eggs, yogurt for sour cream, whole-grain
cereal crumbs for bread crumbs, vegetable oil for shortening.

When you eat out make changes. Stay away from deep fried foods. Watch
your salad dressings. Lime and lemon juice or cocktail sauce are good low-fat
substitutes. Order vegetables cooked without fat seasonings like butter, sour
cream, or cheese sauce, and get broiled chicken or meats.

Take a walk. Exercise causes you to have a diet less and stimulates the
production of a protein called HDL that removes fat from the blood. A brisk
half-hour walk four or five times a week will increase your HDL level (good
cholesterol).

*Lord, help me to eat only food
that is good for my body and to
feed my soul on Your Word.*

❖ December 27 ❖

Go Slow   Read: 2 Corinthians 6

> . . . as servants of God we commend ourselves in every way:
> in . . . patience and kindness . . . (2 Cor. 6:4,6;NIV).

Why is it that every time you go on a diet it gets harder and harder to take the weight off? First you don't want to take weight off that you can't keep off. Yo-yo dieting is not only hard on your health, but it also makes further weight loss more difficult. Why?

The enzyme that is responsible for storing fat (called LPL) found on the surface of fat tissue, has a memory. The LPL of the first-time dieter is ignorant. When it stops getting the amount of fat it's used to getting, it takes a while to realize it needs to produce more enzyme. The more often a person goes on and off diets, the more he is training his LPL to produce enzyme and store fat more quickly and efficiently.

The solution is to lose slowly and exercise. Don't fall prey to weight-loss schemes that promise speed. They don't work. The biggest virtue for a dieter is patience. It is also a virtue for the Christian. Let's learn to be slow to speak up and slow to get angry.

*Lord, give me the patience I need to lose weight and the
patience to treat others with kindness.*

❖ December 28 ❖

When Little Is Better   Read: Exodus 23:27-33

> Little by little I will drive them
> out before you . . . (Exod. 23:30;NIV).

If you cut calories too much, you "downshift" your metabolism. How much is too much? In general, your body does not want to cut back more than 500 calories a day or one pound in a week. Any time you go beyond that you "shock" your system. Then your body kicks into the classical stress response as it prepares for what it thinks to be a time of starvation.

Exaggerated adrenaline production and other stress reactions can make you feel shaky, queasy, and possibly light-headed. If you start feeling this way, you know you have cut down too much on the calories you are taking in. That's why you need to cut back gradually and remember that little is sometimes better.

*Lord, teach me how to lose weight a
little at a time and let me always
eat my meals with love.*

❖ December 29 ❖

Smoking and Weight Gain   Read: Psalm 65

Thou crownest the year with thy goodness . . . (Ps. 65:11).

If you are a smoker, you may want to make this next year, the year that you quit. You may have not quit so far because you are afraid of gaining weight. But that is the devil's lie.

The National Cancer Institute says the average weight gain is 5 pounds! In fact, 10 percent of smokers *lose* weight when they quit. The reason for the weight gain is that people who quit often have a craving for sweets. Gaining a few pounds is a small price to pay compared to the risks from smoking.

To avoid weight gain when you quit, eat low-fat foods like raw vegetables, limit sugar intake, and drink six to eight glasses of water a day to leach any remaining nicotine out of the body. A program of diet and exercise can eliminate weight gain. Stop smoking, exercise, and give up fried foods and sweets. This could be the year you stop smoking!

Lord, crown this year with Your goodness and
help me stop smoking so I can bring glory to You.

❖ December 30 ❖

Bad Habits or Sin?   Read: Numbers 32:20-42

. . . you may be sure that your sin will
find you out (Num. 32:23;NIV).

Have you ever thought about the fact that two major causes of death for Americans are heart disease and cancer and that we often bring them on ourselves? How? By our lifestyle choices and habits. Some people don't understand the link between health and the way we choose to live. Others do understand but continue thinking they are immune to illness. "It will never happen to me!" they say.

Your lifestyle choices ultimately dictate the health and longevity you will have. What kinds of choices am I talking about? *Diet:* what and how much to eat; *exercise:* whether or not you will be physically active on a regular basis; *stress:* whether to manage or ignore it: *smoking:* whether or not to start, continue or break the habit.

All of these are controllable aspects of your lifestyle, and they count either for or against your good health. The decisions you make each day can actually extend and improve the quality of your life. That's why it is a sin not to take care of your body.

Lord, forgive me for not taking care of my body.

❖ **December 31** ❖

Not the End   Read: 1 Thessalonians 5:23-28

> . . . May your whole spirit, soul and body be
> kept blameless . . . (1 Thess. 5:23;NIV).

I recently met a lady who had been listening to my program every day on the radio. She told she suffered from adult-onset diabetes and as a result of this, her doctor had put her on insulin. Each day, as she listened, she got under conviction about eating the low-fat way and exercising. Finally, she started to do a video exercise program and to walk. After a while her lifestyle completely changed.

Today, she is 17 pounds lighter and hooked on exercise. As she told me her story, tears trickled down her cheeks. She said, "Beverly, my doctor was thrilled about my weight loss and new lifestyle! I thank God for giving me the strength to do this, and I thank you for your daily program on radio." To God be the glory!

Nothing would thrill me more than to receive a letter telling me that you were healthier after reading these devotions. And don't stop reading today. This is not the end. You can start the new year off right by letting me be your health coach again next year. Now let me end by praying for you.

Lord, bless this dear reader in spirit, soul, and
body both now and in the years to come.

A Final Word

Plan of Salvation

Throughout this book, we have talked about how important it is for you to have a personal relationship with God by accepting Jesus Christ as your Saviour. If you have never asked Jesus Christ into your heart and you want to do this, permit me to share with you the plan of salvation.

First, read each of these passages and meditate on them.

"For all have sinned, and come short of the glory of God" (Rom. 3:23).

First, we have to see ourselves as sinners, confess that we are sinners, and realize that in no way do we measure up to the glory of God.

"For the wages of sin is death; but the gift of God is eternal life through Jesus Christ our Lord" (Rom. 6:23).

We know that sin brings death to us. As a believer we have eternal life by asking Jesus Christ into our hearts. He, the righteous One, paid the debt of all of us at Calvary when He went to the Cross in payment of all our sins.

"For by grace are ye saved through faith; and that not of yourselves: it is the gift of God" (Eph. 2:8-9).

The grace of God saves us. This is a free gift from God. Our salvation was paid for by Jesus on the Cross. We cannot work for salvation, but through faith in Jesus Christ we have this free gift of God.

"For God so loved the world that he gave his only begotten Son, that whosoever believeth in him should not perish, but have everlasting life. For God sent not his Son into the world to condemn the world; but that the world through Him might be saved" (John 3:16-17).

Jesus came into this world not to condemn people like you and me, but to save people like us. Whoever believes in Jesus will not perish in hell but will have everlasting life in heaven. Jesus came to bring eternal life to the world.

"For I am persuaded that neither death, nor life, nor angels, nor principalities, no powers, nor things present, nor things to come. Nor height, nor depth, nor any other creature, shall be able to separate us from the love of God, which is in Christ Jesus our Lord" (Rom. 8:38-39).

Once we ask Jesus Christ to come into our hearts, nothing can ever separate us from God.

"That if thou shalt confess with thy mouth the Lord Jesus and shalt believe in thine heart that God hath raised him from the dead, thou shalt be saved. For with the heart man believeth unto righteousness; and with the mouth confession is made unto salvation" (Rom. 10:9-10).

With your mouth you must confess Jesus to be the Son of God whom God raised from the dead. If you believe this in your heart, you will be saved.

"For he saith, I have heard thee in a time accepted, and in the day of salvation have I succored thee: behold, now is the accepted time; behold, now is the day of salvation" (2 Cor. 6:2).

Today is the day for you to receive salvation. Don't put it off any longer because you never know what tomorrow may bring.

Now that I have shared with you Scriptures showing you how and why you can be saved, pray this prayer from your heart:

Dear God, I know I am a sinner. I know that Jesus paid the price for my sins on the cross at Calvary. Lord Jesus, please come into my heart and be my Lord and Saviour.

Through this simple act of accepting Jesus Christ by faith, you are now a child of the Living God and you have eternal life.

The next step is to tell someone what you have done. Find a Bible-believing church if you don't have one, and talk to the pastor. Tell him how you came to accept Jesus Christ as your Saviour.

Once you have made public your decision to follow Christ, it is scriptural for you to be baptized. Baptism is a symbol of our "new life" in Christ. Through this act of water baptism, others will see that you have truly committed your life to following Jesus.

Then you need to attend a regular church fellowship, read your Bible, and pray. That's how you will start growing in the grace of God, and your life, for the first time, will have meaning.

Although I had attended church all of my life, I wasn't truly saved and born again until I was thirty-five years old. That's when someone shared this same plan of salvation with me. I want you to know the joy and peace and love that comes from knowing Jesus Christ as your Saviour.

Feel free to write to me if you have any questions about this new life in Christ.

God bless you, my precious friend.

Love in Jesus,
Beverly

BEVERLY'S PRODUCTS

Below is a listing of items available for purchase from Beverly Exercise.

Book:

Easy Low-Fat Cooking, by Beverly Chesser with Gale R. Cox, New Leaf Press. Over 400 low-fat recipes, plus nutrition tips and guidelines. — $15.

Your Health Coach, by Beverly Chesser with Gale R. Cox, Whitaker House. A general nutrition book which teaches low-fat eating and benefits of exercise. Cost — $15.

Videos:

Total Body Workout — A one-hour exercise tape (done in two, 30-minute segments) with exercises for the entire body. These ballet-type, stretching exercises are designed to shape the body, improve posture, and increase flexibility. Cost — $39.95.

Hip and Thigh Workout — A one-hour exercise tape (done in two, 30-minute segments) for the hip and thigh area (inner and outer thigh and derriere). These ballet-type, uplifting exercises will firm and shape the hips and thighs. Cost — $25.

Audio Cassettes:

Exercise Audio Cassette Tapes — Exact photo instructions included.

Total Body Workout — An exercise program for the entire body. Floor exercises only. Low impact. No aerobics. Cost — $8.95.

Hip and Thigh Workout — Hip and thigh exercises only. Floor exercises. Low impact. No aerobics. Cost — $8.95.

Nutrition Teaching Tapes — Beverly speaks on diet and exercise. These tapes are designed to teach proper nutrition and the benefits of exercise. Cost — $5 each. (When you order 8 at a time, they come in a binder. Cost for eight — $40.)

— Tape 1: Introduction to Health
— Tape 2: More on Eating Right
— Tape 3: Health Helpers
— Tape 4: Selficide (Eating Disorders)
— Tape 5: Food Abuse and Diet Pills
— Tape 6: Fighting Fat
— Tape 7: Where's the Fat?
— Tape 8: Lose the Fat
— Tape 9: Cholesterol
— Tape 10: Fiber and Starch
— Tape 11: Fat and Breast Cancer
— Tape 12: Mono Fats
— Tape 13: Diabetes
— Tape 14: Weight Loss
— Tape 15: Bad Fats
— Tape 16: High Blood Pressure & Cholesterol
— Tape 17: Sugar Abuse
— Tape 18: Water and Coffee
— Tape 19: Starvers, Stuffers and Skippers
— Tape 20: How Many Fat Grams
— Tape 21: Stress Relief
— Tape 22: Healthy Bones
— Tape 23: PMS
— Tape 24: HDL Cholesterol

For further information or to order, write or call:

Beverly Exercise
P.O. Box 5434
Anderson, SC 29623
(803) 225-5799 or (803) 224-2498